HARVARD
HISTORICAL
MONOGRAPHS

LI

Published under the direction ·
of the Department of History
from the income of
The Robert Louis Stroock Fund

PUBLIC OPINION, PROPAGANDA, AND POLITICS IN EIGHTEENTH-CENTURY ENGLAND

A Study of the Jew Bill of 1753

by THOMAS W. PERRY

HARVARD UNIVERSITY PRESS

Cambridge, Massachusetts · 1962

Library of Congress Catalog Card Number 62–17222
Printed in the United States of America

PREFACE

IN ITS conception—though not in its basic assumptions—this work departs from the customary analytical-biographical approach to eighteenth-century English politics; it examines a dispute over a question of policy, and the presentation is largely narrative in form. Instead of asking how this Parliament was composed or how that ministry was constructed, I have looked at what a Parliament *did,* and at how a ministry chose to *use* its power with respect to a particular controversial issue. That issue, Jewish naturalization, will interest two quite distinct groups of readers—specialists in eighteenth-century politics and specialists in Anglo-Jewish history—each of which may well skip over the basic background information intended for the other.

Throughout this work, I refer most often to the Jewish Naturalization Act of 1753 as the "Jew Bill," a name that is open to question, first, because the nominal adjective grates harshly; and second, because the Bill, once passed, became an act. My reason, quite simply, is that this was the name most generally applied to the measure at the time, and consequently the one that appears most frequently in my quotations. The solecism involved in speaking of "repealing the Bill" apparently did not trouble eighteenth-century men. Nor did the word "Jew," used as an adjective, then have the derogatory overtones it has today, a fact recognized by various modern authors (such as G. B. Hertz) who, in their accounts of the episode, adopt this eighteenth-century usage as I have done.

Except where there was a particular reason for doing otherwise, I have, in reproducing quotations, corrected the worst irregularities in spelling and punctuation, and modernized the more unfamiliar

and obsolete examples of eighteenth-century idiom. I have, however, retained everything that was either self-explanatory or familiar.

I am indebted to many persons for advice and assistance, and should like in particular to express my gratitude to the secretarial staff of the Department of Humanities, Massachusetts Institute of Technology; to the Photographic Service of the British Museum; to the Secretaries of the Jewish Board of Deputies and of the Spanish and Portuguese Synagogue in London; to Mrs. Dorothea Reeves, of the Kress Room at Baker Library, Harvard Business School; to Mr. John A. Riggs, Assistant Librarian, Harvard College Library, for innumerable acts of kindness performed both in his official capacity and as a friend; to Mr. Elliott Perkins, both for his thoughtful and invariably helpful criticism of the present work when in progress, and, more generally, for all he taught me, in the course of an association of ten years, about eighteenth-century English politics; and finally, to my wife, whose contribution to this work was, in its way, quite as great as my own.

T. W. P.

Watertown, Massachusetts
March 1, 1962

CONTENTS

PUBLIC OPINION,
PROPAGANDA, AND POLITICS
IN EIGHTEENTH-CENTURY ENGLAND

NOTE ON CITATIONS

Periodicals are cited in the following manner: with the magazines, which are numbered serially through each year, first the year, and then the page number; with the newspapers and weeklies, the issue number and then the page (*Gent. Mag.*, 1753:208; *World*, 50:2). The following abbreviations are used throughout.

Add. MSS.	Additional Manuscripts in the British Museum
DNB	*Dictionary of National Biography*
Gent. Mag.	*Gentleman's Magazine*
Hist. MSS. Comm.	*Historical Manuscripts Commission Reports*
Jackson	*Jackson's Oxford Journal*
LEP	*London Evening Post*
Lond. Mag.	*London Magazine*
P. Hist.	Cobbett's *Parliamentary History*
TJHSE	*Transactions of the Jewish Historical Society of England*
WEP	*Whitehall Evening Post*

Unless otherwise indicated, all dates are for the year 1753.

I

INTRODUCTION

ON December 6, 1753, Horace Walpole wrote, in a gossipy letter to his friend George Montagu, "I tell you nothing of Jew bills and Jew motions, for I dare say you have long been as weary of the words as I am." [1] Weary of them Walpole doubtless was, since that topic had been the chief conversation of politically-minded Englishmen for over six months.

It had all begun in the spring of 1753 when, with the Pelham ministry's blessing and support, the Jewish Naturalization Bill—more often called the Jew Bill—was introduced in the House of Lords. The measure was a modest one, technical in nature and merely permissive in its effect. It actually naturalized no one: all it did was to modify the statutory requirements for naturalization so that Parliament *in future cases* could, if it wished, naturalize professing Jews, a thing impossible under existing law. Any foreign Jew wishing to be naturalized would still have to obtain passage of a private Act of Parliament. Since this was an expensive proceeding, there were certain to be few applicants; and of course future Parliaments were in no way bound to accept all or even any of these.

This insignificant bill was approved by the Lords without a debate, and in the Commons it was finally passed by a comfortable margin, though not without arousing considerable opposition both in the House and among the merchants of London. The opposition to the Bill did not subside, however, with the passage of the measure. Instead it grew into a full-voiced religious and political clamor

[1] *The Letters of Horace Walpole,* ed. Mrs. Paget Toynbee (Oxford, 1903–1905), III, 199.

which spread throughout the kingdom and increased in intensity until it became "perhaps the loudest and fiercest, while it lasted, of all the church cries of the eighteenth century." [2]

Naturally the Pelhams were alarmed when this outcry against the Jew Bill—and, more pertinently, against *them* for supporting it—persisted into the autumn without abating. Their concern was heightened by the fact that a general election would have to be held by the spring of 1754 at the very latest; indeed, in many constituencies the campaign had already begun, and in most of them the Jew Bill was the principal argument advanced by the opponents of the Court. In this situation the ministers decided to jettison this political Jonah, and accordingly, when Parliament reassembled in November for its final session before the dissolution, they took the lead in rushing through both Houses the repeal of this measure whose enactment they had supported in the spring.

And so the Jewish Naturalization Act of 1753 was removed from the statute book in the year of its passage, before it had been resorted to in a single instance. The political storm stirred up by the Act died out in most places soon after the repeal; and the results of the general election (which took place some five months later) were on the whole more than satisfactory to the Ministry.

Such, in rough outline, is the story that this work will examine in detail. Of course the whole anticlimactic episode, like the short-lived Jew Bill itself, amounts to no more than the merest transient ripple on the broad stream of English political history. As a thoughtful contemporary accurately predicted, "the domestic politics of this summer will make but a contemptible figure in history, which can record nothing else than the art employed by faction to swell a most inoffensive Bill into a national grievance." [3]

Yet the story of the Jew Bill, though inconsequential in itself, is unquestionably a curious one in several respects. Surely a violent

---

[2] C. J. Abbey and J. H. Overton, *The English Church in the Eighteenth Century* (London, 1878), II, 396. Lecky's language is equally strong: "England was thrown into paroxysms of excitement scarcely less intense than those which followed the impeachment of Sacheverell" (W. E. H. Lecky, *The History of England in the Eighteenth Century,* New York, 1878, I, 285).

[3] Add. MSS. 35398, f. 168 (Philip Yorke to Thomas Birch, Oct. 4).

politico-religious controversy is one of the last things we should expect to find in the tolerant and sleepy 1750's—a time when, according to no less an authority than G. M. Trevelyan, religious and political passions were "stone-cold." [4] And what are we to make of the undignified spectacle of Parliament, in the period of the Whig supremacy, scrambling to repeal an act that it had solemnly passed only six months before? Certainly that is not in keeping with the notion of an oligarchic trusteeship resting upon an unrepresentative and corrupt electoral system, and hence largely immune (at least in time of peace) from popular pressures.

Therefore, although this work is at bottom a history of the Jew Bill and of the controversy the Bill aroused, it has a purpose and, I believe, a value and interest, beyond the mere narration of a particular episode of the year 1753: for a thorough examination of an episode that appears, at least at first glance, to be so out of the ordinary, could hardly fail to enlarge our general understanding of English life and thought in the mid-eighteenth century. Specifically —if I may anticipate one of my conclusions—an understanding of the controversy over the Jew Bill should help us avoid the common but erroneous belief that Whig and Tory doctrines and loyalties were wholly meaningless or even nonexistent in the 1750's: as we shall see, these were—or could be at times—rather more vigorous and significant than is generally supposed. The story of the Bill also suggests that the mid-eighteenth-century Whig oligarchs were more concerned about public opinion, and that individual members of Parliament were more sensitive to popular pressures, than most historians have believed. Finally, there are other topics, such as mid-eighteenth-century propaganda methods, religious attitudes, constitutional theory, and economic notions, which a study of this episode should illumine, even where it tends to confirm, rather than to question, received opinion.

With a view to general questions, then, as well as to particular details, let us turn to the history of the ill-fated Naturalization Act, beginning with a brief look at the social and legal position of the English Jews in 1753.

[4] Trevelyan, *England under Queen Anne, Vol. II: Ramillies and the Union with Scotland* (London, 1932), p. ix.

THE GRAND CONFERENCE or the JEW PREDOMINANT

"Printed for Israel de Costor in Bevis marks near the Synagogue"

[October 1753]

Shown are Samson Gideon; Henry Pelham, attended by a good and an evil genius; his brother, the Duke of Newcastle; a bishop; and looking on "from Obscurity"—that is, unseen by the others—John Hill, a quack doctor and opposition journalist who signed himself "The Inspector."

Gideon, having produced a bag of money, says:
"Dare Gentlemen, & my very good Friends, Dis be de Puss collected by our Tribe for de great Favour."
At his feet lies a list of "Collections from the West Indies, Portugal, Holland, Metz, Prague, England &c, Total . . . 200,000L."

Pelham, ignoring his good genius and told by his evil genius to "Take the Cash . . . at all Events," does so, saying: "The Perquisites always prevailing."

Newcastle, reaching for his share: "It comes

seasonably to me at this Juncture Circumcision or any thing,"

Bishop, dismayed: "We have done those things which we ought not to have done."

Dr. Hill, to the bishop: "Don't mind that my L[ord], the Right of presenting is vested in You & Your Brethren, it's so decreed."

[Beneath the picture are verses:]

See G[ideo]n, C[ommon]s, L[ord]s, and B[ishop]s
by,
Speak then, *Inspector*, from Obscurity.
'Tis such, that pass your L[i]b[er]y away—
Borrow by Br[i]b[er]y, and by V[ic]e they pay,
As Judas did for pelf betray our Lord,
Grant Heav'n that they may meet their just Reward!

II

ENGLISH JEWRY
IN 1753

IN 1753 there were perhaps 8000 Jews in England; they constituted a tiny minority, amounting to about one tenth of one per cent of the total population.[1] Their religious beliefs and observances set them apart from the rest of the community, of course, in an age when, to a greater extent than is generally appreciated, Christian traditions, Christian institutions, and Christian forms of thought were still significant to most men, whether they were positive believers or not. The Jews were "different" in another way, too, in that as a group they were but recent arrivals in England. About half of the estimated 8000 had been born abroad; and of those who were native-born, few could claim more than three generations of Englishry. No known Jewish family—or almost none, for genealogy is always controversial —had been settled in England for more than a century.[2]

There had been Jews in England earlier. They had first come there in the wake of the Conquest, and at their medieval high point the English Jews were established in more places than they were in 1753.[3] Theirs had been the usual tragic history of royal protection

[1] Philo-Patriae, *pseud., Considerations on the Bill to Permit Persons Professing the Jewish Religion to be Naturalized by Parliament* (London, 1753), p. 17. D'Blossiers Tovey, in his *Anglia Judaica* (Oxford, 1738), p. 302, estimated their number at that time to be "near six thousand." For the total population see Basil Williams, *The Whig Supremacy, 1714–1760* (Oxford, 1939), pp. 118–119. The percentage of colored immigrants in Britain today is almost ten times that of Jews in 1753.

[2] G. B. Hertz, *British Imperialism in the Eighteenth Century* (London, 1908), p. 63; H. S. Q. Henriques, *The Jews and the English Law* (Oxford, 1908), pp. 233–234, 80–81, 119n.

[3] Cecil Roth, *A History of the Jews in England* (Oxford, 1941), pp. 11–12; Roth, *The Rise of Provincial Jewry* (London, 1950), Appendix.

alternating with royal exploitation, all of which came to an end in 1290 when Edward I expelled the Jews from his kingdom. This cruel action, which utterly ended the history of medieval English Jewry, was the first of its kind in Europe, and served as an unhappy precedent for later expulsions from other countries, notably France and Spain. It is therefore ironic that modern English Jewry should be derived from a nucleus of refugees expelled from Spain and Portugal two hundred years later.

The readmission of the Jews to England dates from the late Cromwellian period, when certain Jewish leaders in Holland convinced the Protector that the entry of Iberian (or "Sephardic") refugees should no longer be prohibited. There was sufficient public opposition to this, especially from the merchants and the clergy, to cause Cromwell to draw back from any official act of authorization; but he was willing, as Cecil Roth puts it, "to 'connive' at the settlement of the Jews without formally authorizing it." [4] Soon the community was numerous enough to establish a synagogue and to require its own cemetery; and when the restored king showed his willingness (in spite of some public protest) to continue the policy of "toleration by oversight," a steady trickle of Sephardic immigrants began arriving.[5]

At first the number was very small: in Charles II's time there were probably not 500 Jews in England. But closer intercourse with Holland after 1688 resulted in a large influx of Jews from Amsterdam. Most of these were Sephardim who had originally come to Holland as refugees from Spain and Portugal; some, however, were Ashkenazim—that is, Yiddish-speaking Jews from central and eastern Europe. During the eighteenth century these Ashkenazic Jews arrived in increasing numbers, so that by 1753 English Jewry had for some time been split into two groups which, in spite of certain basic similarities, were quite distinct from each other. Both were foreign in origin, but they had come from different regions; both

---

[4] *Jews in England,* pp. 163, 166; *Hist. MSS. Comm., Egmont Papers,* vol. I, pt. 2, pp. 573–574.

[5] Roth, *Jews in England,* pp. 166, 170–173.

were recent arrivals, but the Ashkenazim were the more so by a significant margin. Furthermore, though they shared one faith, still there were differences—mainly over matters of liturgy—which were sufficient to necessitate separate synagogues and cemeteries for each community.[6]

Socially, too, there was a world of difference between the Ashkenazim and such great Sephardic financiers as Joseph Salvador (alias Rodrigues) and Samson Gideon (originally Abudiente). Their relative standing is suggested by the fact that while the Sephardim almost never intermarried with the Ashkenazim, marriage between persons of Sephardic Jewish origin and upper-class Englishmen was not uncommon.[7]

The status and condition of the Ashkenazim are not difficult to describe. Like the Polish and Russian Jews who migrated to western Europe and America around the turn of the present century, these people were as a rule refugees from a wretched ghetto existence. Their lowly past condition and the fact that they were such recent immigrants—and immigrants too distinct from the rest of the community to be quickly assimilated—combined to force them into the lowest strata of English life.

The overwhelming majority of them settled close together in London, where, except for the very few who were substantial merchants and brokers, they found employment in petty retailing and handicrafts, in domestic service to wealthier Jews and, sometimes, in the underworld.[8] But more important to this study, in spite of their small number, were those Ashkenazic Jews who wandered about the countryside hawking spectacles, penknives, buttons, pins, and similar articles.[9] Outside the metropolis practically nothing was known of the Jews: many eighteenth-century

[6] L. D. Barnett, ed., *Bevis Marks Records* (Oxford, 1940–), pt. I, pp. 31–32; Roth, *Jews in England*, pp. 184, 196–199.

[7] Roth, *Jews in England*, p. 199 and note; G. E. C[okayne], *The Complete Peerage*, new ed., ed. Vicary Gibbs *et al.* (London, 1910–), s.v. "Gage."

[8] E. N. Adler, *London*, in Jewish Communities Series (Philadelphia, 1930), p. 150; Roth, *Jews in England*, pp. 199, 223.

[9] *Gentleman's Magazine*, 1753:385; *Jackson's Oxford Journal*, 16:2.

Englishmen had never *seen* one. Therefore, except in Bristol and one or two other towns, the only part of public opinion toward Jews that was not based on folk memories[10] had to be derived from intercourse with these pedlars or from stories about them.

Though their wares, even when suspect, were attractive and useful to people who lived what we would now consider a humdrum existence, still the pedlars themselves must have seemed strange, even mysterious, to their rustic customers. They generally spoke but little English, and that with an unfamiliar accent; in an age of clean shaving, they wore beards; their hair was worn long, and their dress was often both ragged and unorthodox.[11]

From the record of a contemporary criminal case involving one Henry Simons, "a Polish Jew merchant," we can get some idea of the impression that Ashkenazic Jews must have made on ordinary Englishmen. (Simons had been beaten and robbed; after a complicated series of trials justice was done, and Simons' assailant was forced to pay him damages.)[12] Simons had a beard and long, disorderly hair; he wore a skullcap.[13] One witness described his appearance as "outlandish," and told of being "struck with his visage and the oddity of his garb." He knew only a few words of English, a handicap which had contributed materially to his difficulties.[14]

The opening question in one of the trials—"Do you know Henry Simons, a Jew?"—shows that these people were thought of not as individuals, but as members of a distinct group. In subsequent

[10] E.g., frightening tales of ritual murder. One pamphlet written against the Act of 1753 spoke of the Jews' "frequently crucifying Christian children on Good Friday." [William Romaine], *An Answer to a Pamphlet* (London, 1753), p. 23. The memory of this myth is being kept alive even in our own day: see Gerald L. K. Smith's magazine, *The Cross and the Flag*, Jan. 1956, p. 24.

[11] Roth, *Jews in England*, pp. 226–227; and various prints, e.g., that in Adler, *London*, facing p. 142.

[12] *The Case of Henry Simons, a Polish Jew Merchant; and his Appeal to the Public thereon* (London, 1753); *The Case and Appeal of James Ashley* (London, 1753). Ashley was the convicted assailant.

[13] From the frontispiece of *The Case and Appeal;* it is not a caricature.

[14] *Case of Henry Simons*, pp. 23, 96, 87. One of Simons' supporting witnesses, Israel Levi, "a Polander," also knew so little English that he had to testify through an interpreter.

questions and answers Simons was often referred to simply as "the Jew," at times in an almost brutally impersonal manner: "Q. How near was you to the Jew? A. I was almost touching the Jew's chair." One statement by a witness suggests the air of mystery that surrounded these strangers, and shows the kind of things men believed of them: "Then it was dark; then the constable said to me, these wicked Jews carry about with them snickersnee knives and very mischievous weapons, as I have heard." [15]

The unfortunate Henry Simons is mentioned here only as a type; no other Ashkenazi will be named in the remainder of this work. For though the Ashkenazim played perhaps the larger part in forming the image called up in the English mind by the word "Jew," the Sephardim were of far greater weight in English society, politics and finance;[16] and it was at their request and for their benefit that the Naturalization Bill was passed. They were mainly brokers and merchants of substantial wealth, and seem to have moved in much the same social circles as their non-Jewish counterparts. We have already noted their tendency to intermarry with good English families, which was but part of a trend toward nearly complete social assimilation. The Sephardim largely shared the easygoing religious attitudes of many Englishmen of the time, and this fact combined with social ambition to make apostasy to the dominant faith quite common.[17]

Unlike the Ashkenazim, the Sephardim were clean-shaven and dressed in conformity to fashion.[18] In a print attacking the Naturalization Bill, a Sephardi—Samson Gideon—is shown seated at a table offering money to several great politicians from whom he is

---

[15] *Ibid.*, pp. 55, 85, 59.

[16] In 1733, for example, 11 of the 12 licensed "Jew brokers" were Sephardim (*Britannia's Fortune-Teller*, London, 1733, p. 51).

[17] Most modern Anglo-Jewish historians admit (and deplore) this tendency. E.g., Barnett, *Bevis Marks Records*, I, 33; Roth, *Jews in England*, p. 285, note "d"; Adler, *London*, p. 150.

[18] Alfred Rubens, *Anglo-Jewish Portraits* (London, 1935), *passim;* Roth, *Jews in England*, p. 209.

distinguishable only because the artist has deliberately coarsened his features.[19] This print is certainly inaccurate in its accusation of bribery; but in a larger sense it truly represents the position and importance of the Sephardic financiers as respected advisers to ministers and as supporters of the Government.

Perhaps a brief sketch of Gideon's career will give an idea of the activities and standing of these men; he was the greatest of them and so cannot be said to be typical, but the differences are of degree only. Gideon was born in England in 1699, his father being an immigrant of Portuguese extraction who had changed his name from Abudiente. Samson did very well speculating in lottery tickets and stocks—an activity viewed with great suspicion by the public—and became sufficiently rich and influential to have his support sought by ministers offering government loans for public subscription. His investments in the public funds increased both his wealth and his political influence, and by the end of the War of the Austrian Succession he had become a close associate of Henry Pelham and one of the Government's chief financial advisers. In Lucy Sutherland's opinion, he was the most important English financier of his time.[20]

Gideon's social rise (or rather that of his family) paralleled the increase in his fortune, and was accompanied by a gradual estrangement from Judaism. He married a Christian and had all his children baptized at birth, although he never took this step himself, and was buried, at his own request, as a Jew. Wishing, like other City men, to set himself up as a landed gentleman, in 1747 he obtained a grant of arms and purchased a country house which had formerly belonged to a peer. In 1757 he gave his daughter Elizabeth in marriage to Viscount Gage, with a dowry of £40,000. In 1758 Gideon formally requested a baronetcy; he was

---

[19] Israel Solomons, "Satirical and Political Prints on the Jews' Naturalisation Bill, 1753," *TJHSE*, 6 (1908–1910), facsimile facing p. 217, reproduced above, facing p. 4.

[20] "Samson Gideon: Eighteenth Century Jewish Financier," *TJHSE*, 17:79–85 (1953).

refused, but very gently, and when he pressed the matter again the next year, that honor was conferred on his (baptized) son Sampson, then a boy at Eton. The young baronet eventually became an M.P., a member of White's, and an Irish peer under his Christian wife's name of Eardley.[21]

This impressive but not quite perfect success story suggests that in the mid-eighteenth century there was still a certain ambiguity about the social position of even the most fortunate English Jews. The same note appears in the *London Evening Post's* announcement of a wedding that took place (as it happened) on the day when the Jew Bill was first debated in Parliament: "This week was married," it reads, "—— Stratford, Esq., of Argyll Buildings, to Miss Greviere, daughter of Solomon Greviere, Esq., an eminent Jew merchant."[22] Both the wording and the fact that only one other wedding was mentioned in that issue of the paper may be taken as signs of the acceptance of Jews in good society. Yet against this evidence of recognition and acceptance must be placed the fact that the Grevieres were identified as Jewish, and thus set apart.

So—to conclude on a negative note—the Jews of England were *in* the community, but not yet wholly *of* it. The religious difference was important of itself, and cannot be assumed, when we find reference to it in an argument, to be merely an ideological façade covering uglier or more selfish opinions. Besides this, the Jews were marked out from the rest by their recent foreign origin—and eighteenth-century Englishmen had no love for foreigners of any sort, even good Protestant Christians.[23] Finally, the occupations of many of the Jews were such as were bound to incur public disapproval. This was true not only of the poor Ashkenazim, but also of the wealthy and successful Sephardim, many of whose financial activities, however essential to the economy, were nevertheless regarded as bordering upon the unethical, at best: most eighteenth-

---

[21] *Ibid.*, pp. 81–90; Hertz, *British Imperialism*, pp. 100–101.
[22] *London Evening Post*, 3985:1; *Gent. Mag.*, 1753:248.
[23] See the discussion of the "poor Palatines," in Chapter IV.

century Englishmen disliked stockjobbers and speculators on principle, regardless of their religion.[24]

The English Jews of 1753, then, lived at peace with their neighbors. But on several different counts they were potentially a subject of controversy and a target of animosity, should anyone be either so thoughtless or so ill-disposed as publicly to agitate fundamental questions concerning their position in the community.

The Legal Position of the Jews in 1753

As is so often true in the history of English law, we must look to a fact rather than to a concept in order to understand the legal position of English Jewry in 1753; in this instance we must go back to the circumstances of the Readmission, almost a century earlier. It will be recalled that Cromwell, prevented by public opinion from making any open, official concessions to the Jews, still was willing to allow a few of them to settle in England without any express authorization. This informal policy was continued after the Restoration, and for some time the royal dispensing power was the Jews' sole protection against legal harassment.[25]

If the readmission of the Jews had been brought about as a result of an open and formal act of the Government, it would certainly have been accompanied by a further enactment precisely defining their legal position. The Jews would unquestionably have been placed under severe restrictions, and in fact they themselves seem to have been prepared to accept such terms.[26] But fortunately this did not happen, and the first Jewish immigrants found themselves living in a country whose statute book ignored their very existence. In 1753 this was no longer true: by then the Jews had been

[24] Dr. Johnson defined a stockjobber as "a low wretch who gets money by buying and selling shares in the funds." Even a strongly philo-Semitic pamphlet of 1753, in attacking the Jew Bill's City opponents, sneered ironically at the stockjobbers among them: "proper judges, sure! . . . of the good of the nation" (*Considerations*, p. 28).

[25] Both Charles II and James II stopped prosecutions brought against the Jews under the provisions of the Conventicle Act. See Barnett, *Bevis Marks Records*, I, 9 (1664), and I, 15 (1685).

[26] Roth, *Jews in England*, pp. 171–172.

singled out in a few Acts of Parliament. Some of this legislation was favorable to the Jews; rather more of it was unfavorable; but none of it was important.[27]

This does not mean, however, that except for a few pinpricks the law did not discriminate against British subjects who happened to profess the Jewish religion; in fact the Jews lay under several serious disabilities, especially with respect to political rights. Along with certain other groups, Jews could neither hold office in a municipal corporation nor occupy a place of trust under the Crown; they could not sit in Parliament or vote in parliamentary elections; they were denied entrance to the universities. But the main weight of these disabilities fell, as was intended, on Catholics and Protestant Dissenters; that the restrictive statutes also affected the Jews was purely accidental, as in the case of the test and oaths required by the Corporation and Test acts. The denial of the right to vote for members and to sit in Parliament resulted from a similar "accidental discrimination"; for the required anti-Jacobite oath of abjuration contained the words "upon the true faith of a Christian," a formula whose purpose was not to exclude non-Christians, but rather to make the oath absolutely proof against popish equivocation.[28] Another fortuitous legal technicality—the requirement that an oath be taken on the New Testament—made it impossible for Jews to acquire the freedom of the City of London, without which they could not engage in retail trade within the City.[29]

But in 1753 the disabilities that weighed most heavily upon the

[27] For example, both the Blasphemy Act (1698) and the famous Marriage Act (1753) allowed exemptions in favor of the Jews. On the other side we find an act of 1702 intended to encourage conversions to Protestantism, and certain short-lived discriminatory tax laws and proposals—in the reign of William and Mary (Henriques, pp. 164–167, 170–171; Roth, *Jews in England,* p. 187).

[28] Henriques, pp. 246, 267, and 224, n. 2. It must be noted, however, that when Parliament removed *some* of these accidental discriminations against Jews, as was done by an Act of 10 Geo. I, in a sense it rendered the remaining prohibitions deliberate. (For that act, see Henriques, p. 170.)

[29] Henriques, pp. 198–201. Wholesale trade was permitted them; and twelve Jews—though no more at any one time—could also (for a handsome fee) obtain licenses on carry on business as commodity brokers.

Jews—with the possible exception of the denial of civic freedom—were not those to which all of them were subject as religious recusants, but those which fell upon that part of their number, about one half, which was foreign-born. These people, *not because they were Jews but because they were aliens,* could not hold land or real property of any description; and if they wished to rent, they were restricted by law to the more precarious degrees of tenure.[30]

Even more irksome were the commercial discriminations against aliens. Aliens could not own, or share in the ownership of, a British vessel. The Navigation Act of 1660 flatly excluded them from the profitable colonial trade. And even in those branches of commerce permitted them, foreign merchants were required to pay various extraordinary charges called "alien duties," which included special port fees and discriminatory customs rates on many enumerated commodities. Sometimes these alien customs rates were twice as high as those paid by native merchants, so the competitive disadvantage was considerable.[31]

These disabilities weighed heavily upon the foreign-born Sephardic merchant-financiers of London, and no doubt many native-born Jews, though not themselves subject to these duties, still sympathized with those—in many cases business associates or relatives—who were forced to trade at such a disadvantage. Also, since many of these families were international, it is quite possible that some English Jews had relatives abroad who were discouraged by the alien duties from settling in England; during the controversy over the Naturalization Bill much was made of this argument. At any rate, it is clear that the alien duties and disabilities were a real annoyance to many members of the Sephardic community, including some who were not directly subject to them. To learn what one could do about this problem, let us turn to a brief examination of the ways in which British nationality could be obtained in the eighteenth century.

[30] *Ibid.,* p. 230. Certain exceptions, however, were allowed in favor of merchants.
[31] *Gent. Mag.,* 1753:351n; Henriques, pp. 230–232, 231, n. 2. According to *Gent. Mag.,* 1753:352, many aliens avoided these duties by making out their manifests in the name of some British subject; but this was hardly a comfortable solution. (The alien duties were repealed in 1784.)

NATURALIZATION AND DENIZATION IN THE EIGHTEENTH CENTURY

The normal way, for an alien to be fully quit of the discriminatory provisions of English property and commercial law was to apply to Parliament for a private naturalization act. This recourse was not available to a professing Jew, however, because of a statute of 1609 that required every petitioner to receive the Sacrament before his bill was introduced. The act stated that naturalization was a matter of "grace and favour . . . not fit to be bestowed upon any others than such as are of the religion now established in this realm"; like most of the acts mentioned above, it was aimed at Papists rather than Jews.[32]

There was, indeed, an act of 1740 which provided an easier, extra-parliamentary method of naturalization for foreigners who had resided for seven years in the American colonies, and which contained special provisions exempting Quakers and Jews from the obnoxious parts of the regular procedure.[33] It is possible that a few London Jews may have gone to the colonies, served their time, been naturalized, and returned to England.[34] But in all only 189 Jews obtained British nationality under this act, an overwhelming majority (151) being residents of Jamaica, where there was a flourishing congregation;[35] on the whole the Plantation Act, as it was called, was of little benefit to the Sephardic merchants chafing in London under the alien duties.

Although naturalization was all but impossible for the London Jews to obtain, a next-best choice was open to them, for there was no impediment to their being made "free denizens" by the purchase of royal letters-patent; and in fact since the Restoration many had

---

[32] Henriques, p. 238.

[33] For this act (13 Geo. II, c. 7) see Henriques, pp. 240–241. It was also technically possible for a Jew to be naturalized under the provisions of special acts intended to recruit sailors in wartime and to encourage the manufacture of linen cloth and tapestries; but these exceptions were of no practical importance (*ibid.*, p. 239).

[34] Add. MSS. 33053, ff. 56–57. (Reprinted in Cecil Roth, ed., *Anglo-Jewish Letters, 1158–1917*, London, 1938, pp. 129–130.)

[35] Adler, *London*, p. 121; James Picciotto, *Sketches of Anglo-Jewish History* (London, 1875), p. 94.

availed themselves of this rather costly privilege.[36] Probably the most valuable benefit conferred on them by denization—and no small benefit—was the right to engage in the colonial trade. But in certain other respects denization was a poor substitute for naturalization. For example, denization was not retrospective, so that if a denizen's children had been born abroad before the date of his patent, they remained aliens and so could not inherit his real property.[37]

But worst of all, from the standpoint of the Sephardic merchants, was the fact that denization did not, in the period with which we are concerned, grant exemption from the alien duties.[38] Under Charles II and James II denizens had been forgiven certain of these, but not without greatly annoying the native merchants, who finally succeeded in 1690 in obtaining an Order in Council requiring denizens to pay the full alien rate henceforth.[39] Thus a patent of George II, by which seven Portuguese Jews were made denizens, commanded them "to pay to us . . . the like customs and subsidies for their goods and merchandizes as aliens do and ought to pay." [40]

So we, and the foreign-born Sephardic merchants, are driven back to the point at which this discussion began: only by being naturalized could they obtain full property rights and commercial equality; but so long as the sacramental test was required for naturalization, that sole recourse was denied to professing Jews.[41] The only solution to their problem was to obtain an Act of Parliament that would modify the naturalization procedures so as to allow Jews to be exempted from the Test, after the manner of the Plantation Act. And that, simply stated, was the purpose of the ill-fated Jew Bill of 1753.

[36] The privilege was most frequently resorted to under Charles II, when it was most valuable. Roughly 150 Jews were made denizens between 1660 and 1700. Barnett, *Bevis Marks Records*, I, 7, n. 3; Roth, *Jews in England*, p. 212.

[37] Henriques, pp. 234–235.

[38] *Ibid.*, p. 238.

[39] Tovey, *Anglia Judaica*, pp. 287–295; Cobbett's *Parliamentary History*, XIV, 1386; Roth, *Jews in England*, p. 182.

[40] Barnett, *Bevis Marks Records*, I, pl. xii (facsimile).

[41] With the insignificant exceptions noted above, of course.

III

THE GENESIS
OF THE JEW BILL

OF course the Jew Bill of 1753 did not come into existence simply because the London Sephardim suddenly perceived in that year that their problems with regard to naturalization and the alien duties could be solved only by such legislation. As early as 1746 the Spanish and Portuguese Synagogue had appointed a standing "committee of deputies" to lobby, as we say nowadays, for a change in the naturalization laws; and doubtless the subject had been discussed in the community long before that.[1]

The formation of the committee was occasioned by the recent failure of a Jewish Naturalization Bill in the Irish Parliament; it had been defeated by a narrow margin, and the congregation felt that with greater exertions on their part it might have passed. In the next year the effort was renewed, and this time the bill would have become law but for the intervention of the primate, who caused it to be dropped in council without receiving the royal assent.[2]

Since the Jewish community in Ireland was so inconsiderable, it is likely that the London synagogue's chief interest in promoting this

[1] Barnett, *Bevis Marks Records,* I, 39; A. M. Hyamson, in *The Sephardim of England* (London, 1951), p. 128n, says that as early as 1742 the community was paying a solicitor (P. C. Webb) for services "in relation to the applications to Parliament concerning naturalization." (Barnett's work is a narrative history of the Spanish and Portuguese community of London, interspersed with selections, in English translation, from the records of the Bevis Marks Synagogue. The records of the synagogue and of the board of deputies are very scant for this period; the unpublished parts contain nothing about the Bill, I am informed, beyond what has already been published by Barnett, Roth, Hyamson, and others.)

[2] Picciotto, *Sketches,* pp. 113–115; Leon Huehner, "The Jews of Ireland," *TJHSE,* 5 (1902–1905), 236–238; *Hist. MSS. Comm.,* 4th Rept., App. I, p. 299.

bill lay in its usefulness as a precedent for a similar measure in England.[3] That had for some time been the goal of the London Jews, and they felt that they had good reason, in the late 1740's, to be sanguine about attaining it. Even as the Irish Jew Bill was being debated in Dublin, the Parliament at Westminster was considering a bill to permit foreign Protestants to be naturalized without being put to the trouble and expense of a private act. Opposition from the City caused this "General Naturalization Bill" to be defeated, but its persistent promoter, Robert Nugent, reintroduced it in 1751. This time the Sephardic community asked Nugent to add to his bill a clause in their favor. Though he was personally sympathetic to the request, Nugent refused, lest his already battered bill be encumbered with fresh difficulties which might endanger the whole project.[4]

Even so, the bill aroused such violent opposition that it again failed to pass. Oddly enough, the Jews, though excluded from the bill, were brought into the debate by opponents who asserted, of all things, that the want of a clause permitting the naturalization of Jews was one of the bill's most serious defects. If immigrants were to be enticed to settle in England, these men argued, surely a few rich Jews would be preferable to a horde of impoverished Protestants.[5]

Plausible as it is, we may suspect that this argument was in large measure a mere debating point, since most of the opponents of the bill were men who at bottom disapproved of all immigration. Still, it must have been sincere with some: we know that at least one prominent opponent of this bill supported the Jew Bill of 1753.[6] At any rate, the London Sephardim, taking encouragement from such talk, renewed their application for what would now have to be a separate act repealing the existing impediments to Jewish naturalization.[7]

[3] Picciotto, p. 114; Roth, *Jews in England*, p. 213.
[4] William Coxe, *Memoirs of the Administration of the Rt. Hon. Henry Pelham* (London, 1829), I, 386–387; *P. Hist.*, XIV, 136; Philo-Patriae, *Considerations*, p. 23.
[5] *P. Hist.*, XIV, 136; *Considerations*, pp. 23–24.
[6] Humphrey Sydenham, M.P. for Exeter (*P. Hist.*, XIV, 971, 1431n).
[7] *Considerations*, p. 24.

Although the details of the negotiations are not known, the outlines of what happened are clear. On January 14, 1753, Joseph Salvador, a wealthy and prominent Sephardi,[8] sent a memorandum to the Duke of Newcastle. It began with a plain statement of the Jews' request: "It is desired that it be enacted, that any person professing the Jewish religion whom it may in future be thought proper to naturalize, shall in lieu of taking the Holy Sacrament, take the oaths of Supremacy and Allegiance, or such other oaths as may be thought proper, on or before the second reading of the Bill for naturalizing him in either of the Houses of Parliament."[9] This was followed by seven brief "reasons" why such a measure would be a just one, and would be in the interest of both the nation at large and the present Government. (There was no explicit reference to the Jews' more particular reasons for wishing the law changed, namely, the alien duties and the shortcomings of denization.)

This concise, unsigned memorandum, so unlike the inflated "may-it-please-your-Grace" petitions that Newcastle was accustomed to receiving, presupposes the occurrence of earlier negotiations with the duke or some other prominent politician. No doubt Joseph Salvador played a large part in these discussions, but the point is unimportant. For Salvador, in submitting the memorandum, was certainly acting for the committee of deputies, as had been the person—whether Salvador himself, another Jew, or a Christian intermediary—who first raised the question of naturalization with those in or close to the Ministry.[10]

Actually, in spite of the strong official backing this effort received from the Wardens and Elders of the Synagogue, it later transpired that Jewish opinion was not uniformly favorable to the attempt.[11] We know the views of Samson Gideon, and there were no doubt other native-born Jews who concluded, as he seems to have done, that at best the measure could confer no benefit on them personally,

---

[8] Salvador was himself a native-born subject. Picciotto, pp. 162–163.

[9] Add. MSS. 33053, ff. 56–57. (Reprinted in Roth, *Anglo-Jewish Letters*, p. 129.)

[10] P. C. Webb, the community's solicitor, was also active in these negotiations (Hyamson, *Sephardim of England*, p. 128n).

[11] Barnett, *Bevis Marks Records*, I, 40–41; *LEP*, 3979:1 (May 19).

and at worst it might stir up a clamor (as had Nugent's general naturalization bills) and so bring trouble down upon them and the entire community. Gideon, in fact, became so angered at the Wardens for representing the whole community, and apparently Gideon himself by name, as being in favor of the Bill, that he formally severed his connection with the synagogue. But particular circumstances had much to do with Gideon's dramatic retirement from the congregation; we must not exaggerate the significance of this incident or make too much of the divisions of opinion within the synagogue.[12]

More important and more interesting, if we but knew something of them, would be the views of the various politicians with whom the Jews consulted on their bill and its prospects. Unfortunately we do not know for certain who these men were. Robert Nugent was one, in all likelihood; he was among the Bill's most strenuous advocates in the House of Commons; and probably Lord Halifax, the enlightened president of the Board of Trade: he introduced the Bill in the Lords, and several of his personal friends were prominent supporters of the Bill in the lower house.[13]

But welcome as the support of such men must have been, the Jews needed still more the backing of the Triumvirs—Henry Pelham, the Duke of Newcastle (Pelham's brother), and Lord Chancellor Hardwicke—who could assure the success of the Bill by putting the Government's majority behind it; and this backing they obtained without apparent difficulty.

Although assuredly both the politicians and the Jews honestly believed that the proposed change in the naturalization laws was sound public policy, we may reasonably assert, without in the least disparaging either group, that their negotiations rested upon a

[12] Sutherland, "Samson Gideon: Eighteenth Century Jewish Financier," p. 85. See Gideon's letter of resignation in Roth, *Anglo-Jewish Letters,* pp. 131–132; and for another version of the story see Add. MSS. 35398, f. 158 (Birch to Yorke, Sept. 8).

[13] The fact that Salvador's memorandum was addressed to Newcastle does not necessarily indicate that the duke was the central figure in the first consultations; such matters fell within his official purview as secretary of state (northern). On Halifax's friends, see Richard Cumberland, *Memoirs* (London, 1807), I, 160.

narrower base. As the *Gentleman's Magazine* later put it, the intention of the measure was to confer a favor: "the Bill was intended for private purposes, which alone it seems calculated to answer." [14] No doubt the petitioners were sincere when they spoke of encouraging rich foreign Jews to come to England. The removal of any legal disability must have meant something to them in terms of prestige as well. But clearly the primary purpose of the Bill was to make possible the naturalization not of prospective immigrants, but rather of foreign-born Jews already resident in England. Such persons, as we have seen, were subject to the alien duties, even if they had been made denizens; and it was from this commercial discrimination that they wished to be set free. [15]

The ministers, for their part, were obliged to the Jews for their frequent and valuable cooperation in official financial matters. And more generally, the ministers appreciated the fact (of which Salvador reminded them in his memorandum) that the Jews had always been firm supporters of both the Hanoverian dynasty and the Whig interest. Their loyalty had been conspicuously demonstrated in the late rebellion, as even their worst enemies could not wholly deny. [16] So when the Jews solicited support for their bill, the Ministry had every reason to be sympathetic. The favor requested was a small one; it was no more than just; it was consistent, as we shall see, with long-standing Whig policy on immigration; and from the point of view of these Whig politicians, it was eminently deserved.

[14] *Gent. Mag.*, 1753:354.

[15] That relief from these duties was the principal aim of the Bill was flatly stated in two public defenses of the measure. (*Gent. Mag.*, 1753:280, 352.) Another advocate mentioned that among those who were soliciting the Bill, "partly for themselves," were certain deserving aliens who had resided in London "upwards of forty years." These men wished to be naturalized, he said, chiefly for disinterested and patriotic reasons, but also partly in order to obtain the "several private advantages, which naturalized subjects enjoy, that aliens cannot." That the alien duties were meant is made clear in another part of the same pamphlet, where the author, in attempting to show how harmless the Bill was, pointed out that it would not convey "the least right in the City, *except a trifling exemption of duties in the Custom House*" (Philo-Patriae, *Considerations*, pp. 47, 39; my emphasis).

[16] [Romaine], *Answer*, p. 81; *P. Hist.*, XIV, 1402.

Such, then, were the reasons for the Ministry's accession to the Jews' request; and given our knowledge of later developments, the terms and extent of the ministers' commitment can be reconstructed with equal confidence. The ministers were willing to recommend the Bill to their friends and to support it openly themselves; but lest things should go wrong, they limited their involvement in two important respects, just as they had with Nugent's General Naturalization Bill of 1751. First, they did not adopt the Bill as a formal measure of Government; and second, they were prepared to drop it, as they had actually done with Nugent's, if it should arouse enough opposition to threaten them with serious political embarrassment.[17]

In this spirit the Pelham government accepted limited sponsorship of the Jews' proposal. A bill was drafted;[18] Lord Halifax, after carefully considering how the measure stood "with regard to policy, law, and religion," agreed to introduce it;[19] and on April 3, 1753, toward the end of a dull parliamentary term whose quiet nobody expected it to disturb, the Jew Bill was read for the first time in the House of Lords.

[17] Add. MSS. 35606, f. 77 (quoted in Chapter VIII, below); *Considerations,* p. 54.
[18] Apparently by Thomas Sewell, a lawyer who took an especial interest in the rights of religious minorities. L. B. Namier, *The Structure of Politics at the Accession of George III* (London, 1957), p. 371; *Hist. MSS. Comm.,* 15th Rept., App. VI, p. 207 (*Carlisle papers*).
[19] Add. MSS. 32733, f. 239 (Halifax to Newcastle, Nov. 12).

IV

THE POLITICAL SCENE
OF THE EARLY 1750's

EVERYTHING seemed to point to the Bill's easy and quiet passage. Of course this appearance proved to be deceptive: so before examining the Bill and recounting its enactment into law, we shall pause and look more closely at the political situation, noting especially—with the benefit of hindsight—the existence of certain adverse portents and possibilities.

The chief characteristics of the English political scene of the early 1750's were first, the continuing ascendancy of the Whigs under the leadership of the Pelham brothers, who were backing the Bill; and second, the remarkably peaceful or even dull state of public affairs in general. The two were interconnected, of course, and were soon to be overturned together, with the coming of the Seven Years' War, the rise of Pitt, and the new reign. But the historian as much as the poet has need of what Keats called "negative capability," and in this instance he must put out of his mind all consciousness of these great events, which were as yet unforeseen.

"In the course of this whole session," wrote Lord Chesterfield in early 1753 to a friend traveling abroad, "there has hardly been a debate in either House of Parliament. You have therefore lost nothing . . . by your absence from this idle and inactive scene at home." [1] Not quite a year later Horace Walpole echoed Chesterfield's observation: "The House of Commons is become a mere quarter sessions, where nothing is transacted but turnpikes and poor rates. If it were not for some little storms that now and then

[1] *The Letters of Philip Dormer Stanhope, 4th Earl of Chesterfield,* ed. Bonamy Dobrée (London, 1932), V, 2021 (May 17, to the future Lord Huntingdon).

blow over from Ireland, one should scarce distinguish London from York or Bristol." [2]

Fundamental to this general political peace was the fact that the old two-party order of things had all but completely broken down. Though there were occasional skirmishes between Whigs and Tories, doctrinal struggles of the sort that had convulsed England in Queen Anne's reign had long been unknown.

There were two reasons for this. The more obvious was the failure of the Tory party to recover as an organized political force from the disastrous collapse of 1714–1722. By 1753 the parliamentary Tories had dwindled to a mere remnant of the once-great party of Oxford and Bolingbroke. In large measure, then, the prevailing peace was one that had been imposed as the result of a tactical triumph. But the long lull in Whig and Tory warfare reflected, and grew out of, deeper realities as well. After all, the traditional doctrinal differences between Whigs and Tories were largely irrelevant to the political actualities of 1753. The great issues over which the parties had been formed—the prerogative, the succession, the rights of the Dissenters and the position of the Established Church—these had long ago been either settled definitively or compromised at points of accommodation where matters were likely to stand for a long time in the future. The Tories in particular were discomfited, for events had totally destroyed the consistency of their traditional position. As Feiling says, "their stately ship of 'Church and King' had sunk beneath them," leaving the survivors clinging to a few unconnected bits of flotsam. [3]

Both the Tory collapse and the ideological truce contributed, each in its own way, to bring about the opportunism and the factional scrambling for power and patronage that characterized mid-eighteenth-century politics. The long monopoly of office by one party naturally led to disunity in both, so that by 1753 political competition had become, as Chesterfield put it, a matter "chiefly [of] Whig against Whig, for the Tories are pretty much out of the

[2] *Letters*, III, 208 (Feb. 10, 1754).
[3] K. G. Feiling, *The Second Tory Party, 1714–1832* (London, 1951), p. 55.

question." [4] The absence of doctrinal contention likewise tended toward the fragmentation of politics: for "where great questions end, little parties begin." [5]

But in the early 1750's even the maneuvers and intrigues of the "little parties" were at a minimum. Not only was the political scene free of major doctrinal battles; it was also largely undisturbed by minor factional skirmishes.

In part this was the result of a deliberate policy of appeasement on the part of the Pelhams, who, once in office, found political calm very much to their interest and inclination, and did all they could to preserve it. Like Sir Robert Walpole, whose direct political descendants they were, they followed the maxim *Quieta non movere,* aiming at conciliation and retrenchment both at home and abroad, and avoiding contention and controversy of all sorts wherever possible.[6] This policy was so successful that the bitter-end opponents of the Court, deprived of genuine handles for controversy, were forced either to make shift with inflated trifles or, even more tenuously, to pretend, as did one pamphleteer, that the policy of conciliation was itself a subtle danger to English liberty: "For whereas the unmasked tyranny of Jeffreys and his associates only served to exasperate and rouse the nation to defend itself, the mild and gracious measures of our present exalted and idolized Triumvirate might, on the contrary, lull us into a false security, dangerous to ourselves, and fatal to posterity." [7]

It was also to a particular piece of good fortune, as well as to their own exertions, that the Pelhams owed this period of comparative immunity from factional threats to their power. In accordance with the unhappy tradition in the House of Brunswick, the chief and willing focus of the opposition to George II and his ministers was the heir to the throne, Frederick, Prince of Wales. Around Frederick

[4] *Letters,* V, 2059 (Nov. 16).

[5] Walter Bagehot, *The English Constitution* (London, 1952), p. 231.

[6] Coxe, *Pelham,* II, 301–303. When Henry Pelham died, George II exclaimed, "Now I shall have no more peace!"

[7] [James Ralph], *The Protester,* 3:16 (June 16).

had gathered an ill-assorted faction composed largely of men who either from nice calculation or plain necessity had placed their hopes in the next, rather than the present, reign. Naturally the attractive power of this rival court was tending to increase as the king grew older and men began, as the saying was, to turn from the setting to the rising sun. In the 1740's Frederick had even begun to enter his own parliamentary candidates against those of the Court. While these attempts were not highly successful, the prince's popularity and prestige—greatly enhanced by the universal dislike of his brother, "Butcher" Cumberland—were clearly rising, and provided the Ministry with a constant source of concern.[8]

Then in 1751 Frederick suddenly died; anticipated places, pensions, and peerages vanished into air, and with them the unity of the principal opposition to the Pelham ministry. "What an event," exulted a Court Whig in reporting the news: "How many dreams of greatness ended at once! Their imagined splendours, and their meditated vengeance hereafter, all undone and vanished! Well, I will only say, that *worthy honest* men may now do what is right, and meet with no thwartings and difficulty, in making the latter part of his Majesty's life and reign, easy, happy and glorious to him." [9]

Of course the death of the prince did not banish forever all the difficulties of the "worthy honest" Court Whigs; but it did have a decided tranquilizing effect on the politics of the next three or four years—that is, until the war threw up new problems and a new leader. Chesterfield, writing almost two years after Frederick's death, confirmed the continuing influence of that event: "Publick matters here continue in the same quiet and inactive state in which the death of the late Prince of Wales put them, and are likely to continue so some time longer. For though private interest wants no spur, faction wants a head to conduct it." [10]

So much, then, for the general political climate of the early 1750's;

[8] Coxe, I, 379, and II, 50–51; Feiling, *Second Tory Party*, pp. 38, 52–54; J. B. Owen, *The Rise of the Pelhams* (London, 1957), p. 79; and Romney Sedgwick, "Frederick, Prince of Wales," *History Today*, June 1961, 410–416.

[9] Mr. Harris to Sir C. H. Williams, Mar. 22, 1751, in Coxe, *Pelham*, II, 165–166.

[10] *Letters*, V, 1978 (Nov. 21, 1752).

and about the exact alignment of forces at the time the Jew Bill was introduced, little need be said. Disregarding the Jacobites and certain lesser "connexions" whose existence had no effect upon the history of the Bill, we can divide the politicians of 1753 into three broad categories: supporters of the Pelham ministry, disaffected Whigs, and Tories.

The ministerialists formed by far the largest group. Most of them were Whigs of the "old corps" that had provided Sir Robert Walpole with his majorities. But the conciliatory and prudent Pelhams had strongly reinforced the old corps with converts from earlier oppositions such as Pitt, erstwhile "Patriot" and now paymaster-general, and Nugent, formerly a supporter of the prince.[11] They had also welcomed back to the fold, often upon the very slightest indication of regeneracy, Whigs who had previously deserted the old corps for the prince's or some other opposing faction; the opportunist Dodington was typical of these.

The disaffected Whigs formed a category, but not a single unified group. It was they who had been hardest hit by the death of the prince; without this rallying point, and with their ranks sadly thinned by defections to the forgiving Pelhams, they were now little more than an irritant to the Ministry. In 1753 the only considerable unified body of opposition Whigs was a hungry faction whose half-hearted and tractable "leader" was the Duke of Bedford, an enemy of the Pelhams.[12]

Although in 1753 the Tories were, as I have said, a mere shadow of what they once had been, they were by no means extinct. Their voting strength in the House of Commons was far from contemptible, and their weight was disproportionate to their numbers: for the Tories made up a majority of the knights of the shire, a group that enjoyed an undoubted prestige based upon both the large size and the reputed independence of the county electorates.[13] Even one of

---

[11] Claud Nugent, *Memoir of Robert, Earl Nugent* (Chicago, 1898), pp. 31–41.

[12] Horace Walpole, *Memoirs of the Reign of King George the Second* (London, 1847), I, 240.

[13] Feiling, p. 55; Owen, *Pelhams*, p. 259.

their stoutest Old Whig enemies granted that in the country as a
whole the Tories were "not inconsiderable in numbers," but were
rendered ineffective by the want of leadership and of a viable unify-
ing principle. It is in this sense, and with these qualifications, that
we should understand Chesterfield's remark about the Tories' being
"pretty much out of the question." [14]

In 1753, then, the Pelhams were in an enviable position. They had
the complete confidence of George II; their majority in the sitting
Parliament was more than ample, and with the opposition so weak
and divided, the prospects for the future were even brighter. Chesterfield, for example, looking to the approaching general election, predicted that the worst the Pelhams had to fear from the result was
an excess of good fortune: "After the new Parliament shall be
chosen, the greatest difficulty upon the administration will be, to find
pasture enough for the beasts they must feed." [15]

Thus far this brief sketch of the politics and parties of 1753 has
not departed from the views of most contemporary scholars, who,
led by the late Sir Lewis Namier, have come to agree upon the
essentially factional (or even personal) and nondoctrinal nature of
mid-eighteenth-century politics. With the addition of some remarks
on the position and personality of the king, the foregoing summary—
based, as I say, on orthodox or "Namierite" views—provides a suitable *mise en scène* for almost every political episode of 1751–1754.

Such a summary is not, however, adequate to lay the groundwork
for a thorough understanding of the history of the Jew Bill. True,
the orthodox approach is highly relevant to much, or even most,
of that history. But certain features of the episode were out of the
ordinary, and if we are to understand them rightly we must give
more attention than is usually done to the continuing existence, even
in the Pelham era, of Whig and Tory attitudes and loyalties.

[14] Add. MSS. 35606, f. 79 (H. Walpole, Sen., to Yorke, July 23). Trevelyan speaks
of "the latent strength of disorganized Toryism" in this period ("The Two-Party
System in English Political History," in *An Autobiography and Other Essays*, London,
1949, p. 192).

[15] *Letters*, V, 2059 (Nov. 16).

My differences, at bottom, are not so much with Sir Lewis Namier himself as with the tendency to simplify or distort his observation that the old party denominations were rarely of much consequence in this period—which is correct—into the assertion that they were totally meaningless—which is wrong. In insisting upon this distinction, one must be careful not to make too much of what is by far the lesser part of the truth; but that part ought not to be overlooked altogether. For the words "Whig" and "Tory" were far from devoid of meaning or of emotional potency, even in the 1750's.[16]

This survival need not surprise us overmuch. It is true that the old issues were dead or dormant: but new ones had not yet arisen to replace them and efface their memory. It is true that the last real Whig and Tory struggles were far in the past: but political memories were longer than they are in our day, when more frequent and more fundamental changes thrust upon us a succession of greatly varying problems and crises, each of which crowds off the stage many of the attitudes that grew up about its predecessor. In that very different age, then, memories—especially of the reign of Queen Anne—sufficed to keep the old distinctions alive and (as many people still thought) meaningful.

The extent to which the events of the latter half of Anne's reign influenced the political attitudes of forty years later is truly remarkable, and has not been sufficiently noted. The speeches, controversial literature, and even private letters on the Naturalization Act of 1753 are full of references to the Sacheverell Case, for example; and in one of the debates on the repeal of the act, the House of Commons found itself involved in a lengthy and heated argument over the merits of the Peace of Utrecht.[17] The violence of the partisanship that could still be aroused by those remote events is suggested by this passage from a private letter written in 1753 by a Whig stalwart, Horace Walpole, Sen.: "I have in the heart to look back into past transactions, and to unmask that wicked impostor B[olingbroke],

[16] For a more thorough and somewhat more critical discussion of the Namier position on party in this period, see Appendix A.

[17] *P. Hist.*, XV, 143–153. (See Chapter VIII, below.)

whose villainous ministry and measures have been the source, from whence all the difficulties, debts, and distresses, that have embarrassed this nation, both in domestick and foreign concerns, ever since the Peace of Utrecht, have directly flowed."

He then sputters on about the works of "that charlatan," and "the falsehoods advanced in almost every page." [18] No doubt we must allow for the fact that Walpole had himself participated in those affairs; but we must not suppose that the Whig and Tory struggles of Anne's reign were meaningful only to crabbed and tiresome veterans. For example, when the conduct of the Bolingbroke ministry came under discussion in the debate referred to above, the Tory case was argued by a member who had been born only in 1722. [19]

So far were they from thinking that party was dead, the men to whom these memories were most vivid believed that it was as alive as ever, and that the present political calm was temporary and deceptive. Thus after the party clamor against the Jew Bill had begun, old Horace Walpole—who blamed all the trouble, in his outspoken fashion, on "a worthless set of Jacobites"—professed to be not at all surprised at its intensity and extent: "I did not at all wonder that it spread with such violence among all sorts of people of a certain denomination and principles, in politicks, for gentlemen of that complexion, as well as the vulgar, though otherwise of good sense, are strangers to all moderation when they have any the least handle, to asperse and calumniate the present government and administration, and although certain circumstances too long to explain, had spread a face of calm and tranquility over the nation, yet the minds of a certain party are not at all altered: the apparent dead ashes cover sparks, that the least breath will kindle into flame." [20]

Of course this was an exaggeration: forty years had moderated the

---

[18] Add. MSS. 35606, f. 80 (Walpole to Yorke, July 23). None of this anger is attributable to Bolingbroke's heterodox posthumous philosophical works, which had not yet been published.

[19] William Northey. *P. Hist.*, XV, 147–148; G. P. Judd, *Members of Parliament, 1734–1832* (New Haven, 1955), p. 290.

[20] Add. MSS. 35606, ff. 84–85 (Walpole to Yorke, Sept. 29).

partisanship of most men, even if not of Walpole and some of the more passionate of the Tories. But the controversy over the Naturalization Act of 1753 indicates that although attenuated by the passage of time and usually dormant for want of an occasion, the old passions were still present in many breasts, ready to revive or to *be* revived whenever a question touching upon the traditional party positions arose.

Renewals of Whig and Tory hostilities were rare by 1753, as I have said; and such partisan conflicts as did occur[21] were concerned, as a rule, not with current policies or legislation, but with past events or disputes over Jacobitism. In addition, however, there was at least one fairly important and as yet unsettled question of policy that retained enough vitality to reanimate the old feelings of party. This potentially explosive topic was the question of immigration and naturalization, on which the main bodies of both parties had maintained consistent and directly conflicting views through four parliamentary encounters, the earliest of them dating back to the reign of William and Mary. Then, and ever since, Whigs had been the champions of what we would call a "liberal" policy, Tories of an "exclusionist" one.

The first major encounter between Whig liberals and Tory exclusionists occurred in the session of 1693–94, when a Whig member brought in a bill for the naturalization of foreign Protestants.[22] The cities of northern Europe then swarmed with exiled Huguenots and

[21] E.g., the Oxfordshire election of 1754 (see Chapter IX) and the allegations of Jacobitism in 1753 against the governors of Prince George. The latter affair was, to be exact, partly factional as well as doctrinal—like the controversy over the Jew Bill itself (Coxe, *Pelham*, II, 238–239; Walpole, *George II*, I, 298–332).

[22] The exact provisions of the bill are not known, but probably were the same as those of the act of 1709. For this episode see T. B. Macaulay, *History of England* (London, 1913–1915), V, 2424–2426; *P. Hist.*, V, 849–857; *Journals of the House of Commons*, XI, 28–129, *passim;* and the contemporary publications cited below. Actually there were at least three earlier general naturalization bills (in 1667, 1672, and 1680; see Anchitell Grey, *Debates of the House of Commons*, London, 1763, I, 56, II, 154–157, and VIII, 225–226). But though those debates in some respects foreshadowed the later ones, the controversy did not assume its full-blown partisan aspect until after the revolution.

with Protestant refugees from the devastated Palatinate. These people, it was argued, would make respectable and industrious subjects. The war had cost many thousands of English lives, and to make up the deficiency not only would be objectively beneficial to the economy but also, by adding to the total strength of the kingdom, would be a "mortification to our grand enemy at Versailles."[23] Besides, Protestant England owed these refugees her charity and protection. Finally, there is no doubt that politicians of narrower views reasoned that since these people would all be Dissenters, their admission would benefit the Whig party.

Tories, on the other hand, opposed the bill for reasons of religion, party advantage, and ultrapatriotism. They were not slow to perceive that any foreigner, however irreproachable in his Protestantism, could hardly, by definition, be a thorough Church of England man, much less a High Churchman. Thus a Tory broadside urged the exclusion of foreigners in order that "the Protestant religion [might be] kept pure and undefiled";[24] and a pamphlet expressed fears that the influx of aliens might "corrupt [Christianity] to a kind of mungril religion."[25] And to the Tories, as to the Whigs, the political corollary of this religious "peril" was obvious.

In addition to these religious and party reasons for opposing immigration, the Tories were influenced by attitudes that one can characterize only as nationalist or even jingo. One pamphleteer feared that a general naturalization "would in a little time surcharge the Kingdom with aliens, and either drive out, streighten, consume, or quite blot out the *English* Nation."[26] Our chief parliamentary memorial of this episode is in the same vein. It is a fiery rant against all foreigners by Sir John Knight, a Jacobite member, who concluded his remarks with this elegant motion: "that the Serjeant be com-

[23] *Some Seasonable Queries on . . . a General Naturalization* [London?, 1694], p. 3.
[24] *A Brief and Summary Narrative of the many Mischiefs and Inconveniencies . . . Occasioned by Naturalizing of Aliens* [London?, 1694?]. Not paged.
[25] *Sundry Considerations touching Naturalization of Aliens* [London?, 1695?], p. 11.
[26] *Ibid.*, p. 7.

manded to open the doors, and let us first kick the Bill out of the House, and then foreigners out of the Kingdom." [27] This speech, printed by the tens of thousands and widely circulated, had a great effect, and though the bill had a majority at the early stages, the opposition gained such strength that the proposal was dropped.

The question next came to the fore in 1709, when a Whig bill was introduced to permit the naturalization, without a private act, of foreigners who took the necessary oaths to the Government and received communion in any Protestant church.[28] The parties re-occupied the old battle-lines; Whig majorities in both Houses easily beat down Tory amendments specifying the *Anglican* Sacrament as the test, and went on to enact the original bill into law.[29]

In the year following over ten thousand German refugees migrated to England to take advantage of the act. Two thousand of them had to be sent home when they were found to be Papists, and most of those who were allowed to remain were hardly more welcome. Almost all of them were destitute—indeed, this seems to have been the chief reason why many of them came to England—and the "poor Palatines," as they were called, became a serious burden upon the English economy in a notoriously hard year.

A general outcry arose against them, abetted, with a view to the approaching elections, by the Tories. One pamphlet flatly gave its opinion "that whoever advised the bringing over [of] the poor Palatines into this Kingdom, was an enemy to the Queen and King-

[27] [Sir John Knight], *The following Speech being spoke off hand upon the Debates in the House of Commons . . .* [London?, 1694]. Not paged. (Reprinted in *P. Hist.*, V, 851–857.)

[28] For this episode see Trevelyan, *England under Queen Anne, Vol. III: The Peace and the Protestant Succession* (London, 1948), pp. 35–38; Gilbert Burnet, *History of His Own Times* (Oxford, 1823), V, 398–399; *P. Hist.*, VI, 780–783; *Commons' Journals*, XVI, 108–143, *passim; Journals of the House of Lords*, XVIII, 660–668; and the contemporary pamphlets cited below in notes 29–33.

[29] Swift called Burnet a "Dog" for opposing the amendment (Burnet, *History*, V, 399n). A purported division list was published in a Tory pamphlet entitled *A View of the Queen and Kingdom's Enemies in the Case of the Poor Palatines* [London?, 1711?], pp. 14ff.

dom." [30] Embarrassed Whig notables who had taken the lead in raising money to relieve the distress of these people found even their charity turned against them by uncompromising Tory controversialists: "Happy was he amongst the Whig-Party that could most distinguish himself by his bounty to these strangers that were come to devour the land, when he had no bowels of compassion for the wants of his fellow-subjects . . . While our own native poor were starving without any manner of provision made for them, [wealthy Whigs preferred to bestow their alms upon] . . . a parcel of vagabonds who might have lived comfortably enough in their native country, had not the laziness of their dispositions, and the report of our known generosity drawn them out of it." [31]

After their smashing electoral victory of 1710 (to which, according to Trevelyan, the discontent over the Palatines contributed) the Tories repealed the Whig act.[32] But in spite of this disappointment and defeat, Whigs continued to advocate a more liberal naturalization policy. A Whig pamphlet of 1714, for example, not only defended the repealed act as "public-spirited," but went on to recommend the naturalization of the Jews. The author doubted whether this proposal would prove very popular, but he brought it forward all the same, feeling, he said, that he could best serve his country by "the promoting of humanity, and the doing good to all mankind." [33]

The issue was next raised in Parliament as the War of the Austrian Succession was drawing to a close. There was much talk at that

[30] *A View of the Queen and Kingdom's Enemies,* p. 9.

[31] *Ibid.,* pp. 6, 7. This pamphlet, cited above as the source of the names of those who supported the bill, also contains (pp. 10–11) a list of the (Whig) trustees of the fund to assist the poor Palatines. As this quotation shows, the author's purpose was something other than to celebrate the charitable actions of his political opponents. Cf. Burnet, IV, 34: "All the Tories declared against the good reception that was given them, as much as the Whigs approved of it."

[32] Burnet, VI, 35; *P. Hist.,* VI, 1000, 1088–1089; *Commons' Journals,* XVI, 470–472, and XVII, 26–34; *Lords' Journals,* XIX, 215. The repeal was first passed by the Commons in 1711, but was summarily rejected by the Lords. Twenty-six peers registered formal dissents against the rejection. In 1712 the Commons sent up a second repealing bill, and the Lords acquiesced.

[33] *Reasons for Naturalizing the Jews in Great Britain and Ireland* (London, 1714), pp. 5, 8.

time (as in 1693 and 1709) about the need to encourage immigration in order to make good the losses incurred in the war, and thus help England hold her own in the unrelenting commercial rivalry which mercantilist thought decreed to be the essence of international relationships in time of "peace." [34] In consequence, Robert Nugent introduced, in 1747 and 1751, the proposal to naturalize foreign Protestants, which was mentioned in the preceding chapter as having encouraged the Jews to apply for changes in the law as it affected them.

The arguments for and against the proposal were couched largely in economic terms, and to some people the issue was in fact primarily one of economics rather than of party politics. But in spite of the long interval since the last party struggle over naturalization, others regarded the measure in a political light, viewing it not as mere *ad hoc* economic expedient, but as a renewed Whig effort on behalf of a traditional and favorite party scheme. Thus Horace Walpole, in recounting the history of this attempt at a general naturalization, referred to the measure as "a favourite Whig point, overthrown in the Queen's time by the narrow ignorance of the Tories";[35] the City of London, in its petition against the bill of 1747, specifically mentioned the two earlier naturalization proposals and condemned them in strong partisan language;[36] and at an important Tory banquet, the bill was honored with a derisive toast that employed almost the exact words of Sir John Knight's famous speech and broadside of 1694, "that the Naturalization Bill may be kicked out of the House, and the foreigners out of the Kingdom." [37]

Nevertheless, because of a particular circumstance quite irrelevant to the naturalization controversy, the bill of 1747 failed to obtain the firm support of the Ministry and so did not survive its second reading. At first Henry Pelham had encouraged the bill—"from

---

[34] *P. Hist.*, XIV, 133–140, and 133n.

[35] Walpole, *George II*, I, 44–45.

[36] *P. Hist.*, XIV, 133–135. Coxe also points out the relation between the Whig bills of 1709 and 1747. (*Pelham*, II, 179–180.)

[37] Joseph Grego, *A History of Parliamentary Elections and Electioneering* (London, 1892), p. 108, quoting the *London Evening Post*.

party principle," says the Whig chronicler Coxe, as well as from considerations of political economy. But when the City protested so vehemently against the proposal, the minister professed himself indifferent to the fate of the bill, even though he still approved of it in principle.[38] This retreat, according to Walpole, was a consequence of Pelham's determination not to offend Sir John Barnard, the leader of the City's opposition to the bill. Barnard's support of several government loans to carry on the war had been invaluable, and his continued cooperation with the Ministry was essential to the success of Pelham's great project of reducing the interest rate on the national debt, which undertaking was not completed until 1750.[39]

In 1751, with this impediment removed, Pelham gave his "cordial concurrence" to Nugent's decision to reintroduce his bill. Again the measure was strongly opposed; according to Walpole, "the Tories to a man were against it"; and as in 1747 the City of London petitioned against its passage.[40] But this time the influence of the minister was behind the bill. When it was first attacked, Pelham "strenuously supported" it, and his influence carried it at the second reading, in spite of the City's strong petition. The bill's majorities decreased at each successive stage of its progress, however, and the protests without doors kept growing louder. The death of the Prince of Wales caused the third reading to be postponed; then there was a second postponement, and during the interval petitions opposing the measure came in from eight provincial towns—most of them Tory strongholds.[41]

At this point the prudent and peace-loving minister again withdrew his support from the unpopular measure. Pelham's retreat resulted in further defections and these, together with the desertion

---

[38] Coxe, *Pelham,* I, 386–387, and II, 179–180; *Commons' Journals,* XXV, 499. Nugent was at this time a member of the prince's faction, and the Pelhams were in no way obligated to him.

[39] Walpole, *George II,* I, 45; L. Sutherland, "Samson Gideon and the Reduction of Interest, 1749–50," *Economic History Review,* 16:24 (1946).

[40] Coxe, II, 180; Walpole, *George II,* I, 92; *P. Hist.,* XIV, 971.

[41] Coxe, II, 180; *P. Hist.,* XIV, 971–972. There were petitions against the bill from Bristol, Thetford, Rochester, Southampton, Oxford, Salisbury, Reading, and Gloucester. There were also two petitions in favor of the bill, both from Bristol.

of the Bedford Whigs (see below), were sufficient to sink the bill. A motion for its being immediately accorded a third reading was narrowly defeated, and the bill, postponed for a third time, "was no more heard of." [42]

The history of the Naturalization Bill of 1751 is enlightening in several respects which bear importantly upon that of the Jew Bill of two years later. First, it shows how this traditionally controversial issue still retained the power at least briefly to infuse new life into old party animosities, and how, given an occasion, Whigs and Tories could still rally about the badly faded standards behind which, in days now distant but well remembered, they or their ancestors had marched into battle. Thus we see such Whigs as Pelham and young Horace Walpole regarding the bill chiefly in party terms, and the Tories for their part opposing it "to a man." [43]

Yet these events also convey a clear warning against making too much of this point, by providing, as they surely do, strong confirmatory evidence for Namier's thesis concerning the diluted strength and diminished importance of party doctrines and party loyalty in this period. For against the momentary awakening of party spirit must be set the fact that in the end "a strong Whig Parliament"—the words are those of the chancellor[44]—refused to carry this "favourite Whig point."

Indeed, it is altogether possible that the bill would have fared not worse, but better, if the Tory opposition in the House had been more numerous. As a result of the Tory collapse, the nominal Whig majority was so massive that factional maneuvering within it had replaced the old two-party conflict as the essential stuff of politics.[45]

---

[42] Coxe, II, 180; *P. Hist.*, XIV, 972.

[43] Note also the title of a pamphlet in favor of the bill: *Some Thoughts upon a Bill for General Naturalization: Addressed to Those of all Denominations who act upon Whig Principles* (London, 1751).

[44] P. C. Yorke, *The Life and Correspondence of Philip Yorke, Earl of Hardwicke* (Cambridge, Eng., 1913), II, 82 (Hardwicke to Abp. Herring, Oct. 20, 1747).

[45] The parallel with the Democratic party in the southern United States hardly needs mentioning.

Thus a leader such as Henry Pelham (of whose cautious tactics this episode provides a good example) regarded a victory for Whig over Tory principles as far too dearly bought if for any reason the struggle to achieve it placed much strain upon the bonds that held his current coalition together.

Similarly, each of the factions that made up the so-called Whig majority was always ready to prefer a particular competitive advantage over party principle whenever the two conflicted. Thus at the time of the debates over Nugent's second bill, the Bedford Whigs were formally allied to the Pelhams, but were, for various reasons, in the process of loosening the ties that bound them to the coalition. As one step in their maneuvers (and one that incidentally gave them a chance to gain support among the bill's enemies) the Bedfords quit the House before the final and crucial division, in which the motion for the bill was defeated by only thirteen votes.[46] So in the end such Whig party zeal as the bill had attracted at its early stages faded before the centrifugal tendencies of the politics of the Pelham era, and the measure was lost.

At the same time, this episode shows how the Tory remnant, as a result of its different situation, could, at least on occasion, behave far more like a true doctrinal party than could the Whigs. For where the several Whig factions would naturally ignore party principle in order to gain or hold power, the main body of the Tories, like all oppositions without prospect of office, were able to stick to their principles at all costs—or rather, at no cost. Held together almost entirely by memories, personal relationships, and by a sentimental zeal for causes most of which had long ago been rendered nugatory by events, the Tories welcomed battles over issues that touched upon those parts of their traditional faith which still retained relevance and meaning, because such battles "gave them something to be Tories about."[47]

Finally, there remains the question of why the City of London

[46] Coxe, II, 163; Walpole, *George II*, I, 92.
[47] The phrase within quotation marks is adapted from Richard Pares, *King George III and the Politicians* (Oxford, 1953), p. 72.

should have joined the Tories in opposing these naturalization projects, and whether there was any reason to expect the merchants to
assert themselves in the same strenuous manner against the Jew Bill.

To a certain extent, and in certain people, the City's anti-immigration stand was part of the Tory tradition, or was at least closely
related to it. Namier, for example, uses the word "Tory" to describe
the City's politics in this period;[48] loyal Whigs were in the habit of
classifying leading City politicians as Tories or even Jacobites;[49] and
a City M.P. could speak out quite as strongly as any country Tory
about the need to defend the Established Church and the Test Act.[50]

Still it will not do to make too much of this, since the City's
Toryism seems to have been not so much a positive political creed
as a medium through which the lesser merchants gave voice, under
a Whig regime, to the same antipathy toward the central Government that was expressed by violent Whiggism in the Restoration
period, and by Radicalism in the reign of George III.[51] So in
describing the relation between the City and the Tory positions on
immigration and naturalization, we should speak more of coincidence than of identity: for the City's thinking on these subjects was
chiefly influenced by economic considerations—that is, by various
interests, theories, and prejudices—whose effect was to bring most
of the merchants into agreement with the exclusionist policy of the
nationalist and High Church Tories.

The assumption that underlay the merchants' arguments was the
widely accepted conception of the national economy as more or less
static (except in its relation to the economies of competing mercantile powers). From this, and from the general belief that each

[48] *England in the Age of the American Revolution* (London, 1930), p. 211.

[49] E.g., in the Duke of Newcastle's analysis of the Parliament of 1754, three of
the four City members are listed as opponents of the Government, two of them
being specifically called Tories. The fourth (Barnard) is listed as "doubtful" (Add.
MSS. 33034, ff. 178, 179). For "Jacobite," see Add. MSS. 35606, ff. 79, 84, 85 (H.
Walpole, Sen., to Yorke, July 23, Sept. 29).

[50] *P. Hist.*, XIV, 1389.

[51] Namier, *England in the Age of the American Revolution,* pp. 211–212; Lucy
Sutherland, "The City of London in Eighteenth-Century Politics," in *Essays presented
to Sir Lewis Namier,* ed. R. Pares and A. J. P. Taylor (London, 1956), pp. 54–55.

particular branch of trade was already "overstocked," [52] it followed that the entry into the market of additional competitors could only result in a smaller share for everyone, at first in the trades that attracted the most newcomers, and ultimately throughout the economy as a whole. Thus we find the most prominent City M.P. of this period arguing that "it is madness, if not worse, to put . . . foreigners upon an equal footing with natives, because it only enables the former to take the bread, or part of the bread, out of the mouths of the latter, without increasing in the least the national trade or commerce." [53]

A more particular consideration, but one which for that reason operated very strongly where it operated at all, was the feeling that it was necessary to maintain the present barriers to naturalization as part of the outer defenses of other interests nearer home, such as the privileges of the great monopoly companies and the countless other chartered corporations of every kind. For many of the arguments or precedents for freeing more foreigners of the alien duties and thus admitting more persons to equal participation in the English economy in general could just as well be brought to bear against the particular restrictions and discriminations that set apart various privileged sectors within that economy. [54]

Now in the 1750's these orthodox opinions—exclusionist with regard to the whole economy, and restrictionist with regard to movement within it—were under attack, and so were all the more tenaciously held and alertly defended. The criticism came principally from a school of protoliberal pamphleteers who insisted that the economy would benefit both from an infusion of new blood, as it were, and from a freer internal circulation. [55] The debate also had

[52] E.g., *P. Hist.*, XIV, 1409. Cf. the concept of the "mature economy" that was current in the 1930's.

[53] *P. Hist.*, XIV, 1391 (Sir John Barnard).

[54] Restrictions both on naturalization and on movement with the economy seem to have had the same attackers and the same defenders. See, for example, the works of Jonas Hanway and Josiah Tucker in the Bibliography. Also see the *Whitehall Evening Post*, 1198:1, where the alien duties are attacked as a device of "a few monopolists" who wanted to keep prices high.

[55] In one important respect these men were closer to the old mercantilism than

a political aspect, since most of these writers seem to have been Whig partisans, and since Henry Pelham himself was on record as favoring, at least in principle, not only a general naturalization but also the "repeal [of] every law, tending to establish a monopoly, in any quarter of the realm." [56]

Pelham was hardly the minister to put such a radical plan into effect; but the debate on these issues was still not wholly academic. Early in 1753, for example, at the very time that the Jew Bill was being drawn up, a bill was introduced in the Lords to abolish all restrictions whatever on the choice of occupations and of places of work. The liverymen of the London companies struck back at once with a petition that swamped the bill.[57]

More interesting, and more substantial, was the debate over the Turkey (or Levant) Company, which also took place just before the passage of the Jew Bill. The Turkey trade had long been languishing, and attacks on the monopoly, both from economists and from excluded merchants, had been building up for several years. Finally in 1753, over the protests of the company, Parliament passed an act which in effect terminated the monopoly by making the freedom of the company cheap and easy to acquire.[58]

By coincidence, the debate over opening the Turkey trade occasioned discussions about both naturalization and the Jews. The

---

they were to the free-trade liberalism of the nineteenth century, with its belief in a universally beneficial open international market. These eighteenth-century men still viewed international commerce as an intense competitive struggle between national economies, and favored immigration and *internal* economic freedom in the belief that these would improve England's position vis-à-vis her commercial enemies. Thus one pro-immigration pamphleteer spoke of the importance of encouraging new methods and techniques: without such improvements by us, he argued, "the improvements of other nations will continually beat us out of what we have" (Philo-Patriae, *pseud.*, *Further Considerations on the Act* [London, 1753], p. 77). Another argued for free immigration on the charmingly simple grounds that "we want at least eight millions more of people, to be upon an equality with France" (*Some Thoughts upon a Bill*, p. 5).

[56] Coxe, *Pelham*, II, 83 (a parliamentary speech of 1749).

[57] *WEP*, 1097:1 (Feb. 22).

[58] A. C. Wood, *A History of the Levant Company* (Oxford, 1935), pp. 153ff.; *London Magazine*, 1753:376–377.

question of naturalization arose incidentally, as a result of the connection between external and internal economic barriers; and the
Jews were brought into the argument because of the particular
conditions under which the Turkey trade was conducted. At that
time all transactions in the Levant between English factors and
Turkish customers had to be carried out through a group of powerful Jewish brokers; and an understandable fear that these middle-
men might favor Jewish over Christian merchants, if given a choice,
had long caused Jews to be excluded from membership in the
company. By the act of 1753 this prohibition was removed, but only
on condition that no Jewish factor be employed by a Jewish
merchant-adventurer.[59]

Thus it happened that the Jewish Naturalization Bill was brought
forward during the last stages of a complicated public debate which
at once touched upon particular economic privileges, naturalization,
and even the Jews themselves.[60] Yet the backers of the Bill, being

[59] Wood, pp. 156, 214–215.

[60] The extent to which these topics were lumped together in the economic thought
of the time is suggested by a pamphlet occasioned by the Turkey Bill of early 1753,
and significantly entitled *Reflections upon Naturalization, Corporations, and Companies.* The immediate purpose of the work was the termination of the privileges of
the Turkey Company: the author hoped that Parliament would "allow every man a
free and open trade to Turkey, *whether he be Jew or Gentile,* a pedlar or a merchant" (p. 41; my emphasis). But the pamphlet went well beyond this particular
controversy, asserting that *all* restraint was "hurtful to commerce," and broadening
its attack to include the guilds and the "monopolish spirit" in general (pp. 26, 22,
29–30). In this connection the author specifically endorsed the short-lived bill mentioned above "to enable any person to follow any trade which his natural genius shall
incline him to" (p. 7). He also spoke out for a general naturalization of foreign
Protestants such as that lately defeated, and criticized the narrow views of so many
of his countrymen on that head: "Like savages," he wrote, ". . . [we] hate foreigners,
though we ourselves are an olio of the dregs of all nations" (pp. 5, 22).

Finally, in an arresting passage which is more than anticipatory of nineteenth-
century liberalism, he summarized and gave coherence to his total position: "Monopolies," it reads, "are equally dangerous in trade, in politics and religion. A free
trade, a free government, and a free liberty of conscience, are the rights and the
blessings of mankind" (Appendix).

A pamphlet supporting the Naturalization Bill of 1751 linked these three doctrines
even more closely: "From [a single set of] causes narrow notions in religion, narrow

without the benefit of hindsight, must have seen in this fact not a potential danger to their proposal, but rather a further reason for assuming that it would be quietly approved. After all, the upshot of the controversy over the Turkey Bill, as far as the Jews were concerned, was that they were accorded without serious objection a legal privilege which had heretofore been deliberately[61] withheld from them. In the face of such a precedent, the likelihood of a strong City opposition to the Jew Bill must have seemed remote. And there was another reason for optimism as well, in the fact that lately, thanks to Pelham's policy of accommodation and appeasement, relations between the City and the Government were less hostile than they had been for years.[62]

So, to sum up, the Jew Bill was introduced in Parliament at a time when the political scene was remarkably peaceful and when the Pelham government, which was supporting the measure, seemed unshakably secure. A keen observer, however, could have detected several potential dangers to the Bill in this apparently ideal situation.

To begin with, there was to be a general election within fifteen months at the very most: in some places the nominating and canvassing had already begun.[63] Opposition candidates were desperate for an election cry; and the very policy which was keeping things quiet by denying the opposition large issues could only force them, *faute de mieux,* to pitch upon small ones and make of them what they could.

The Jew Bill, because of its extreme insignificance, was a most unlikely candidate for this unwelcome distinction. Yet if we put aside the fact that the practical effect of the Bill was so slight, and look in the abstract at its "nature and tendency," we shall observe

---

notions in trade, narrow notions in policy are derived; and persecutions, monopolies, and exclusion of foreigners flow from the same tenets, religious, commercial, and political" (*Some Thoughts upon a Bill,* p. 4).

[61] Wood, p. 155 and n.

[62] Sutherland, "The City of London in Eighteenth-Century Politics," p. 54.

[63] Most notably in Oxfordshire. R. J. Robson, *The Oxfordshire Election of 1754* (Oxford, 1949), pp. 16ff.

that it was well qualified in several respects to become the subject of a partisan wrangle. Most obviously, the Bill rested upon the Whig doctrine that immigration and easier naturalization were good things —a doctrine that had proved, only two years before, to be still highly controversial. The Bill was Whiggish in its religious implications, too, since it further reduced the comprehensiveness of the sacramental test, and tacitly reaffirmed the extension of the principle of toleration to include even non-Christians. So the Tories, with their exclusionist immigration policy and their jealousy for the privileges of the Church, were likely to think ill of the measure in proportion as they thought it important; many City merchants would surely be averse to the tendency of the Bill, for the economic reasons discussed above; and if the Bill proved sufficiently unpopular, the most cynical and opportunistic among the opposition Whigs could be counted on to howl with the pack.

Only the practical insignificance of the Jew Bill, then, stood between it and the kind of attack that had defeated Nugent's bills. For this measure touched upon the same traditionally controversial political and economic questions as Nugent's had, and had in addition a manifest religious aspect which was certain, if the Bill became widely known, to attract to it the enmity both of those who loved the Church and of those who hated the Jews. In particular, there was nothing that could so effectively revive the partisan zeal of the Tories as an opportunity to cry "The Church in danger!" as they had done forty-three years before, with such great consequences.

So if the Bill should come to be regarded not as a harmless private favor, but as a matter of public policy; if it should become, either by accident or design, sufficiently notorious and inflated to cause its trifling practical effect to be lost sight of amidst the shouting; in short, if the Bill's general principles, rather than its actual intention, became the ground of a public debate, then there was every likelihood that it would arouse a formidable opposition, and that the enemies of the Ministry would seize upon it as an election cry.

V

THE PASSAGE OF THE JEW BILL
AND THE ORIGINS OF THE
PUBLIC CLAMOR

THE early part of the Jew Bill's parliamentary career was fully in keeping with the measure's essential insignificance. It seems to have passed the Lords without the least public notice being taken of it: not until the second week of May, when it was in the middle stages of its journey through the Commons, was it mentioned explicitly in the newspapers. Yet less than a fortnight later, this uninteresting and unimportant bill had become the object of a full-voiced public clamor.

The unmistakably partisan character of this belated outcry against the Jew Bill, and the suddenness with which it rose to such intensity, have quite naturally inclined most historians to presume that the whole episode had been deliberately planned and artfully conducted from the very first in order to serve the political ends of a desperate and unprincipled opposition. Here is a typical account: "The Bill passed through the House of Lords without a division, and without any serious opposition. When the Bill came down to the Commons, it was soon perceived that political capital might be made out of it by an unscrupulous opposition. The Parliament was then nearly six years old, and there was bound to be a general election in the course of the following year. It was therefore determined to make a party cry out of the introduction of [this] piece of legislation." [1] This explanation has the great virtue of simplicity. Moreover, it appeals

---

[1] Henriques, *Jews and English Law,* p. 242. This is also a good example of the unfortunate serviceability of the passive voice.

to both the rationalizing and the moralizing tendencies in most of us: to the former, by providing a partisan cause for a partisan effect; and to the latter, by enabling us comfortably to assign to bad men the responsibility for a bad thing.

But unfortunately the evidence, when closely examined, will not sustain this convenient explanation of the origin of the public clamor over the Jew Bill. Rather than being deliberately contrived by far-sighted politicians, the clamor arose out of a concatenation of unforeseen circumstances and events that attended the Bill's parliamentary career, and in which purely partisan considerations played but a small part until almost the last moment. It will be the function of this chapter not only to recount the passage of the Jew Bill but also, in doing so, to make clear when and why the political controversy over the Bill really began.

THE HOUSE OF LORDS

On April 3, 1753, the Earl of Halifax presented to the Lords a bill entitled "An Act to permit persons professing the Jewish religion to be naturalized by Parliament." The Bill, which was not in the technical sense a Government measure, was read for the first time, apparently without comment. On April 6 it had its second reading, and on the 10th and 12th it was discussed "for some time" by the committee of the whole House, which "made several amendments thereunto." The next day those amendments were accepted by the House, and on the 16th, not quite two weeks after it had been introduced, the Bill was approved without a division and sent to the Commons.[2]

Even with the amendments the Bill was simple and fairly short.[3] The preamble cited the act of 1609, which provided, among other things, that no person could be naturalized without first taking the Anglican Sacrament; whereby, it was observed, "many persons of considerable substance professing the Jewish religion are prevented

---

[2] *Lords' Journals,* XXVIII, 73, 80, 84, 88, 90, 91, 93; Add. MSS. 35606, f. 77.

[3] Since the House of Commons made no further amendments, this is the form in which the Bill was finally enacted. The quotations that follow are from an authorized reprint of the text of the act (26 Geo. II, c. 26) in the *WEP,* 1150:1 (June 26).

from being naturalized." Next the preamble referred to the Plantation Act of 1740 which, as was explained earlier, granted exemption
from the sacramental test to certain colonial nonconformists, including Jews, and thus furnished a precedent for the further intended
breach in the restrictive provisions of the act of 1609. Then came the
substance of the present Bill: "Be it therefore enacted . . . that persons
professing the Jewish religion may, upon application for that purpose, be naturalized by Parliament without receiving the Sacrament
of the Lord's Supper, the said Act of the seventh year of the reign
of King James the First, or any other law, statute, matter, or thing
to the contrary in any wise notwithstanding."

Then followed what are undoubtedly the "several amendments"
that were added to the Bill in committee. They were four in number,
but only the last—the so-called "advowson clause"—was at all interesting or important.[4] Apparently a question was raised in committee
about the incongruity of having ecclesiastical patronage fall into the
hands of Jews who purchased landed estates.[5] To counter this objection Lord Chancellor Hardwicke inserted a clause in the Bill prohibit-
ing professing Jews from purchasing, inheriting, or exercising the
right of presentment to any living. It will be observed that this clause,
unlike any other part of the Bill, affected the legal rights of native-
born Jews—and affected them *adversely*.[6]

[4] The first provided that every act of naturalization passed under the enabling
provision of the present act must contain a clause expressly declaring the beneficiary
subject and liable to the political disabilities laid upon all naturalized persons by the
Act of Settlement (1701). Probably this requirement, which merely reiterated legal
restrictions already in force, was added in order to assure some noble questioner in
committee. The second added clause provided that no person might be naturalized
under this act unless he should have resided in Great Britain or Ireland for three
years without being absent for more than three months at any one time. The third
clause required each applicant to furnish proof by two credible witnesses that he
professed the Jewish religion, and had done so for three years. This provision doubtless
reflects the concern of some noble lords that the act might be used by crypto-
Catholics to avoid the sacramental test (*Considerations*, p. 49).

[5] Cf. the attitude of Secker, Bishop of Oxford, a friend of both the Ministry and
the Bill: "We have laws against Popish patronages: and though the danger from
Jewish may not be so great, yet the shame of them is much greater" (Add. MSS.
35592, f. 192: Secker to Hardwicke, Nov. 12).

[6] In the propaganda against the Bill this fact was almost universally ignored, which
rather exasperated the chancellor: "The objectors are gainers by the clause I inserted

Thus far the Bill had met no opposition, nor does it seem to have attracted the least public notice.[7] Its final passage was unanimously approved by the Lords, and while there had been "discussions" in committee, which caused the original bill to be amended, strictly speaking there was no debate.[8] In old Horace Walpole's words "[it] passed with all imaginable formality and deliberation in the House of Lords, without the least murmuring or opposition within doors or without." [9]

That the Lords were not much excited by this bill is also suggested by the attendance lists for early April, when the Clandestine Marriage Bill was at roughly the same stage in the parliamentary process as the Jew Bill, and so may be used for purposes of comparison. The Marriage Bill came up in committee on April 5 and 9 and on both days attracted a fuller house than did the Jew Bill, which was discussed twice in committee during the following week. The differences are too small to be conclusive, but they do suggest, as does all the other evidence, that the Marriage Bill, which in a few weeks was quite eclipsed in the public mind by the Jew Bill, aroused the greater interest at this stage.[10] In particular it is obvious that the bishops as a group showed more solicitude over the Marriage Bill than over the other; later, when the Jew Bill came under public attack, they

---

in the Bill, which disables all persons, professing the Jewish religion, from purchasing livings, or presenting to them. The *London Evening Post* has not given me my due merit on this head; for this *de novo* disables even Jews born in England" (Add. MSS. 35351, f. 248: Hardwicke to P. Yorke, July 29). The *London Evening Post* was the bitterest newspaper opponent of the Bill and the Ministry.

[7] The evidence does not support Coxe's assertion that "before the Bill was brought into the Commons, it had excited . . . general alarm" (*Pelham*, II, 244).

[8] Philip Yorke, M.P., the chancellor's eldest son, referred to the Bill as "an affair which was not debated in the House of Lords" (Add. MSS. 35398, f. 125: Yorke to Birch, June 28).

[9] Add. MSS. 35606, f. 85 (Walpole to Yorke, Sept. 29).

[10] The following table, from *Lords' Journals*, XXVIII, under the dates cited, shows the number of peers present at those four committee sessions:

	Marriage Bill		Jew Bill	
	April 5th	9th	10th	12th
Bishops present:	15	14	10	9
Temporal peers:	53	40	37	40
	68	54	47	49

were roundly berated for their failure to make a stand against it. Thus we read in a letter written during the later controversy that "the Bishop of Norwich, who thought proper to plead his absence when the Bill was under consideration of the House of Lords, could not escape the insult of some of his Suffolk clergy, who frankly told him, that this was no excuse, since it was his duty to have attended and opposed." [11]

Of course the fact that the Bill was not openly opposed in the Lords hardly proves that all those present positively favored the measure. Even allowing for the effect of retrospective wisdom on later statements, it seems clear that at least a handful, especially among the bishops, were cool toward the Bill. For example, among those present when the Bill unanimously passed its third reading was the Bishop of Lincoln, who later expressed his real views in a letter to an author who had submitted a pro-Jewish pamphlet to him. "My sentiments with regard to the Jews are not so favourable as yours. I was for granting them all kinds of franchisements in relation to trade and even denization, but I was by no means for naturalizing them or incorporating them into our nation. I did not indeed oppose the Bill, because I was then extremely deaf and in no condition to oppose, *nor did I choose to be singular,* but I was in my heart against it." [12] But surely in this case the exception confirms the rule, and Bishop Thomas's reluctance to be "singular" supports the assertion that the Jew Bill's journey through the House of Lords was quiet and uneventful. It was destined to be otherwise in the Commons.

THE HOUSE OF COMMONS AND THE PETITIONS

The Bill came down from the Lords on April 16 and had its first reading in the Commons the next day. No further action was taken on it until May 3, on which day its second reading was ordered for May 7.[13] This lack of haste bespeaks the confident attitude of the

[11] Add. MSS. 35398, f. 128 (Birch to Yorke, July 7).
[12] *Hist. MSS. Comm.,* 10th Rept., App. I, 448 (Bishop Thomas to E. Weston, Dec. 29). My emphasis.
[13] *Commons' Journals,* XXVI, 770, 775, 803.

managers of the Bill: surely if they had expected a serious opposition to develop, either within or without doors, they would hardly have allowed the Bill to lie dormant for three weeks while its enemies aroused others against it. Old Horace Walpole, one of the Bill's leading supporters, recalled this overconfidence—for such it proved to be—in a letter written a few months later. "I must own that after it had passed the Lords' House so quietly, I did not expect it would have raised such a general flame . . . [It was] received at first in the House of Commons as so innocent a thing, that no debate was expected from it." [14]

The second reading took place on Monday, May 7, before a House which was rather thin in spite of the fact that the members had been on notice since the preceding Thursday that the Bill was to come up at this sitting. Now for the first time the Bill came under attack. At least five members spoke against it, offering arguments drawn mainly from economics, religion, and legal precedent; there were replies from at least five supporters of the Bill.[15] When the House divided, the Bill was carried by 95 to 16, and was scheduled for discussion in committee of the whole on May 15.[16]

The five members who spoke against the Bill represented between them the two groups from which opposition to any naturalization measure was to be expected—the Tory gentlemen and the London merchants. The Tory speakers were Sir Edmund Isham, Charles Cholmondeley, Nicholas Fazakerley, and William Northey.[17] Two of the four were knights of the shire, and all but Fazakerley were country gentlemen.[18] Isham, at least in the barest outlines of his biography, was the very type of a mid-century Tory M.P.: he was a baronet—the sixth of his line—and sat continuously for Northamptonshire from his elder brother's death in 1736 to his own death

[14] Add. MSS. 35606, ff. 84, 85 (Walpole to Yorke, Sept. 29).

[15] The *Parliamentary History* contains four speeches on each side, taken from the *London Magazine;* the latter also mentions two other members as having spoken (*P. Hist.,* XIV, 1365–1417; *Lond. Mag.,* 1753:422).

[16] *Commons' Journals,* XXVI, 808–809. The speeches will be summarized and discussed in the next chapter.

[17] All four are listed as "Against, Torys" in the Duke of Newcastle's analysis of the next Parliament (Add. MSS. 33034, ff. 177–178).

[18] *Ibid.,* ff. 169–171. Fazakerley was a barrister.

thirty-seven years later.[19] Cholmondeley was the same sort: from 1710 to 1715, and then from 1722 until his death in 1756, he sat for Cheshire, as did others of his family after him.[20] Fazakerley, the most prominent of the four, was "a Jacobite of the cautious type." He was of an old Lancashire family and represented the borough of Preston, where he resided, for a term similar to Isham's and Cholmondeley's: thirty-five years, from 1732 to his death.[21] Northey, a hotheaded young highflier, was at this time sitting for the borough of Calne.[22]

The fifth speaker who opposed the Bill on May 7, and the one who seems to have made the greatest impression, was a respected and capable independent member, Sir John Barnard.[23] He was the idol of the lesser merchants of the City of London, which turbulent constituency he represented from 1722 to 1761. Barnard had been a prominent opponent of Nugent's earlier naturalization schemes and now, against a somewhat similar though far more modest measure, he once again allied himself with the country Tories.[24]

Of the five members who spoke in favor of the Bill, the last and most important was Henry Pelham himself; and as if to leave no

[19] Eric Forrester, *Northamptonshire County Elections and Electioneering, 1695–1832* (London, 1941), pp. 58, 85. Judd, in his *Members of Parliament*, p. 190, gives slightly different dates for Isham's tenure.

[20] Judd, p. 150.

[21] *Ibid.*, p. 191; the quotation is from the *Dictionary of National Biography*.

[22] Judd, p. 290. It is interesting and perhaps significant that all these Tory members except Northey (born in 1722) were old enough to have clear personal recollections of the great party struggles of Queen Anne's last years. Fazakerley and Cholmondeley were born in 1685, and Isham in 1690. Indeed, Cholmondeley had sat in the last Tory Parliament, and had no doubt given his vote to repeal the Whig naturalization act that had admitted the "poor Palatines" to England. The Court speakers in the debate were markedly younger: Pelham was born in 1696, the other four in 1699, 1702, 1710, and 1717.

[23] A letter published in a provincial newspaper six weeks after the debate asserted that Barnard had been the *only* member to oppose the Bill. *Jackson*, 8:2 (June 23). See also *P. Hist.*, XV, 150.

[24] Judd, p. 113; Walpole, *George II*, I, 45; *DNB;* Sutherland, "Samson Gideon and the Reduction of Interest," p. 13. The implication in Roth, *Jews in England*, p. 215, that Barnard opposed the Bill simply on account of his private quarrel with Gideon, is both inaccurate and unfair.

doubt of the ministerial backing of this technically non-Government measure, the other four speakers were all prominent Court Whigs. There was Nugent, known for his interest in immigration policy, but also, since the death of the Prince of Wales, as a friend of the Pelhams.[25] There were Lords Dupplin and Barrington, both well-known politicians and officeholders of the second rank. Dupplin was a personal friend of Newcastle and Hardwicke, and a member of the Board of Trade;[26] Barrington held a post at the Admiralty.[27] The other advocate of the Bill, Nicholas Hardinge, was less important, but still conformed to the pattern: he was a secretary of the Treasury, and a recent recipient of Pelham's patronage.[28]

Thus in the debate of May 7 we see the emergence of the same basic alignment of forces and interests that had characterized the struggles over earlier naturalization measures and was to characterize the later public controversy over the Jew Bill. On the one side were the Tory gentlemen and the London merchants;[29] on the other, the pro-immigration Whigs, most of them friends of the Government. Most, but not all: for the Jew Bill also had the support of such men as Thomas Potter and, in the other House, Lord Temple[30]— men who remained Whiggish in their attitudes toward immigration, even though they were currently either in outright opposition to the Pelhams or more or less independent. It will be recalled, too, that Nugent had been in opposition when he brought forward his earlier bills; and thus it can be said that he spoke on May 7 not primarily as a Courtier, but as a sincere enthusiast for liberal immigration measures.

But while hindsight allows us to say that the battle-lines were already discernible on May 7, it would be wrong to suppose that the great controversy over the Bill had truly begun. Actually the debate

---

[25] Nugent, *Memoir of Nugent*, pp. 41, 201–203, 252–256.

[26] *DNB* s.v. "Hay, Thomas"; Yorke, *Hardwicke*, III, 449n.

[27] *DNB*. Both Dupplin and Barrington were intimate friends of Lord Halifax, the original sponsor of the Bill; this relationship may well have played a part in their active support of the measure (Cumberland, *Memoirs*, I, 160).

[28] *DNB;* Coxe, *Pelham*, II, 221.

[29] They were later joined by the Bedford Whigs (see Chapter VI).

[30] For these men, see Chapter VIII.

of May 7, though it naturally stands out in a selective narration such as this one, caused very little stir at the time, either within doors or without. It was ignored by the newspapers, including those opposition journals which a few weeks later had almost no topic but the Jews and their notorious bill. In August, when the agitation against the Bill was at its height, one of these papers, the extreme Tory *Jackson's Oxford Journal,* made this enthusiastic comment on one of the speeches of May 7, several of which had by then been published: "The speech of N[icholas] F[azakerley] in the Political Club, inserted in the *London Magazine* for July last, deserves to be wrote in letters of gold, and sent to every free borough in the Kingdom; for it bespeaks the lawyer, the scholar, the gentleman, and the lover of his country." [31] But at the time the debate occurred in which this noble speech was delivered, the *Oxford Journal* had taken no notice whatever; indeed, the paper did not even mention the Bill until May 19.

This negative evidence indicates clearly that the general clamor against the Bill had not yet begun. It also strongly suggests that the opposition of May 7 cannot have been a part of any organized attempt to arouse public opinion against the Bill.[32] For if this were true, surely the opposition newspapers, so eager later on to print the merest trifle about the issue, would have carried some report of the debate.

The general public, then, was still unaware of the existence of the Jew Bill.[33] As for the House of Commons, there the Bill's supporters were no doubt vexed that their modest measure had drawn fire from the traditional anti-immigration bloc. Yet they could find ample justification for continued confidence in both the low total and the one-sided margin of the division (95–16).[34]

---

[31] *Jackson,* 16:2.

[32] Coxe implies this (II, 246).

[33] A ministerial pamphleteer unwittingly confirms this when he asserts that by May 9 the Bill was well known to *many*—not all—of the *magistrates* of London, who had "proper officers to advise them of every occurrence in Parliament" (*Considerations,* pp. 26, 28).

[34] On May 8, 118 members divided on a local highway repair bill, seven more than had voted on the Jew Bill the previous day (*Commons' Journals,* XXVI, 810).

A week later, on May 15, the Bill was discussed in committee of the whole; in spite of renewed opposition, it was approved without further amendment.[35] But by now the Jew Bill was beginning to attract attention without doors. The violent Tory *London Evening Post,* which, like the rest of the press, had ignored the debate of May 7, printed explicit attacks against the Bill on May 12 and 15.[36] On May 17 and 19 respectively the ministerial *Whitehall Evening Post* and the Tory *Oxford Journal* mentioned the Bill for the first time, both papers carrying straightforward reports only one sentence long and almost identical, saying that on the 15th "a great number of Jew merchants [had] attended at the House of Commons, about their Naturalization Bill now depending there." [37]

Never again, however, did these two opposing papers treat a story about the Jew Bill in the same way. By the time the next week's issue of the *Oxford Journal* appeared, the controversy over the Bill had become a matter of great interest to the public and had entered a new phase, in which the fundamental considerations were those of practical politics and in which the primary target was no longer the Bill but the Pelham ministry.

The story of how the debate over the Jew Bill suddenly widened from a minor doctrinal skirmish within Parliament to a major partisan clamor without is essentially the story of the four petitions— two on either side of the question—that were presented to the House of Commons between the second and third readings of the Bill.[38] The first of these to be set in motion was an appeal from "certain merchants and traders of London," who alleged that passing the Bill would have harmful effects upon foreign trade, particularly with Spain and Portugal. The petition was probably drawn up shortly after the debate over the second reading (May 7), when

---

[35] *Lond. Mag.,* 1753:422.

[36] The *London Evening Post* had in fact printed an isolated implicit reference to the Bill on April 26, but in a passage so obscure and whimsical that few readers can either have understood it or concerned themselves about it (3978:1).

[37] *WEP,* 1133:1; *Jackson,* 3:2.

[38] The texts of the petitions are in *Commons' Journals,* XXVI, 827, 829.

the Bill first began to be talked of. There is no reason to suppose that politics had any considerable part in its inspiration. "Philo-Patriae," a ministerial pamphleteer who had as keen an eye as any for unmasking sinister motives and devious behavior in his political opponents, said simply (as did the petition itself) that the signers were mainly traders to Spain and Portugal who wished "to overset the Bill." He continued: "The conduct of the merchants who opposed the Bill, is easily accounted for; narrow principles, and a view to their own private interests, were the incentive; they are disgusted at seeing the Jews trade in the same countries with them, and think their trade would be more profitable, by there being fewer traders; never reflecting on the generous and certain maxim, that the most extensive trade is the most beneficial." [39]

This orthodox restrictionist attitude was reinforced by fears that any official favor shown the Jews might cause offense to be taken by Spain and Portugal—nations where the Inquisition was still active and which, in the words of one who signed this petition, "hate the Jews out of measure." In those days of mercantilist controls such resentment could easily be translated into discriminatory commercial regulations whose weight would fall directly upon these native English merchants; fears were expressed in particular for Great Britain's unique and valuable "most favored nation" privileges in Portugal.[40]

The petition was drawn up at a private meeting and then placed near the Royal Exchange. For the first few days a degree of secrecy attended the soliciting of signatures, the purport of the petition apparently being divulged only to those whose concurrence was taken for granted.[41] Probably these merchants, knowing that their appeal would have more weight if it was the only one presented to the House, wished to keep their intention from becoming known to the friends of the Bill, lest the latter, being alerted, should get up

---

[39] *Considerations*, pp. 26, 52–53.

[40] [Jonas Hanway], *A Review of the Proposed Naturalization of the Jews* (London, 1753), pp. 87–88; *P. Hist.*, XIV, 1425. Today somewhat similar considerations complicate American commercial and diplomatic intercourse with Saudi Arabia.

[41] *Considerations*, p. 27; [Romaine], *Answer*, pp. 67–68.

a counter-petition which might offset the effect of the original one.

If this was in fact the merchants' hope it was disappointed in the event, for the Bill was strongly backed by not one, but two, petitions. The first and more important of these was signed by 102 London merchants and traders,[42] all of them Christians,[43] who asserted that the Bill, if enacted, would "increase the commerce and credit of [the] nation." There is little doubt that this petition was inspired by the Ministry itself. All the evidence[44] points in that direction, and common sense would seem to support the same conclusion. For the Jew Bill could confer no direct benefit whatever upon these 102 Christian merchants, or on the 200-odd who signed the second favorable petition. What motive, one may ask, other than a sense of obligation to the backers of the Bill, and what initiative other than that of the Ministry, can have caused these men to organize and to assert themselves so positively in favor of the measure?

As for the ministers, probably they had got wind of the petition of the Portugal merchants, and moved to counter its effect; or perhaps they wished to offset whatever impression had been made on the House of Commons by the attacks against the Bill on May 7. But whether or not it had originally been intended as a counter-measure, this effort by the friends of the Bill soon was competing directly with that of the Portugal merchants, who by now were pressing their petition openly. The solicitation of signatures in favor of the Bill began on May 17.[45] On May 18 the *London Gazetteer* carried an insertion in support of the Portugal merchants' petition; Philip Carteret Webb, the Jews' solicitor, immediately replied with an anonymous leaflet attacking the piece as a mis-

---

[42] Cecil Roth, ed., *Magna Bibliotheca Anglo-Judaica* (London, 1937), p. 222.

[43] This is asserted, in capital letters, by "Philo-Patriae," and is not contradicted by his opponents (*Considerations,* p. 31).

[44] E.g., John Entick, *A New and Accurate History and Survey of London* (London, 1766), III, 88; *Free and Candid Remarks on a Paper Published in Defence of the Jews* (London?, 1753), quoted in *Gent. Mag.,* 1753:346; and [Hanway], *Review,* p. 100.

[45] *Considerations,* p. 30n.

representation of the Bill and asserting that the various petitions would show that the greater part of the mercantile interest favored the measure.[46]

By this time the second petition in favor of the Bill had been initiated; it was ultimately subscribed by over 200 merchants and shippers,[47] who alleged that the Bill, if enacted, would increase the nation's foreign trade, especially the export of woollen goods. This petition, too, seems to have been inspired by the Ministry, and probably was set in motion when it began to appear that the other two competing petitions might simply cancel each other out. Indeed, the timing of the presentations to the House of the two favorable petitions (which will be recounted presently) leaves little doubt that the managers of the Bill were lying in wait, as it were, for the opposing petition of the Portugal merchants, intending to box it in on either side and thus ensure that the advocates of the Bill would have both the first and the last word.

The first part of the plan was put into effect shortly after nine o'clock Monday morning, May 21, when the first favorable petition was laid before the House of Commons. Note that this was done not on Tuesday, when the Bill was to be debated, but the day before. What is more, it was done at about the earliest possible moment on Monday: for the *Journals* show that the House had got through only a few matters of detail before the petition was presented.[48] Upon motion several of the names subscribed to it were read aloud, "that the House might see what sort of men the petitioners were," and the petition was ordered to lie upon the table until the third reading; the House then turned to its main business of the day, a committee on the Marriage Bill.[49]

---

[46] *Gent. Mag.*, 1753:278–280.

[47] *Considerations*, p. 32.

[48] *Commons' Journals*, XXVI, 827.

[49] *Ibid.*; *P. Hist.*, XIV, 1417. Coxe, *Pelham*, II, 252, and Tobias Smollett, *History of England* (Philadelphia, 1822), II, 107, assert that the reading of the names discredited the petition by revealing the signers to be "mostly foreigners, or descendants of Jews" (Coxe). Contemporary enemies of the Bill did not attack the petition on this ground, however. Probably it is no more than an inference based upon an incident

In thus placing the favorable views of these 102 London merchants on record before both the House and the public, the friends
of the Bill had gained a clear tactical advantage. The City opponents
of the Bill had not been idle, however, and before the day was
over they delivered a heavy counterblow in the form of a vehement
official protest against the Bill from the Lord Mayor, aldermen,
and Commons of London, in Common Council assembled. This
City petition burst onto the scene with almost no warning and
therefore with all the greater effect; and literally overnight it
broadened the scope and heightened the intensity of the whole
controversy.

At first glance this protest may not seem very unusual; after all,
the Corporation had also petitioned against both of Nugent's
earlier naturalization bills. Yet there were differences. First, the
Jew Bill was a rather small target to draw such heavy fire; and
second, there was the fact that the Corporation's fire had been
held until the last moment. For the City petition against the Jew
Bill was submitted only a day before the Bill was to be finally
passed into law, while those of 1747 and 1751 had both been brought
in soon after the bills they were attacking had been introduced.[50]

The wording of the protest was also remarkable: in spite of its
official derivation, the City petition was far more sweeping in its
assertions and more immoderate in its language than any of the
others on either side of the controversy. The others, it will be recalled, considered the Bill solely in an economic light; none of
them so much as suggested that it had a religious or political aspect.
The City petition, too, objected to the Bill on economic grounds;
but it did so last of all, only after expressing, in phrases bearing
the unmistakable impress of the City's Toryism, the petitioners'
apprehension that the Bill would "tend greatly to the dishonour
of the Christian religion, [and] endanger our excellent Constitution."

Opposition turns of expression were only to be expected from

that occurred when Nugent's bill of 1751 was before the House (see *P. Hist.*, XIV,
971).
[50] *P. Hist.*, XIV, 133–134, 970–971.

the Common Council; but the extravagance of these phrases might seem to suggest that the petitioners were looking beyond the Bill to the coming election.[51] During the later election clamor this interpretation of the City's action was widely accepted by embattled supporters of the Bill and the Ministry. Old Horace Walpole, for example, attributed the petition simply to the "malignant spirit of a worthless set of Jacobites in the Common Council." [52] No doubt some of the petitioners were motivated by a desire to make trouble for the Ministry, but clearly politics played only a minor part in the affair. Rather, the Corporation's protest grew out of the agitation begun a fortnight before by the Portugal merchants and other private persons who were opposed to the Bill.

Little need be said about the various motives (some of them not a bit more creditable than outright faction would have been) that informed this growing opposition to the Jew Bill, since essentially they were the same as those which had prompted the City to oppose Nugent's earlier bills. Most important, surely, were the economic reasons—exclusionist theories, and fears for monopolies and privileges—that have already been discussed. Such views may have been ill-founded or narrow, but even an unfriendly pamphleteer admitted by implication that they were honestly held and had nothing to do with either religious bigotry or party politics.[53]

In addition there were men (no doubt of every political persuasion) who opposed the Bill on religious grounds ranging from sincere doctrinal scruples[54] to virulent anti-Semitism.[55] Others

---

[51] Actually this language, though extravagant, was by no means unprecedented. The City's petition against Nugent's naturalization bill of 1747 had warned starkly against admitting foreigners who, having "grown up under arbitrary government, [might] be fittest to answer arbitrary purposes." And in 1751 a petition from Bristol expressed concern that Nugent's second bill might "endanger the subversion of our Constitution" (*P. Hist.*, XIV, 135, 972).

[52] Add. MSS. 35606, f. 79 (Walpole to Yorke, July 23). Another ministerial partisan referred to the petition as a "covered battery" that had been suddenly "unmasked" according to plan (*Considerations*, pp. 30–31).

[53] *Considerations*, pp. 52–53. The passage was quoted above on p. 55.

[54] *Ibid.*, p. 57.

[55] See the discussion of the pamphlet literature, in Chapter VI.

among the Bill's opponents were simply xenophobic ultra-Tories, men whose kind had vehemently opposed every naturalization measure since the time of William and Mary.[56] Finally, many persons entertained mistaken or exaggerated notions of the Bill's actual provisions, either because of deliberate obfuscation on the part of its most zealous enemies, or because of an honest confusion between the pending measure on the one hand and Nugent's recent and more sweeping proposal, or the Plantation Act of 1740, on the other. Consequently all sorts of objectively irrelevant fears and prejudices must be assumed to have contributed to both the size and the intensity of the opposition to the Bill.[57]

Behind the City agitation, then, lay a dislike of the Bill which was unquestionably genuine, even if largely interested, wrong-headed, ill-informed, and disproportionate to its object. And this protest belatedly assumed the form of an official petition not because of a farsighted plot against the Ministry, but because of the increasing heat of the controversy, and because of the disadvantageous tactical situation in which the opponents of the Bill found themselves as the final debate approached.

It is clear that during the third week of May the public controversy over the Jew Bill began to pick up momentum sharply. The debate and division in the Commons on May 7, it will be recalled, was not even reported in the newspapers. The Corporation of London met two days later, but did not protest against the Bill or even (it would appear) discuss it at the meeting.[58]

But on Saturday May 12, the Bill was attacked for the first time in the *London Evening Post;* on Tuesday the 15th the *London Evening Post* carried another, and stronger, attack. On Thursday the first petition in favor of the Bill was opened, to be followed in a day or so by the second. The *Gazetteer* article in support of the

---

[56] *Considerations*, p. 53.

[57] *Gent. Mag.*, 1753:279; "Philo-Patriae," *Considerations*, pp. 27–28, 34; see also the same author's *Further Considerations*, p. 92.

[58] *LEP*, 3984:1 (May 10); *Considerations*, p. 26.

Portugal petition appeared on Friday and was answered immediately by Webb's leaflet defending the Bill and accusing its opponents of misrepresenting it.

As the weekend came on and the third reading, scheduled for Tuesday, drew near, "the Bill . . . became the public talk of every company." [59] The City opponents of the Bill must have felt that their tactical position was weak. They had counted on making a strong impression on the House of Commons with the Portugal petition. But against not one, but two, petitions in favor of the Bill, they could expect to do little more than hold their own—and they knew that merely to hold would not be enough.

After all, they were asking the House of Commons not only to turn its back on the unanimous approval given the Bill by the Lords, but also to reverse its own favorable actions on the measure. Since these included a division in which the Bill had carried by over six to one, its City opponents clearly had their work cut out for them. Their strength without doors was increasing—Webb either was deceived or was whistling in the dark when he implied that only a small minority of the merchants disliked the Bill—but if the House was to be prevailed upon to reconsider its stand at this late stage in the Bill's parliamentary career, then that strength would have to be demonstrated by something more telling than a mere private protest.

Impelled by such considerations, some of the more strenuous opponents of the Bill who happened also to be Common Councillors had begun urging that a special Council meeting be convened to take more effective measures against the Bill. Not until Saturday the 19th, however, were these men able to win over the number of Commoners requisite to submit a request for such a meeting. Since the Lord Mayor had already left town for the weekend, it was necessary to send to his country seat in order to obtain his authorization for a special session on Monday. Consequently the summons could not be issued until Saturday afternoon and thus

[59] *Considerations*, p. 29.

failed to reach many who, like the Lord Mayor, had already left for the country.[60]

But in spite of the meeting's having been called "at the shortest notice," the assemblage on Monday was quite impressive, there being present the Lord Mayor, the two sheriffs, several aldermen (two of them Members of Parliament), and 125 of the 230-odd Commoners. A fiery resolution condemning the Bill was passed and given to a committee with instructions to draw up a petition based upon it. The committee withdrew briefly and returned with a petition which (with one amendment) was all but unanimously agreed to; "only one gentleman spoke in favour of the Bill, or held up his hand against the petition." [61]

The meeting took less than two hours. When it was over, the sheriffs set out for Westminster with the petition, no doubt hoping that its prompt delivery would help offset the effect of the favorable petition that had been brought in earlier that day. Since the House sat late that evening on the Marriage Bill, they arrived in good time and presented their petition. Like the other, it was ordered tabled until the next day's debate.[62]

On Tuesday, May 22, the eagerly anticipated third reading of the Jew Bill took place. The proceedings began with the presentation of the two remaining petitions—that of the Portugal and other merchants opposed to the Bill, and the second petition in favor of it. The City petition submitted on Monday was also read, although by now its phrases about dishonoring the Christian religion and endangering the Constitution must have been well known to all the town, let alone to the House of Commons.

Next, as they had requested in their petition, some of the merchants who opposed the Bill were permitted to come to the bar

[60] *Ibid.*, p. 33; *LEP*, 3980:4 (May 22).

[61] For accounts of the meeting, see previous note; also *WEP*, 1135:1 (May 22), and *Gent. Mag.*, 1753:246. The last quotation is from the *London Evening Post;* but the ministerial *Whitehall Evening Post* admitted that the motion "was almost unanimously agreed to."

[62] *Considerations*, p. 33; Walpole, *Letters*, III, 158; *Commons' Journals*, XXVI, 827.

of the House, where they argued their case more fully and submitted to questioning by members. The House was generous with its time, allowing the merchants not only to speak at some length but also to examine several witnesses who gave evidence to support the contention that the Bill would injure English trade, especially with Portugal.[63]

But the indulgence of the House toward the merchants was strictly limited to this grant of a hearing; the questioning was sharp, and on the whole the petitioners were roughly treated by the friends of the Bill.[64] One of these, taking somewhat captious exception to an answer elicited by one of his questions, remarked impatiently that the petitioners were ignorant of the nature of the Bill. This same gentleman (who was also a member of the Administration) disparaged the opposition to the Bill, attributing it to the insidious exertions of some factious and designing men in the City; these men he rather inelegantly termed "scabby sheep," thus earning the gratitude of the opposition propagandists, who saw to it that this epithet was not soon forgotten.[65]

By the admission of one who took a prominent part in it, the merchants' presentation was poorly prepared, which no doubt intensified the ill-humor of the House.[66] But though the private merchants were the ones who felt the sting, it was not *their* petition but the City's that had occasioned the annoyance and exasperation which so many members clearly felt; the friends of the Bill conceded that the private petition was "decent," but the City petition in their view amounted to nothing less than an affront to the dignity of Parliament.[67]

The City petition gave offense both by what it said and by the timing of its presentation. Its assertion that the Jew Bill would

---

[63] *P. Hist.*, XIV, 1418, 1419, 1425. One petitioner spoke for half an hour.

[64] *P. Hist.*, XV, 138.

[65] *P. Hist.*, XIV, 1419. See also the *Protester* (an opposition weekly) for Aug. 4 (10:59), and *LEP*, 3995:1.

[66] [Hanway], *Review*, p. 104; *Gent. Mag.*, 1753:291.

[67] *P. Hist.*, XV, 144–145. Of course these private merchants were the persons chiefly responsible for the offensive City petition.

dishonor Christianity and endanger the Constitution was felt to disparage the piety and patriotism of both Houses (and especially the reverend Bench), who had, after all, given their overwhelming approval to this allegedly shocking measure.[68] Henry Pelham went so far as to say (in a later speech) that such broad topics had no place in a petition. If a man feared injury to his *private* rights or property as a result of any depending measure, it was proper that his protest should be heard. "But in matters of a public concern, no body of men, how respectable soever, have a right to come here and tell us what we ought or ought not to do: to attempt it, is an attack upon the dignity of this House." [69]

The fact that the City petition was brought forward so late in the Bill's parliamentary career was also resented; even the City's hired apologist later admitted that this did appear to be disrespectful of the House of Commons.[70] After all, as a simple matter of good form it behooved any body as important as the Corporation of London to make its objections known before a bill progressed to a point where Parliament could not gracefully let it drop.[71]

As we might expect, the members whose sense of decorum was most outraged happened also to be those who were placed in a politically embarrassing position by the City's last-minute protest. They were the members who had provided the Bill with its majorities thus far—men who had gone along with it, thinking it a good measure but of no great moment, and not expecting it to be strongly opposed. As will be recalled, this was the attitude of the Ministry as well, whose original commitment to the Bill, while sincere enough, did not extend to a willingness to carry the measure

---

[68] The petitions of 1747 and 1751 were far less offensive, in spite of their strong language, because they referred to new bills to which the Commons were committed but slightly, and the Lords not at all. (It was probably the minor importance and technical nature of the Jew Bill, combined perhaps with its religious aspect, that caused it to be introduced, unlike the earlier naturalization measures, in the upper house.)

[69] *P. Hist.*, XV, 144. Surely the ancient notion of Parliament as a court of law is implicit here. Cf. the legal doctrine of "standing."

[70] [Romaine], *Answer*, p. 73.

[71] *Considerations*, p. 28.

against a considerable opposition, or to incur any substantial political risks on its account. But now at the third reading the City petition had the unwelcome effect of forcing both the Ministry and its individual followers to choose between repudiating their reiterated approval of the Bill on the one hand, and appearing on the other to disregard the solemn warning of a city which was not only the greatest in the kingdom, but also the one most nearly affected by the Bill.

From the harsh treatment of the petitioning merchants and from the debate that followed, it became clear that the friends of the Bill were determined not to back down; in fact, their embarrassment seems to have strengthened their resolve.[72] It was also obvious that they were in the majority;[73] so when it was finally moved "that the Bill do pass," the opposition presented a substitute motion to adjourn the debate until a month hence. Since Parliament was to be prorogued well before that date, this move would have killed the Bill; the purpose of the motion, of course, was to provide a way in which wavering supporters of the measure could in effect reverse their previous position without loss of dignity.

There being a new motion before the House, the Earl of Egmont [74] seized the occasion to deliver a final attack on the Bill. It was a long speech and a powerful one. He reviewed and answered the arguments put forward by the friends of the Bill, and belabored them for their treatment of the "respectable merchants" who had been questioned at the bar. He painted a dismal picture of the Jew Bill's probable results: religion disgraced, the Portugal trade "greatly impaired, if not totally destroyed," and English landed estates in Jewish hands, with a consequent increase in Jewish political influence.

But the most interesting part of the speech was that in which Egmont spoke of the possibility that the Tory spirit of forty years

---

[72] *Ibid.,* p. 59.

[73] *P. Hist.,* XIV, 1428.

[74] An Irish peer, M.P. for Weobley; a prominent supporter of the late Prince of Wales and still in opposition (*DNB* s.v. "Perceval, John").

ago might still be revived. Recalling the Sacheverell impeachment, he warned that the Jew Bill, if persisted in by the Ministry, would provoke a general clamor that would be certain to have an effect on the approaching elections:

Sir . . . our ministers are certainly not aware how national, how general [the opposition to this Bill] may probably become, which, from the times in which we stand, and from the tendency it may probably acquire, it is neither wise nor honest to provoke.

The present Administration are some of them the same men, others bred at least in the same school, most if not all of them able to remember the spirit that rose against their connection, and overthrew them, towards the end of the reign of Queen Anne. The origin of that was a silly measure which jarred the same string with this. It is true they recovered their ground again, by the accident of the Queen's death, and the accession of the present royal family to the throne. But let them take care now: if they overthrow themselves by the same wantonness, the same presumption, the same inattention to, or ignorance of, the true temper of the people, they possibly may fall never to rise again.

For my own part, dead as all spirit appears to be throughout the whole nation, I do verily believe that this Bill will rouse it, but in a way, of all others, in which I should least like to see it rise. I detest the race the nation was hurried to run by that spirit which I have just now mentioned, and I rejoice that I know . . . that a moderation, and a fair disposition to the present royal family, does exist (as much as they are traduced) in far the greater number of those who are descended from the warmest actors of those times. Nothing but your folly and extravagance in the pursuit of such measures as this, can bring them back into the passionate humours that appeared then.

He did not expect a large minority against the Bill; for that matter, he did not desire to see one, if it became so "merely by the effect which this Bill may have upon the minds of men at the next general election." At the same time, he went on, "I am amazed that this consideration makes no impression, for so sure I am that this Bill will have an effect upon the people which you do not expect, that when that day comes, which is not far off, I shall not fear to set my foot upon any ground of election in the

Kingdom—I who have spoke my sentiments and voted against the Bill—in opposition to any one man among you, or any new Christian who has appeared or voted for it; and so, do I verily believe, any other gentleman may do, who this day in this House shall act and vote with me." [75]

Ignoring Lord Egmont's warning, the House rejected the motion to adjourn by 96 votes to 55, and then passed the Bill without a further division.[76]

During the fortnight when the Jew Bill was awaiting the royal assent, the House of Commons turned its attention to other business. The public excitement over the Bill, however, instead of subsiding with the passage of the measure, actually increased in intensity.[77] Surely no sober person could seriously have expected the king to refuse his assent to a measure that had duly passed both Houses; yet in this brief time the clamor rose to such a pitch that the possibility of his doing so became a topic of discussion, at least among the Bill's more furious opponents. In reporting this extraordinary development, the *London Magazine,* in spite of its dislike of the Bill, could not quite conceal the trifling and futile nature of such talk:

This famous and important Bill having thus passed both Houses, some of the most zealous advocates against it without doors, began to talk of petitioning his Majesty not to give it the Royal Assent; but as it was a question, whether this would have been agreeable to our Constitution, the design was either laid aside, or they had not time to carry it into execution; for as the session ended June 7, the Bill then received the Royal Assent; though, from what has since appeared, it must be presumed, that the Crown could never have had a better or more popular opportunity for exerting that prerogative which is like to fall into desue-

---

[75] *P. Hist.,* XIV, 1427–28. This is not the end of the speech; the political argument was only one of several urged by Egmont, and not necessarily the most prominent.

[76] *Commons' Journals,* XXVI, 829.

[77] In the week following the Bill's enactment, the *London Evening Post,* for example, devoted more space to the Bill, and was more violent in its attacks, than in the week preceding.

tude; and indeed it was perhaps the first time that it could ever have been exerted with any view to popularity.[78]

And so, after having begun its parliamentary career without any public notice whatever, the Jew Bill was finally enacted into law amidst an intense general clamor that was to continue until the act was repealed—and after.

The chain of events that brought about this unexpected result can be said to have begun with the petition of the merchants who were concerned, selfishly but nonpolitically, over the Bill's presumed effect on the Portugal trade.[79] Soon the two favorable petitions entered into direct competition with it for the City's support, and the Bill became for the first time a topic of public discussion and controversy.

The success of the favorable petitions, which was clearly misleading as to the true sentiments of most of the City, both alarmed and angered the opponents of the Bill, who had hitherto been fairly confident that it would never reach final passage. Instead of being a subtle political stroke, the City petition was a desperate and hasty counterblow: the evidence seems to bear out the contention put forward at the time, "that the Corporation would never have petitioned against the Bill, had it not been for the petitions in favour of it." [80]

In addition to simply adding fuel to the fire, the City petition made two particular contributions to the controversy that require specific mention. One of these was the new prominence and the official respectability, as it were, that the City petition gave to the religious issue, which henceforth was uppermost in the public clamor against the Bill. As Henry Pelham put it, "It was that petition which first gave a religious turn to the dispute." [81]

The other was the sharp deterioration of relations between the

[78] *Lond. Mag.*, 1753:423; see also *LEP*, 3981:1, and 3987:1.

[79] It was to "that famous petition," says a contemporary account, "[that] we owe the beginning of all this clamor" (Philo-Patriae, *Considerations*, p. 58).

[80] Quoted, and unconvincingly rebutted, in *Considerations*, p. 30.

[81] *P. Hist.*, XV, 145. Without doors, that is. For, as Pelham was sharply reminded

City and the Ministry. The immediate consequence of the petition, it will be recalled, had been to embitter the parliamentary proceedings of May 22; and that unpleasantness, in turn, had its effect. In the later controversy the importance of this bad feeling between the City and the Ministry was so great, and the role of the City petition in contributing to it was so obvious, that one ministerial pamphleteer even suggested that the real intention of the petitioners may have been to anger the House into passing the Bill, so that a clamor could be fomented afterwards.[82] Others with a taste for intrigue have asserted that the opponents were numerous enough to have defeated the Bill at the third reading, but deliberately allowed it to pass in order to treasure it up as an election issue.[83]

Statements of a like nature are so commonly met with in general works that the point deserves reiteration: no person who has studied the evidence in detail can seriously credit the notion that the opposition to the Jew Bill was factitious and opportunistic from the very beginning, or that the controversy was the consequence of an artful and deliberate scheme for injuring the Ministry at the approaching election. If anything, the friends of the Bill appear to have maneuvered with far more competence in the affair of the petitions than did its enemies. The ill-prepared presentation by the merchants at the bar of the House, and the haste attendant upon the convening of the special meeting of the Common Council—recall that the Lord Mayor and many others had already left for the weekend before the summons went out—these facts are hardly compatible with the subtle and farsighted schemes imputed afterwards to the opposition.

And one final objection, hitherto unmentioned, must be met by

---

(p. 157), the opposition had raised religious objections in the May 7 debate (see Chapter VI, below).

[82] *Considerations,* p. 54.

[83] Roth, *Jews in England,* p. 216; based, no doubt, on *P. Hist.,* XIV, 1368n, since there is no substantial contemporary evidence for this assertion. Besides, the motley oppositions of the Pelham era, though doubtless sufficiently Machiavellian, were simply not well enough organized and disciplined to execute such a maneuver. Cf. *Considerations,* p. 58.

those who put forward suggestions of a deliberate party design. This is the fact that three Tory members actually voted for the Jew Bill at some stage (probably thinking the measure unimportant) and so were caught, to their acute discomfort, on the "wrong" side of the ensuing outcry. One of them was unseated in 1754 apparently without even going to the poll;[84] another, though he eventually was returned, was at one point so unnerved by attacks upon him on account of the Bill that he offered to withdraw his candidacy.[85] That these opposition members were as much surprised and discomfited by the later clamor over the Bill as were the friends of the Ministry, clearly tells against the notion that the whole affair was, from the beginning, a carefully laid plot to embarrass Court candidates at the next election.

The correct explanation of how and why the Jew Bill became the subject of a great political clamor is nevertheless a simple one in its general outlines, even if we must forgo the convenient idea of a deliberate design. As was explained in the preceding chapter, the Jew Bill ultimately rested upon basic principles of religious and economic "liberalism" which were incompatible both with the nationalist and High Church opinions of the Tory remnant and with the restrictionist economic views of the City merchants. Since it raised what were to these men genuine issues, the Bill, abstractly considered, was a perfectly proper and natural object of attack from the Tories and the City members. Indeed, it would have been surprising if the Bill had been allowed to pass without at least such a token resistance or gesture of protest as that which was so resoundingly defeated at the second reading in the House of Commons.

The "nature and tendency" of the Bill, then, touched upon genuine and long-standing party differences and questions of economic policy; but the measure itself was too obviously limited in effect

---

[84] Sydenham of Exeter. See Walpole, *George II*, I, 141; *P. Hist.*, XIV, 1431n; *Lond. Mag.*, 1754:246–248; and also below, Chapter IX.

[85] Berkeley of Gloucestershire (Add. MSS. 35398, ff. 166–167). The third was M. Robinson Morris of Canterbury (*ibid.*, f. 151). See below, Chapter IX.

and importance to serve as the burden of an election appeal. Fortunately for the opponents of the Ministry, however, this want of
magnitude was remedied, partly by a blunder committed by the
Bill's advocates (which will be discussed presently), and partly
by the ever-increasing excitement and bitterness, both within and
without doors, that attended the last stage of the Bill's journey
through the House of Commons. The battle of the private petitions
marked the beginning of the latter development, and the events of
May 21 and 22 were its climax. These events—among which the
City petition was the most clearly determinative—stirred into flame
the latent hostility that normally existed between the City and the
Ministry; broadened and intensified the whole controversy by
emphasizing the religious aspect of the Bill; and finally, by thus
enlarging (or rather inflating) the controversy, made it sufficiently
loud and sufficiently general (though no more substantial than
before) to serve as an election cry for the desperate Tories and the
turbulent City politicians.

After May 21 and 22, wrote "Philo-Patriae," "*then* party became
entirely master of the whole affair [and] those without doors, who
opposed the measures of the Administration, joined in the opposition to the Bill." [86] Faction did not create the clamor, then, but
rather seized upon it gleefully after a chain of happenings had
already puffed this trifling bill into a momentary public sensation.
Now the problem of the enemies of the Ministry was to spread this
ridiculously exaggerated clamor throughout the provinces and to
keep it alive long enough to serve their purposes at the general
election, which might not take place for another nine months or
more. Apparently untroubled by scruples of any sort, they undertook to this end the extravagant propaganda campaign that will
be described in the next chapter.

[86] *Considerations*, p. 55. My emphasis.

VI

THE GREAT CLAMOR
OF 1753

THE PARTICIPANTS,
THEIR PRINCIPAL METHOD, AND THEIR OBJECTIVE

AS WE have seen, the clamor that convulsed most of England during the summer and autumn of 1753 originated in London in the week of May 21, after the City petition and the final debate on the Jew Bill had angered many men and opened the eyes of others to the possibility that the excitement and confusion over the Bill might be exploited for political purposes. Two overlapping groups contributed to the growing outcry in the City: those merchants who had disliked the tendency of the Bill from the first, and the antiministerialists among the livery in general, who, now that the Bill was notorious, raised their voices in noisy, though belated, protest.

The merchants, considered as such, were merely continuing the battle that they had begun with their petitioning efforts against the Bill. Some of their propaganda, in consequence, was not political at all, but was rather an attempt to justify their conduct or to enter a last rebuttal. The clearest example of this was the anonymous *Review of the Proposed Naturalization of the Jews*, "by a merchant who subscribed the petition against [it]"—in fact, the busy philanthropist Jonas Hanway, archfoe of tea-drinking, and pioneer of the umbrella. Hanway's pamphlet offered various economic and anti-Semitic arguments against the Bill, but explicitly and with manifest sincerity deplored the party zeal that all too obviously informed many other attacks being made on it.[1]

---

[1] [Hanway], *Review*, pp. 99–106. This is the message with which he concludes the

Several other pieces of City propaganda can be said on the whole to look backward to the parliamentary proceedings, rather than forward to the election. But as the clamor grew (and as the election drew nearer), this distinction lost its meaning: for opposition politicians had made the "Jewish issue" so much their own that any attack on the Jews or the Bill was bound to be political in its effect, regardless of its author's intention. In London, then, the outcry began as a nonpolitical effort to prevent the passage of the Bill. But this was soon joined, and then wholly appropriated, by the politicians, and thus became an outright antiministerial agitation, led by the violent Tory *London Evening Post* and strongly backed by most of the Corporation.

The country Tories were not slow to take up the cry that had been raised by their brethren and allies in the City; and with the adherence of this group the clamor became truly national. Throughout the country, Tory editors and divines fulminated against the odious Bill and its still more odious ministerial sponsors. In particular, the chance to stand forth once more in defense of the Church seems to have acted on Tories everywhere as a veritable tonic: almost joyously, one feels, they reassumed the old attitudes against the old foe.

Thus even before the Bill had received the royal assent, the *London Evening Post* asked mischievously whether passive obedience, "though a long exploded doctrine," might not after all be the only resource of conscientious but law-abiding Christians for so long a time as this obnoxious act should remain in effect.[2] A similar invigorating atavism appeared in the West Country, where the "reigning toast" was none other than the old Tory cry, with

whole work. The pamphlet begins in an equally nonpartisan vein, with an admiring dedication addressed to an unnamed sponsor of the Bill who is clearly meant to be Henry Pelham. According to Hanway, Pelham was led into his mistaken support of the Bill by his "moderation and benevolence." Less charitable opponents were by this time attributing Pelham's action to inducements of a more material nature. (See plate, facing p. 4.) For Hanway himself see *DNB*.

[2] *LEP*, 3985:1 (June 2).

an incidental addition to bring it up to date: "Church and King, without mass, meeting, or synagogue!" [3]

A third group that joined the clamor and worked to propagate it was the opposition Whig faction led by the Duke of Bedford. Bedford was the leading backer of a new political weekly which, as we shall see presently, was one of the most violent and influential outlets of antiministerial and anti-Semitic propaganda.

Since the Tories, the City, and the Bedfords shared little besides a common desire to injure the Ministry, we should not be surprised at the total absence of evidence suggesting that there was any real coordination between the three groups, or that the propaganda campaign against the Jew Bill was in any sense organized or planned. Newspapers of similar political outlook copied from one another, as was common at the time; and as we should expect, the same arguments and conceits kept recurring in the publications of all three groups. But the effectiveness of the campaign is to be sought not in organization or central direction, but in the highly serviceable nature of the raw material available for exploitation, and in the enthusiasm and lack of scruple that individual publicists brought to their work.

Their method was a simple and familiar one; they labored first, to stir up public anxiety and resentment concerning the Bill and the Jews, and second, to channel the resultant explosion in the direction of the Ministry. As we might expect, one of the devices by which they fixed the essential association in the public mind was the substitution of the word "Jew" for the word "Whig." For example, the Pelhams were referred to as the Jewish brothers, and their supporters as the Jewish candidates; or again, a local contest might be described as one between the Jew Interest and the Christian Interest, or between the Jews and the Gentiles.[4] This sort of thing was so common that in the political vocabulary of 1753–54 the words "Jew" and "Whig" became practically synonymous.

[3] Add. MSS. 35398, f. 164 (Birch to Yorke, Sept. 22). See also *P. Hist.*, XV, 95.
[4] *Jackson*, 15:1, 17:2, 53:2; and also [Romaine], *Answer*, the motto, and the preface to the second edition.

In fact, most of the ostensible anti-Semitism of the clamor was aimed wholly at the Court politicians, and was surely understood in that spirit. Take, for example, the seemingly ugly story of a drunken Tory mob (in Oxfordshire) parading with the effigy of a Jew: the incident quite changes its character (and loses much of its distastefulness) when we learn that the so-called "Jew" was named "Ned," after a local Whig candidate who had not even been in Parliament when the Naturalization Bill was passed.[5] As this incident indicates, the "anti-Jewish" clamor of 1753 was meant, even at its ugliest, to prepare the ground not for a pogrom, but for a general election.

The astonishing absence of actual physical violence against individual Jews or their property is the best evidence for the argument that the passions stirred up by the clamor were largely directed, and were by their fomenters intended to be directed, against the Court politicians rather than against the Jews. The absence of violence would not be indicative of much in our day, when public disturbances, though on the increase, are still comparatively rare. But one need only look into an eighteenth-century newspaper (especially in an election year) to learn how common, and how much taken for granted, were riots of the most outrageous sort. In this respect the election of 1754 was no different from any other. We read, to cite only one example, of an election riot at Nottingham which resulted in the destruction of a Dissenting chapel, the smashing (in revenge) of the windows of all the churches, and the deaths of "only two" men.[6] It is against this background that we must place the following deplorable but minor incident in a theater, which is the only instance of actual public unpleasantness toward Jews that I have found in any contemporary source: "After the second musick, some Jew ladies and gentlemen were noticed in one of the balconies, when the cry immediately began, *No Jews, out with them, circumcise them,* &c. &c. and was followed with showers of apples, &c. with great rudeness, till the company were obliged to leave their seats; but upon remon-

---

[5] *Jackson,* 35:1; "Ned" was Sir Edward Turner, Bt.

[6] *Ibid.,* 54:1; see also 23:3, 24:2, and 52:1.

strance from a gentleman that sat next them, to some others in the
pit, a loud clap ensued, the company were reinstated, and met with
no other molestation." [7]

This straightforward account is taken from a Tory newspaper
that contributed one of the shrillest voices to the "anti-Jewish"
clamor. Another opposition paper, though it had printed some most
unpleasant anti-Semitic squibs, commented thus upon the incident
(which took place after the repeal of the Bill): "P. S. I cannot dismiss
this paper, without observing that the turbulence of some part of the
audience in the gallery broke out very unreasonably against a few
gentlemen of a particular sect on the above night. As the people
have carried their point, by a vigorous and noble effort of spirit, in
not admitting them to a naturalization, they certainly should treat
them for the future with that humanity and politeness, which is due
to strangers." [8]

The weight of the evidence indicates, as does this example, that
the opposition publicists meant no real harm to the Jews themselves,
but only to the Pelhams and their friends.[9] In short, these men were
willing to stir up the deepest and most intense emotions and prejudices, in hopes of exploiting them for a short-run political advantage.
Thus the moralist's most material reproach upon the fomenters of
the clamor is not bigotry as such, but extreme irresponsibility, and
a deplorable callousness—a common eighteenth-century failing—
toward the feelings of their ostensible targets. The clamor must have
been deeply painful to the English Jews—even to those who knew
that it was but a part of a political game that did not really concern
them. And if, as Cecil Roth says, the clamor left behind no rancor

---

[7] *LEP,* 4066:4. This sort of disturbance was not unusual in eighteenth-century
London. Cf. Boswell at the opera in 1762 (*Boswell's London Journal,* ed. F. A. Pottle,
New York, 1950, pp. 71–72): "Just before the overture began to be played, two
Highland officers came in. The mob in the upper gallery roared out, 'No Scots! No
Scots! Out with them!,' hissed and pelted them with apples . . . The rudeness of the
English vulgar is terrible."

[8] [Arthur Murphy], *The Gray's Inn Journal,* 11:66 (Dec. 8).

[9] This is also the opinion of G. B. Hertz, *British Imperialism,* pp. 76–77. For a discussion of why the spirit and intensity of the anti-Semitism of the clamor are often
misinterpreted, see Appendix B, below.

and had no significant lasting social effects,[10] surely the greatest share of the credit for this happy result should go to the patience and wisdom of a people which all too often has been forced to call upon those qualities.

The Arguments of Both Sides, and the Grounds of the Bill's Unpopularity

No matter how skillful and uninhibited the opposition propagandists were, probably their campaign would not have been such a great success but for a piece of unintentional assistance from the advocates of the Jew Bill. Of course the initial public outburst over the Bill resulted from circumstances that could hardly have been anticipated. Yet the Bill might have been just another three-day sensation instead of the topic of a protracted public dispute, if its friends had not committed a tactical blunder.

This was their mistake: instead of simply saying that the Bill would have virtually no effect on the community at large, and that it was intended chiefly as a private favor to a few deserving people already resident in England, those who spoke for the measure in the House of Commons, and those who later defended it in print, argued their case in terms of high public policy. Deserting their best ground —namely, the Bill's trifling practical significance—they emphasized the controversial "liberal" [11] principles upon which the Bill ultimately rested, and tried to show that substantial public benefits would all but certainly flow from its enactment.

Such a defense of the Bill was quite unnecessary. As the *Gentleman's Magazine* put it, at the conclusion of its generally favorable discussion of the measure, "The Bill was intended for private purposes, which alone it seems calculated to answer, and which may be answered with safety to the public: Whether they might be thus answered was the only necessary enquiry. It was not necessary, with an affected parade of publick good, to conceal the intention of con-

---

[10] *Jews in England*, p. 221. (Hertz disagrees; see *British Imperialism*, pp. 98ff.)

[11] The quotation marks, here and elsewhere, are meant only as a reminder that strictly speaking this sense of the word "liberal" is an anachronism in 1753.

ferring a favour; for why should a favour be refused that may be granted without labour, expence, or risk?"[12]

But this "affected parade of publick good" was worse than unnecessary: it was positively prejudicial to the cause it was meant to serve. For it not only reopened such traditionally contentious topics as immigration and toleration, but also gave the opposition a reason (or an excuse) for an all-out attack on the Bill. This would have been difficult or impossible if the measure's intention had been frankly avowed; but when its friends asserted that the Bill would do great good, its enemies were enabled to assert, without appearing ridiculous, that it would do great harm. They had a good chance of being believed, too, since the obvious discrepancy between the Bill's apparently limited scope, on the one hand, and its pretended great advantages, on the other, created genuine confusion and alarm in many minds.

It was in the first parliamentary debate on the Bill that its friends made this tactical error, in which they thenceforth persisted. That was on May 7, when the Bill was read for the second time in the House of Commons and was approved by 95 votes to 16. The Tories, realizing that they were certain to be outvoted, seem to have been less concerned with attempting to obstruct the pending measure than with using it as an occasion for reiterating, with appropriate topical embellishments, all of their favorite anti-immigration and antiministerial arguments. But instead of shrugging off this assault as ridiculously disproportionate to its object, the friends of the Bill, as was noted before, replied in kind. (It is quite likely that, provoked by the Tory attack, they partly lost sight of the Jew Bill in their eagerness to vindicate their traditional party position on immigration.) Thus it happened that the May 7 debate, though it was in no sense a part of the clamor—recall that it was not even reported in the newspapers—nevertheless was marked by the same characteristics as the later propaganda battle: from the Tories and the City came an absurdly exaggerated doctrinaire attack, and from the Court Whigs an essentially irrelevant doctrinaire defense.

[12] *Gent. Mag.*, 1753:354.

In addition to setting (or rather foreshadowing) the tone of the subsequent public controversy, the debate brought out all the major arguments that were later raised on both sides of the question. And so, by way of introduction to a more detailed examination of the propaganda battle, I shall summarize the arguments offered by both sides in the May 7 debate, and then attempt to set forth the actual substance of the opposition's point of view, as distinguished from the mere forensic froth.

The members who spoke in favor of the Bill on May 7 argued first, that the legal disabilities to which aliens were subject were so considerable that no rich foreign Jew would ever think of removing to England so long as it remained impossible for him to be naturalized.[13] Second, they contended that it was in England's own interest to modify the naturalization requirements so as to encourage such people to immigrate.

The Jewish immigrants would make loyal subjects, it was asserted; the patriotic behavior of the London community in 1745–46 put that beyond question.[14] Since the Jews always took care of their own poor, there was no reason to fear that any of the immigrants would become a public burden.[15] Besides, this bill would in practice open the door only to the rich, since (unlike Nugent's bills, and the acts of 1709 and 1740) it still required each applicant for naturalization to obtain a private act, a proceeding which would involve him in a great expense.[16] This requirement also left in the hands of Parliament an absolute control over the disposition of each particular case, and consequently over the total number to be admitted.[17]

Together these obstacles ensured that the Bill would result in the naturalization of only a few people: Pelham spoke in terms of "several," or "a few," and, more precisely, of forty or fifty heads of

---

[13] *P. Hist.*, XIV, 1378. Of course these printed speeches must not be taken as anything more than an approximation of what was said in the actual debate.

[14] *Ibid.*, p. 1402.

[15] *Ibid.*, p. 1401.

[16] *Ibid.*, pp. 1375, 1396, 1400. A private act, even when more than one name was included, was said to cost at least £20 or £30 for each applicant (*ibid.*, p. 147).

[17] *Ibid.*, pp. 1376, 1400–1401.

families.[18] But instead of emphasizing this point, the advocates of the Bill obscured it hopelessly by their rapturous dilatations upon the public benefits, mainly economic, that were likely (and some said, certain) to result from the passage of the Bill.

"In my opinion," said the enthusiastic Nugent, "it will bring rich Jews from all parts of the world to settle amongst us."[19] The consumption of domestic manufactures and farm produce would increase, which would stimulate employment.[20] Tax receipts would rise, and at the same time the increase in private capital available for investment would permit a reduction in the interest rate on public loans, with a consequent saving to the Treasury on debt service.[21] Some of these foreign Jews were already holders of government securities; if they could be attracted to England, the interest would remain at home, adding yearly a large sum to the national stock of gold and silver, instead of being spent abroad, perhaps among England's most avowed enemies.[22] There was no question but that the Jews' well-known abilities in matters relating to trade would be beneficial to the whole economy;[23] and the landed interest would be particular gainers by the Bill, since the entry of new Jewish bidders into the market for estates would raise the price of lands over the whole kingdom.[24]

Replying to the religious objections put forward by the opponents of the Bill, its advocates urged, at times eloquently, the usual arguments for toleration. Nor, they added, would the Bill be in any way hurtful to the Christian religion; in fact, it would in all likelihood prove to be quite the opposite. For while the Jews never proselytized, and so could do no injury to Christianity, yet there was a real hope that the natural human tendency to conform to the prevailing

---

[18] *Ibid.*, pp. 1414, 1416.

[19] *Ibid.*, p. 1387.

[20] *Ibid.*, 1387, 1416.

[21] *Ibid.*

[22] *Ibid.*, p. 1376.

[23] *Ibid.*, pp. 1376, 1386.

[24] *Ibid.*, pp. 1387, 1396, 1400. It is surprising that these three speakers should have been blind to the possibility that this argument might backfire. In his heated attack on the Bill in the final debate, Lord Egmont specifically referred to this "imprudent intimation" by the Bill's friends, and used it to show how great a threat the measure was (*ibid.*, pp. 1425–1426).

fashion in religion would lead to the conversion of many of the richest Jewish families, which would of course bring about the conversion of many of the poor.[25]

In sum, the Bill could do no harm; and (as Pelham put it) it would certainly be of some, and might be of very great, advantage to the country.[26] Nugent concluded even more strongly: "I know of no set of men in the Kingdom that will not be benefited by this Bill, except those merchants and shopkeepers who love to deal at an extravagant profit ... Thus, Sir, if we regard our interest, we must, I think, be for passing this Bill into a law." [27]

Tory members, as was said before, were quick to associate the Jew Bill with the other "naturalization schemes" that had been brought forward of late by "some notional gentlemen." They complained of the "prevailing humour of naturalizing foreigners," and criticized the Ministry's recourse to "the quack prescriptions of naturalizing Jews and foreign Protestants," when what the country really needed was a reduction in taxes.[28] Indeed, in the final debate Lord Egmont denounced the Jew Bill as part of an artful design to smooth the way for a reintroduction of Nugent's "hateful" bill to naturalize foreign Protestants, which had been "happily defeated" two years before.[29]

But the members who spoke against the Jew Bill on May 7 affected to believe that the measure was quite capable of ruining the country by itself. They began with the assumption that passage of the Bill would result in a great influx of Jews, an exaggeration to which the Bill's advocates unwittingly lent color with their inflated accounts of the measure's anticipated benefits. "We may, if we please," said

[25] *Ibid.*, pp. 1383–1385. (The speaker, Nugent, was himself a convert from Catholicism to the Church of England.) In the winter of 1751–52 the leaders of the Sephardic and Ashkenazic congregations of London joined in a formal agreement to discountenance proselytizing, which they termed a "pernicious and unlawful" practice. This move may have been intended to help prepare the ground for the later Bill. The documents are to be found in Roth, *Anglo-Jewish Letters*, pp. 126–128.

[26] *P. Hist.*, XIV, 1417.

[27] *Ibid.*, pp. 1387–1388.

[28] *Ibid.*, pp. 1369–1370, 1408, 1405.

[29] *Ibid.*, p. 1430. Egmont, however, was not a Tory. See also *LEP*, 4032:1.

Sir John Barnard, "call it only a Bill for empowering the Parliament to naturalize, but it will in effect be a general naturalization of the Jews." [30] Isham of Northamptonshire made a similar assertion: "Whatever may seem to be intended, every gentleman may foresee, that a general naturalization of the Hebrew nation will be the consequence." [31]

The notion that Parliament retained an effective check on the number of Jews to be naturalized was illusory, Isham asserted; for "if those of true English blood have not now the power to prevent opening this sluice for letting the torrent in upon us, can we hope, that they will have power enough to shut it up, after the torrent is broke in, and the Jews are become possessed, not only of all the wealth, but of many, perhaps most, of the land-estates in the Kingdom?" [32] Nor would the necessity of obtaining a private act restrict the number of applicants. Actually the cost was "very inconsiderable," and besides, rich Jews would pay the expenses of their poorer brethren.[33] Then too, where the rich come the poor must follow; and even if the poorest immigrants could not themselves afford to be naturalized, their children born in England would become English subjects.[34]

Having inflated the Bill into a general naturalization measure and having raised the chimera of a flood of Jewish immigrants, both rich and poor, the opposition proceeded to let its fancy play, with perverse enthusiasm, over the various particular forms which this general menace might conceivably assume. Thus Barnard asserted that the Jews might in time become England's only merchants and shopkeepers. The exclusion of all Christians from such activities would undo not only the former trading classes but the landed classes as well: for younger sons, debarred from going into trade, would deplete, rather than augment, the family fortune; and a family threatened with ruin could no longer look to a wealthy

[30] *P. Hist.*, XIV, 1394.   [31] *Ibid.*, p. 1379.
[32] *Ibid.*, p. 1381.   [33] *Ibid.*, p. 1379.
[34] *Ibid.*, pp. 1395, 1379.

younger son for help, or hope for a timely marriage with a mercantile heiress.[35]

As Jews replaced Christians as the owners of most landed estates, Jewish political influence would grow apace. Jews would soon have the vote and sit in Parliament, where they could join the Dissenters in repealing the Test Act and all the other laws for securing the Established Church.[36] Or they might engage in political action of a more direct sort, by furnishing an ambitious monarch with money to raise a mercenary army by means of which he and his Jewish abettors could enslave the kingdom. And if anything like this should ever come to pass, added the speaker sorrowfully, "God have mercy upon such of the natives as shall continue Christian; for I am sure our rulers the Jews would have none." [37]

The speeches against the Bill were so full of this sort of extravagance and rant that it is impossible to say just how much of the opposition's case was seriously meant, and how much ought to be attributed to partisan ebullition. Yet it is clear that beneath these half-humorous, half-bigoted, baroque elaborations lay a genuine dislike, perhaps not so much of the Jew Bill itself, as of the policy and principles on which it was based.

This dislike rested in its turn upon an opposing set of fundamental assumptions, attitudes, and prejudices, which informed the early opposition to the Bill and also served as the basis of the later propaganda campaign. Most of these opinions and feelings have already been touched upon briefly in the discussions of the motives behind the petitions against the Jew Bill, and behind the Tory and City resistance to earlier naturalization proposals.

The economic objections in particular require little additional explanation. There was, as we should expect, much talk about the Jews' supposed penchant for sharp dealing; it was also argued that the usual economic activities of the Jews were parasitical rather than beneficial, since Jews notoriously preferred usury to honest toil,

[35] *Ibid.*, p. 1393.   [36] *Ibid.*, pp. 1371, 1389.   [37] *Ibid.*, pp. 1408, 1411.

which is the true origin of trade.[38] But essentially the economic case against the Bill, as expounded in the debate by Barnard and Fazakerley and later by City pamphleteers, rested upon the concept of the static economy, and the restrictionist doctrines that followed from it. To the rosy predictions of the pro-immigration Whigs, the opponents replied with the assertion that the Bill could not possibly be beneficial, and was almost certain, indeed, to do harm:

Let us take, for example, Sir [said Barnard], the Kingdom of Portugal: does any man think that we do not now export as many of our manufactures thither as can possibly find a vent, or that our Portugal merchants and their factors, who are so numerous, and so independent of one another, do not sell those goods as cheap as they can be sold? Suppose, then, that we export yearly thither to the value of a million sterling, and that this is the utmost that can be exported: if we should naturalize all the Jews in the world, they could not add to that exportation: they could only come in for a share of it; and suppose that share to be £200,000 worth of goods yearly, is it not evident, that in this case one fifth of our English Portuguese merchants must give up the trade, or all of them together must trade for one fifth less than they used to do? This, therefore, could be of no advantage to our trade or manufacturers: it would only transfer the profit upon £200,000 worth of goods yearly from our native English merchants to our naturalized Jews.[39]

Nor, continued Barnard, could the Bill be expected to be beneficial in its effect on domestic, or internal, trade: "Have we not already as many English shop-keepers of all kinds as can be supported by the consumption? . . . Therefore . . . if Jew shop-keepers should increase, the Christian must diminish in number; so that if in this way the Bill now before us should have any effect, it would only be a transferring of a share of the profit upon our home consumption, from our native Christians to our naturalized Jews." [40]

Fears for particular economic privileges, too, though not mentioned in the May 7 debate, contributed to the strength of the public opposition to the Bill. This objection seems to have been first raised in a letter signed "A Stockholder," in the *Gentleman's Magazine* for

---

[38] *Ibid.*, pp. 1390–1391.   [39] *Ibid.*, p. 1392.   [40] *Ibid.*, p. 1393.

July. The writer presented a complicated and plausible legal argument purporting to show that the effect of the Bill—and its hidden
purpose as well—would be to admit naturalized Jews to offices in
the three great monopoly companies.[41] An answer in the next issue
confirms the weight that this point had with some persons: "The
making way for Jews to preside in our great companies, which one
of your correspondents has shewn to be a kind of concealed design
of the Jew Bill, has alarmed me more than all the objections so
zealously accumulated against it, and has converted some defenders
of the Bill; as it is a consequence which they did not apprehend, by
reason of the obscure wording of it." [42] Indeed, this argument made
such headway that a letter to the *Gentleman's Magazine* for October
assumed, *as the basis for a further objection,* that "rich Jews, in
consequence of this law, [would] become qualified to be governors,
directors, supercargoes, &c. of the three great companies." [43]

Another (and probably more general) source of opposition to the
Naturalization Bill was simply the traditionally strong sentiment
against foreigners, which was in the present instance reinforced and
heightened by anti-Semitism. This composite prejudice, and the relative importance of the two antipathies that constituted it, were explicitly set forth in a letter published in a Tory newspaper shortly
after the Bill's enactment. The writer commended the local Tory
candidates for being "against this Bill . . . [and] against every Bill
that has the least tendency to let in a swarm of *foreigners, especially
Jewish foreigners,* to lord it over Englishmen and Christians." [44]
Fazakerley gave voice to the same feeling in the May 7 debate when
he expressed the hope that British trade could be revived "by means
of our own people, without the assistance of naturalized Jews, or
any other foreigners." [45]

[41] *Gent. Mag.,* 1753:317–318.
[42] *Ibid.,* p. 382.
[43] *Ibid.,* p. 467.
[44] *Jackson,* 6:4 (June 9). My emphasis.
[45] *P. Hist.,* XIV, 1405–1406. It will be recalled that since all the Jews in England
were such recent immigrants, Englishmen would naturally think of Jews as foreigners,
and not just as religious nonconformists: anti-Semitism and xenophobia inevitably
went together. For another example of this, note the promise by a Tory political
association that its members "would exert themselves in the great causes of Chris-

Yet another important source of antipathy to the Bill, and one closely related to this antiforeign and anti-Jewish prejudice, was the fear that a large number of Jewish immigrants would eventually come into possession of landed estates—a kind of property that meant much not only in terms of economic and political power, but of prestige as well. Of course any naturalization measure could be regarded, at least theoretically, as a threat to the land. But the Jew Bill jarred this sensitive string in a particular as well as in a general way, and arguments against it on this head seem to have been especially effective: in fact, the Bill came to be widely regarded as an insidious attempt to grant the Jews (whether naturalized or not) certain valuable and new legal rights with respect to real property.

The rationale of this belief was rather subtle, and was no doubt more widely accepted than understood. It was based on the clause of the Jew Bill that forbade Jews to acquire or hold advowsons. According to the maxim *Exceptio firmat regulam in casibus non exceptis,* this specific restriction with respect to one kind of property implicitly affirmed the capacity of Jews to hold all other kinds, including landed estates.[46]

Now there were those who insisted that all the unrepealed medieval statutes restricting Jewish personal and property rights were still in force; in particular these persons argued that the law as it then stood denied the right of a Jew, even if native-born, to hold land except at the king's pleasure.[47] If this was so, then the Jew Bill's concealed implications were far-reaching indeed.[48] Actually, the best legal opinion held that the old restrictions did not apply to the Jews of 1753; but the question was a nice one, and even the

tianity and national birth-right, against all *Jewish* schemes . . . for the introduction of *foreigners* into this nation." (Add. MSS. 35398, f. 144. First emphasis mine.)

[46] *P. Hist.,* XV, 104. The clause in point, it will be recalled, was not even a part of the original Bill, but was added to it in the Lords to meet a particular objection.

[47] *An Historical Treatise Concerning Jews and Judaism in England* [London?, 1753], reviewed in *Gent. Mag.,* 1753:346; [Romaine], *Answer,* pp. 2ff.; *P. Hist.,* XIV, 1403, 1406; Add. MSS. 35592, ff. 88–89 (Bp. Secker to Hardwicke, June, 1753).

[48] E.g., a satirical print shows one Jew saying to another, "We can buy estates now" (Solomons, "Satirical Prints," p. 225). Surprisingly, Cecil Roth (who complains that the Bill's significance "is generally misunderstood") agrees with its contemporary enemies that the Bill's chief, though concealed, intention was to permit landholding

friends of the Bill took this opposition argument seriously. For example, Carteret Webb at the chancellor's behest searched the original rolls for evidence against it, and later published his findings in pamphlet form.[49]

Finally—though by no means last in order of importance—there was the widespread feeling that the Jew Bill, because of its implicit latitudinarianism, and specifically because of its curtailment of the scope of the sacramental test, was an affront, or even a danger, to the established religion. This sentiment should not be confused with anti-Semitism as such. At bottom it rested upon the medieval concept of the essential oneness of Church and State, which had been the basis of the act of 1609 that was now to be partly repealed. The preamble of that act affirmed that the "grace and favour" of naturalization should not be bestowed on any but "such as are of the religion now established in this realm."

The Jew Bill was by no means the first exception to this rule, but the opposition liked it no better for that. Both in the May 7 debate and in the canvassing for signatures against the Bill, opponents spoke of it as a threat to the Test Act.[50] In the same vein Isham of Northamptonshire took occasion from the Bill to wonder whether too much favor, rather than too little, had been shown to Jewish nonconformists: "I think that instead of resolving to go into a Committee upon this Bill, we should resolve to appoint a Secret Committee to enquire, whether the Jews be allowed to have a synagogue, or other place of public worship in this Kingdom, and if they have, by what authority that indulgence has been granted or allowed." [51]

---

by Jews (*Jews in England,* pp. 214–215, 215n). A. M. Hyamson, in his *History of the Jews in England* (London, 1908), pp. 278–279, makes the same mistake. Lucy Sutherland, in "Samson Gideon: Eighteenth Century Jewish Financier," p. 84, gives an explanation for this persistent error.

[49] Add. MSS. 35592, f. 129 (Webb to Hardwicke, Aug. 22); also, [P. C. Webb], *The Question, whether a Jew, born within the British Dominions, was, before the making the late Act of Parliament, a Person capable, by Law, to purchase and hold Lands to him, and his Heirs, Fairly Stated and Considered* (London, 1753).

[50] *P. Hist.,* XIV, 1389; *Considerations,* p. 27.

[51] *P. Hist.,* XIV, 1382.

In short, some men (mainly Tories) felt that in opposing this bill—or better, in opposing this *kind* of bill—they were making a stand in defense of religion and of the just prerogatives of the Established Church, against abandoned men (mainly Whigs) who cared not a whit for either. Thus Isham implied, in a sarcastic aside, that some gentlemen in the House had never looked into the Bible since they were at school; Barnard of London also deplored the prevailing irreligious tendency.[52] The same attitude was reflected in a print published in the later clamor, which showed a cross being attacked by a mob of Jews and Deists led by Samson Gideon and the late Lord Bolingbroke.[53]

These, then—restrictionist economic views, xenophobia compounded with anti-Semitism, and tutelary fears for the land and the Church—were the chief principles and prejudices on which the original opposition to the Jew Bill was based, and to which the propagandists of the later clamor made their appeal. There can be no doubt that these opinions and attitudes were widely and sincerely held; the success of the clamor is sufficient proof of that.

It is true that the propaganda campaign was almost wholly a matter of opportunistic electioneering by an unscrupulous opposition; but we must make clear exactly what we mean when we characterize their protests as essentially cynical and factitious. For what was artificial or insincere about the clamor was not so much the principles that the opponents affirmed, as their assertion that those principles were materially threatened by this insignificant bill. Or again: the Jew Bill was, in principle, the sort of measure that the

[52] *Ibid.*, pp. 1380, 1389. This Christian (and Tory) gloom deserves more attention than it has generally received: there was more to the intellectual climate of eighteenth-century England than the optimism and smugness of which so much is usually made. Note Oliver Goldsmith's characterization of the Jew Bill as "injurious to that religion which was still left among the populace" (*History of England*, London, 1771, IV, 340).

[53] Solomons, "Satirical Prints," facsimile facing p. 227. Ignoring the conspicuous exception of Bolingbroke, Tories in the 1750's insisted that Whiggism and Deism, if not identical, were at least very closely related. "A true Whig is a Deist," we are told; or again, "I do not say that all Whigs are Deists, but all Deists are certainly Whigs" (*Jackson*, 28:3, 47:3).

Tories and the City genuinely and traditionally disliked; but it was not, in fact, the substantial and far-reaching measure that, for election purposes, they fraudulently represented it to be.

THE PROPAGANDA AGAINST THE BILL

Almost without exception, the arguments used in the propaganda against the Jew Bill rested, explicitly or implicitly, on the false premise that the Bill would bring about an unlimited naturalization of foreign Jews. From there the propagandists proceeded, as we shall see, to discover dangers even more fantastic than those descried by the parliamentary opposition on May 7—which was no mean achievement. As we should expect, the clamor, unlike the debate, was characterized by attacks upon individuals such as Samson Gideon and Henry Pelham. It also rang many changes on the time-worn topic of bribery, now rejuvenated by wild talk of limitless amounts of Jewish gold, which, having purchased the Bill, would now purchase the election unless true Britons awoke to the danger. But otherwise there was little new by way of substance: almost all the arguments ultimately derived from one or another of the basic principles and prejudices already discussed.

Therefore our examination of the propaganda will be organized not around the arguments employed in the clamor, but around the principal methods by which those arguments were disseminated and by which pressure was brought upon Parliament to repeal the Act. A separate section will be devoted to each important propaganda medium (such as pamphlets, newspapers, prints), with descriptions of one or more representative examples. The propaganda in favor of the Bill will be dealt with in a separate chapter.

Pamphlets and Other Occasional Publications.[1] Perhaps the best indication of the magnitude of the clamor over the Jew Bill is the remarkable number of occasional publications that the controversy

---

[1] The pamphlet literature is the one part of the history of the Jew Bill that has been discussed at length in a published source, and I have accordingly chosen to treat it less fully here than it would otherwise deserve. In Hertz's *British Imperialism*

called forth. In the twelve-month interval between the first excitement over the Bill and the general election of 1754, roughly sixty pamphlets, leaflets, and broadsides directly pertaining to the controversy were published.[2] This figure does not include the many election publications that contained incidental references to the Bill, nor does it include the several works on Jewish theology and ritual that were either reissued or hastily got up, in order to take advantage of the sudden widespread curiosity about Judaism. Though the eighteenth-century fondness for irony makes it hazardous to assign unseen works to one side or the other on the basis of their titles, it would appear that those opposed to the Bill were the more numerous by three or four to one.

Most of the pamphlets ran to perhaps thirty octavo pages, but several approached or exceeded a length of one hundred pages. All of them seem to have been published in London; usually they were sold for sixpence or a shilling. One or two pamphlets on each side were widely distributed, but the influence of most of them must have been more or less limited to London, Edinburgh,[3] and the largest provincial towns.

Almost all these works were published anonymously, and we can say very little with certainty about the men and motives behind most of them. Some men with strong feelings on economics, religion, or party entered the controversy quite on their own. For example, Jonas Hanway, in his previously mentioned *Review of the Proposed Naturalization of the Jews,* was clearly breaking a private lance against the Bill.

Others wrote against the Jews and the Bill for hire; and among

---

there is a lively essay which, although it also contains some remarks on the episode as a whole, amounts really to a review of the pamphlets and the arguments they present. It is somewhat marred by a tendency to overemphasize the more outrageous or ridiculous assertions made by the opponents of the Bill.

[2] Roth, *Magna Bibliotheca Anglo-Judaica,* pp. 215–225. This list is incomplete, however; a few additional titles are to be found in the monthly lists of new publications in the *London Magazine* and the *Gentleman's Magazine.* But these in turn are not complete either.

[3] See the book lists in the *Scots Magazine.*

these was William Romaine, a London divine with a peevish and choleric disposition, narrow Evangelical opinions, and a large and fervent following.[4] Romaine undertook the defense of the City's role in the affair of the petitions. A ministerial writer who signed himself "Philo-Patriae" had sharply attacked the conduct and motives of the Portugal merchants and Common Councillors in that affair, and many copies of his pamphlet—Romaine said "several thousands"—had been dispersed throughout the kingdom. This work, entitled *Considerations on the Bill,* had appeared in August or September, and Romaine's *Answer* was published in October as "a proper antidote" to counteract the effect of the earlier piece on public opinion.[5] To ensure to the pamphlet the widest possible circulation the original edition, which sold for sixpence, was followed immediately by a second, which was distributed gratis at the expense of the City of London.[6]

Romaine's *Answer* went far beyond a mere justification of the actions of the merchants and citizens; two thirds of it was devoted to a violent general condemnation of the Jews and the Bill, mostly on legal and religious grounds. Instancing various medieval statutes which he said were still in force, and also certain of Coke's common-law opinions, Romaine asserted that a Jew, even if born in England, could not be a natural-born subject; nor could a Jew hold land except at the king's pleasure.[7]

More interestingly, he put forward (though with dubious sincerity) the medieval concept of England as a Christian society and state ruled over by Jesus Christ, with the king acting as His deputy.[8]

[4] For Romaine's life and singularly unattractive character see the account—often unintentionally amusing—in John Charles Ryle, *The Christian Leaders of the Last Century* (London, 1869). Ryle, an Anglican bishop, praises Romaine for his stand against the Jew Bill (pp. 160–161). That Romaine wrote for hire is only an assumption on my part.

[5] The full title is, *Answer to a Pamphlet Entitled "Considerations on the Bill to Permit Persons Professing the Jewish Religion to be Naturalized."* See the preface.

[6] Add. MSS. 35398, f. 178 (Birch to Yorke, Oct. 20). The title page of the second edition bears the note, "Reprinted by the Citizens of London."

[7] *Answer,* pp. 2ff., 10.

[8] *Ibid.,* p. 56.

Such a state, governed in accordance with Christian teachings and having the salvation of men's souls as its chief end, obviously had no room for Jews: as Coke had said, they were the Devil's subjects, not Christ's.[9] Therefore, declared Romaine—echoing the language of the City's petition—the naturalization of the Jews was a dishonor to the Christian religion, and had been regarded as such "ever since there was a Christian Society"; indeed, he went on, "the present set of [bishops] is the only one since the time of Christ, that would have countenanced so anti-Christian a measure."[10]

This sort of religious virulence was typical of most of the pamphlet. There was little manifest party spirit in the work—though the Biblical motto on the title page alluded (probably) to the current election campaign in London, and characterized the two sides in such a way as to suggest that Romaine was not exactly neutral: "The multitude of the City was divided," it reads, "and part held with the Jews, and part with the Apostles."[11]

Nor was very much space given to economic arguments, which might seem surprising in view of the City's sponsorship of the work. But in putting such considerations second, Romaine's *Answer* resembled the vast majority of the pamphlets opposed to the Bill. Ever since the City petition of May 21, public attacks on the Bill, whatever their source and motive, tended for tactical reasons to be pitched mainly upon the more comprehensive and emotional ground of religion; this was as true of the merchants' propaganda as it was of that of the High Church party.

The shifts of ground were not all in one direction, however: at times we find Tories offering mercantile arguments against the Bill. The fact is, that in spite of the more or less distinct doctrinal bases of each group's opposition to the Bill, both the merchants and the country Tories drew their ammunition indiscriminately from a common store, with each group using the other's arguments according to the needs of the moment.

A second pamphlet that appears, like Romaine's, to have been officially inspired, was the *Modest Apology for the Citizens and*

---

[9] *Ibid.*, pp. 9, 10.   [10] *Ibid.*, pp. 22, 25.   [11] Acts xiv, 4.

Merchants of London, who petitioned the House of Commons against Naturalizing the Jews. Written even before the Bill had received the royal assent,[12] it was among the ten or twelve publications on the Bill—almost all of them opposed to it—that appeared before the end of June. It was sixteen pages long, sold for fourpence, and went through three editions within a month.

The *Modest Apology*'s preface asserted that the Jew Bill was objectionable on both economic and religious grounds. Promising that the economic arguments would soon be collected and laid before the public, the pamphlet limited itself wholly to the second topic, which in its view was the real issue anyway: "The Bill . . . is entirely of a religious nature. It strikes at the root of our present establishment, and affects the very being of Christianity; and because great pains have been taken to make us believe that trade was the principal end in view, and to turn our attention from its malignant influence on our religion, we have therefore drawn these few hints together."[13]

Like Romaine, the anonymous author of the *Apology* argued that England was a Christian nation, "founded upon the doctrine of Jesus Christ," and could not admit these "crucifiers" without becoming involved in their inherited guilt.[14] Nor could any human authority remove this guilt, for it had been laid upon the Jewish nation by God Himself, and had even been made manifest in the Jews' personal appearance: "You know a Jew at first sight. And what then are his distinguishing features? Examine what it is peculiar that strikes you. It is not his dirty skin, for there are other people as nasty; neither is it the make of his body, for the Dutch are every whit as odd, awkward figures as the Jews. But look at his eyes. Don't you see a malignant blackness underneath them, which gives them such a cast, as bespeaks guilt and murder? You can never mistake a Jew by this mask, it throws such a dead, livid aspect over all his features, that he carries evidence enough in his face to convict him of being a crucifier."[15]

This is one of the nastiest anti-Semitic passages to be found in the

---

[12] *Apology*, p. iv.
[13] *Ibid.*, p. 1.
[14] *Ibid.*, pp. 3, 12, 14.
[15] *Ibid.*, pp. 5, 8–10.

literature of the clamor. Even the author seems to have had qualms about it, since he defended himself with the assertion that while his remarks were indeed severe, they were nevertheless true, and "truth cannot be uncharitable." [16] The repulsive performance ends with the hope that "these hints may suffice to set the subject in a clear light, so far as religion is concerned." [17]

The author of the *Apology,* again like Romaine, was content merely to stir up public hostility to Jewish naturalization, without attempting specifically to channel that hostility in the direction of the Ministry. But other hands were at work on that task, among them those of the anonymous author of *The Statesman and Broker,* a four-page libel which appeared, like the *Apology,* very early in the clamor. On July 5 an informant who signed himself simply "Z" wrote to the Duke of Newcastle to call attention to this piece: it was so defamatory, wrote "Z", that even the *London Evening Post* had "refused to print it, though carried . . . [there] by Lord Cornwallis's brother." [18] A few days later an agent forwarded a copy of the work; he had bought it, he said, near Temple Bar, from "an old woman who sells them . . . a miserable old creature with a blanket about her like a mumper." [19]

The work is an awkwardly written ballad telling how Samson Gideon called on Henry Pelham in order to arrange a naturalization bill on behalf of his whole "tribe." Pelham himself was willing to do anything his caller asked, so sensible was he of the past favors Gideon had performed, not only for him, but also for his "late friend BOB." Still, there were serious obstacles: "Barnard would rage"; the bishops would object, and his brother, too.

But surely, answered Gideon, the duke—and the chancellor, should he protest—could easily be bought. A "sweet'ning clause" could be put in for the bishops, forbidding Jews to present to livings on their estates; the prospect of gaining this valuable patronage would

---

[16] *Ibid.,* p. 10.
[17] *Ibid.,* p. 14.

[18] Add. MSS. 35413, f. 202.
[19] *Ibid.,* f. 212.

quickly end all objections from that quarter.[20] And the opposition of Barnard and the City, averred Gideon, was not worth worrying about.

These arguments, reinforced with a bribe of £100,000, thoroughly convinced Pelham:

> The bargain struck, they both withdrew,
>   Each to his occupation,
> G----n the City to undo,
>   And P----m the whole nation.[21]

No doubt to the disappointment of their eager agent, the Ministry chose not to prosecute this libel. And wisely: because, quite simply, if they had set even this as a criterion, and applied it consistently to everything that was published during the clamor, they would have been obliged to bring more actions than the courts could have heard in a year.

An Opposition Newspaper: Jackson's Oxford Journal. Jackson's Oxford Journal was a weekly paper; published Saturdays at Oxford, it circulated also in several nearby counties.[1] It consisted of four pages (one of them almost entirely devoted to advertisements), and sold for twopence. It was not an established paper, having been begun only in May of 1753, amid the rising excitement over the great Oxfordshire election of 1753–54. That famous contest was an old-fashioned Whig and Tory affair;[2] and in the struggle, in spite of his protestations about being a mere printer,[3] William Jackson was clearly on the Tory side, although he did occasionally print letters from Whig readers.

His chief topic, and in some numbers almost his only one, was the Jew Bill. Of course after the Bill's passage, there was almost no substantial news on the subject for over five months. Nor was there

---

[20] The same malicious interpretation of the advowson clause appears in one of the satirical prints. See plate, facing p. 4.

[21] All quotations are from a copy of *The Statesman and Broker* inserted in the Hardwicke papers (Add. MSS. 35413, ff. 214–216).

[1] Robson, *Oxfordshire Election*, p. 29.   [2] *Ibid.*, p. 43.   [3] *Jackson*, 1:3.

anything to report about the iniquitous activities of local Jews, for the simple reason that there *were* no local Jews.[4] But Jackson's ingenuity was equal to the challenge: from May until the end of the year, he managed to include some reference to the Bill or the Jews in every single issue.

This was most easily (and most honestly) accomplished by means of letters to the editor, perhaps most often genuine, but on occasion composed by Jackson himself or reprinted from the violent Tory *London Evening Post*. (In fact Jackson reproduced so many political pieces from the *London Evening Post* that it is to be presumed that some settled arrangement existed between the two papers.)[5]

Some of these pieces purported to convey news, such as the letter signed "Christiana" which informed Jackson's readers that a Jew had been overheard to say, on the Royal Exchange in London, "I hope to live now to see the day not to meet a Christian in this place, or an Englishman in the Kingdom." [6] Others more clearly kept to expressions of opinion, which were often coarse and cruel. "The Bill for naturalizing Jews," wrote "Britannicus," "now stirs our choler, and grumbles in our gizzards." [7] "Old England" declared that "had there been a law to inoculate the leprosy upon every man, woman, and child, throughout his Majesty's British Dominions, there had been less to complain of, than of the impure conjunction with Jewish blood, at the expense of all that can be called Christian amongst us." He went on to urge every freeholder, whether Churchman or Dissenter, to vote only for such candidates as promised to work for the repeal of the Bill.[8]

As will be supposed, Jackson and his Tory contributors more often than not went on from general denunciations of the Jew Bill to explicit attacks on the Whig candidates for Oxfordshire, Lord Parker

---

[4] See Chapter II, above, and Robson, p. 91. Jackson explained this as best he could, saying that "as [the Jews] and their abettors are well known to most of the friends of Christianity and the Old [i.e., Tory] Interest, particularly in Oxfordshire, since a remarkable period few or none of them have strolled that way" (16:2).

[5] E.g., all three passages quoted from *Jackson* in the next paragraph appeared first in the *London Evening Post*. And see Robson, p. 31.

[6] *Jackson*, 12:3. [7] *Ibid.*, 3:4. [8] *Ibid.*, 8:2.

and Sir Edward Turner. Thus "A Christian Freeholder," after speaking of the Jewish threat to the land, and raising the supposedly consequent specter of "a Jewish King upon the Throne, with a Jewish House of Lords, and a Jewish House of Commons," asserted "that the inventors and promoters of this Bill . . . are entirely in the interest of Lord Parker and Sir Edward Turner: and . . . that Lord Wenman and Sir James Dashwood, with their friends, are heartily against this Bill." [9] It did Parker and Turner no good to say that at heart they disliked the measure. In fact "An Englishman, and a Christian" would not even accept in exculpation Turner's plea that he had not been a Member of Parliament when the Bill was passed: "[It is] most probable, that if they did not, they would have voted FOR the said Bill, as (we know) the C--rt M-mb-rs did . . . I am bound to oppose the favourers of infidelity and circumcision." [10] And soon even the subtle distinction between Jews and their Whig "favourers" was totally lost, as in the story of the effigy of the "Jew" called Ned (Sir Edward Turner), or in attacks on "the Gideonites, the Parkerites, the Turnerites, and . . . Briberites of all the tribes of Israel." [11]

Nor did Jackson's news columns remain unaffected by his antipathy to the Jew Bill, to which he referred as "the Act in favour of the enemies of our Blessed Redeemer." [12] He gave prominence to stories about the opposition that the Bill had aroused elsewhere, and reported the brave slogans that candidates were using to show their distaste for it, such as "No Jews; Christianity and the Constitution," or "No Jews, no Naturalization Bill, Old England and Christianity for ever." [13] By such devices the clamor was made partly self-sustaining, and grew as it went.

[9] *Ibid.*, 6:4.

[10] *Ibid.*, 10:3.

[11] *Ibid.*, 13:2.

[12] *Ibid.*, 15:1.

[13] *Ibid.*, 12:2, 6:3. Among these slogans one does *not* find the famous "No Jews, no wooden shoes!" which can be counted on to appear in almost any modern account of the Jew Bill. (G. B. Hertz, for example, uses it for the title of his essay in *British Imperialism.*) Possibly it gained this currency from the piece by a Dr. Taylor (from *Bentley's Miscellany* for March 1848) that one finds prefixed to Isaac D'Israeli's popular *Curiosities of Literature* (e.g., London, 1893). But where Taylor got the slogan, I do not know—for I have met with it in no contemporary source whatever.

Less legitimately, Jackson also sought out news stories discreditable to Jews; he even found room on his front page for such trifles as an unsuccessful attempt by a Jewish pedlar in another county to cheat some young ladies.[14] Sometimes he added a comment of his own, to make certain that the point was not missed. For example, having taken occasion to present, as news, an account of the stolen goods trade in London, he concluded thus: "Numbers of Jews are employed in this vile traffick—pretty fellows indeed, and very proper for naturalization!"[15] A somewhat similar editorial embellishment appears in Jackson's otherwise factual report of the successful canvass of a Court candidate in another county: "By the irresistible influence and weight of the Hebrew wealth, which hath already begun to operate in these parts, [he] has gained his point."[16]

The last of these is not far from outright invention, and we find that, too, in the *Oxford Journal:* for Jackson was perfectly willing to insert totally fraudulent news items among the genuine ones from both home and abroad. Thus his readers were told that the Jews of Algiers were said to be preparing to embark for England to take advantage of the late act.[17] Or again, directly after some verses telling how the Bill was obtained by bribing the Pelhams, there came this not unrelated "news" story from London: "The day the Jew Bill passed, Mr. Fr*nc* [Franco] took out of the bank twenty-seven bank notes for one thousand pounds each."[18] And, playing upon one of his readers' chief anxieties, Jackson printed this report: "We hear A—— F——, Esq., a considerable Jew merchant, has lately bought the Manor of P——, in the County of Leicester, and the estate thereto belonging, for the sum of £41,000."[19]

Perhaps the most improbable of these inventions was a report from Alnwick, in Northumberland, "that a certain curate in that

---

Mrs. M. D. George refers to the slogan in her *English Political Caricature to 1792* (Oxford, 1959), p. 100, but without a specific citation. She informs me that in her opinion the probability that the slogan was used is "very great." For its meaning, see her index, s.v. "Slogans: slavery and wooden shoes."

[14] *Jackson*, 15:1. (Also in *LEP*, 4013:1.)
[15] *Ibid.*, 11:1.
[16] *Ibid.*, 12:1.
[17] *Ibid.*, 15:1.
[18] *Ibid.*, 25:2.
[19] *Ibid.*, 12:3.

neighourhood [had been] sent for to christen a child, instead of which he circumcised him; and being the first time of his performing that operation, the infant died." This would soon become a custom, the curate added. Jackson suggested that this act had been encouraged by the success of the "great Jew [Whig] meeting, held at A[lnwic]k in the beginning of July last." "The above account," concluded Jackson, "though shocking, we are informed is true." [20] In fairness it should be added that some of Jackson's inventions were more whimsical than malicious—such as the report that a group of Whig sportsmen had opened a subscription "for a Jew plate to be run for by circumcised horses." [21]

Once the election was over, Jackson's extraordinary interest in Jews totally disappeared; clearly it had been a matter of opposition politics from the first. This is revealed in two particular ways. One is the straightforward treatment, in the *Oxford Journal* for June 8, 1754, of an incident involving the Jews of Norwich that could easily have been exploited for propaganda if the editor had wished.[22]

The second was the paper's occasional inconsistency in applying its prime criterion of political respectability. Thus it attacked Sir William Calvert of London, a Court member, for voting for the Bill; but at the same time that it denounced Calvert as "the Jewish candidate," the *Oxford Journal* was willing to puff the candidacy (for Westminster) of an opposition worthy who had also voted for the Bill—though of course it suppressed that inconvenient detail.[23] Thus whatever was sincere in Jackson's dislike of the Jew Bill yielded precedence, in this instance, to his far stronger dislike of the Pelhams.

Jackson's propaganda campaign seems to have been remarkably effective; indeed its results were more far-reaching than he can have known. For, as we shall see in a later chapter, it was apparently the "anti-Jewish" excitement in Oxfordshire, which Jackson had done

[20] *Ibid.*, 20:1. [21] *Ibid.*, 19:3. [22] *Ibid.*, 58:1.
[23] *Ibid.*, 47:1, 53:2, 51:3. The second person referred to is the famous General Oglethorpe.

so much to foment, that led to the Ministry's decision to repeal the Bill.

Magazines. Like almost every other kind of periodical publication, the important monthly magazines[1] took sides over the Jew Bill, the *London Magazine* opposing, and the *Gentleman's Magazine* supporting it.[2] The latter's advocacy of the Bill was only moderate, however, and since it opened its columns to both sides, the *Gentleman's Magazine* must have a place alongside its rival and imitator, in this discussion of the magazines' part in the propaganda campaign against the Bill.

These monthly magazines were still for the most part what the name implies: collections of occasional contributions and of pieces that had already been published elsewhere.[3] Therefore, while Jackson can be said, in more than one sense, to have played a creative role in the clamor, the magazines naturally tended to reflect other manifestations of the controversy, instead of contributing much of their own.

This does not mean that they were unimportant, however. For in addition to assuring a wider audience to the pieces they reprinted, the magazines also offered some material that was nowhere else available, such as the reports of the parliamentary debates on the Bill. Between June and September the *London Magazine* published, under the usual patent disguises, eight speeches from the debate of May 7, and Lord Egmont's speech in favor of delaying the third reading. Except for Egmont's speech, which was printed in the *Gentleman's Magazine* and also sold in the form of a broadside, these could only be found in the *London Magazine,* to which source Jackson and other editors referred their readers.[4]

---

[1] I largely pass over such magazines as the *Universal,* which was essentially non-political, and the *Scots,* of Edinburgh, which for the most part took its material on the Jew Bill straight from the *London Magazine.*

[2] *Lond. Mag.,* 1754:213; *Gent. Mag.,* 1753:354.

[3] One of the mottoes on the title page of the *Gentleman's Magazine* was *E pluribus unum.*

[4] *Lond. Mag.,* 1753:257–266, 305–321, 353–356, 401–406: *Gent. Mag.,* 1753:477–481; Solomons, "Satirical Prints," p. 227; *Jackson,* 16:2; *LEP,* 4073:1.

A similar documentary service was rendered by the *Gentleman's Magazine,* which devoted five pages of one issue to reprinting several addresses and instructions on the subject of the Jew Bill from constituencies to their members, together with the members' replies. Since almost all of these, both addresses and answers, vied with one another to see which could denounce the Bill in the strongest terms, their wide dissemination by the magazine, whatever the editor's intentions, can only have added to the strength of the clamor.[5]

Among the published sources on which the magazines depended most heavily for material were the weekly essay-papers written in the tradition of Addison and Steele; for example, in 1753 the *London Magazine* reprinted nine more or less complete numbers of the *World,* and seven of the *Adventurer.* Since these papers occasionally touched upon the controversy over the Jew Bill, the magazines, in bringing them before a new audience, were contributing to the clamor, if only at second hand. Thus a person who was not a regular reader of the *Craftsman*—and nobody could have kept up with *all* these papers—might nevertheless have read, in the *London Magazine* for July, the burlesque "Hebrew Journal" for one hundred years hence, which had appeared in the *Craftsman* of July 14.[6] Here are a few typical excerpts:

At two o'clock this morning died at his house in Grosvenor-square, the right Hon. the earl of Balaam, baron of Zimri, and knight of the most noble order of Melchizedeck.

We are . . . informed, that the statue of Sir John Barnard, formerly father of this City, and a strenuous asserter of Christianity, is ordered to be taken down, and that of Pontius Pilate to be put up in his room.

Last night the Bill for naturalizing Christians was thrown out of the Sanhedrim by a very great majority.

This morning early the Hon. Mendez Gidion, Esq., set out from his house in Arlington-street for Scarborough, for the recovery of his health.[7]

---

[5] *Gent. Mag.,* 1753:467–472. Also *Lond. Mag.,* 1753:473–474. These instructions first appeared in various country newspapers and in the *London Evening Post;* they are discussed in a separate section, below.

[6] The dates are correct: these magazines, unlike ours, were published at the end of the month.

[7] *Lond. Mag.,* 1753:302–303. To this piece the magazine appended an interesting partial disclaimer, commenting that such lampoons were "far from agreeable to the

These excerpts, incidentally, illustrate the way in which Jewish terms and proper names were used in 1753 as a universally understood political jargon or code-language, a development which testifies eloquently to the effectiveness and extent of the clamor. The last item is a perfect example of this: for as every reader knew at once from the other proper names, one had only to translate "Mendez Gidion" to read "Henry Pelham," and the paragraph became a recent and true news story.[8]

The controversy over the Jew Bill even made its way into some of the light verse[9] and songs[10] submitted to the magazines; but this again was more a reflection of the public's fascination with the topic than an intentional or significant contribution to the clamor. In two of the *London Magazine*'s regular features, however, one does find a few examples of the sort of deliberate propaganda tricks that *Jackson's Oxford Journal* employed against the Bill. In the July issue, for example, the magazine found room for only six news stories under "Foreign Affairs," and of these, three—in fact, the first three— concerned Jews. The first of these stories was quite in the grandest manner of the *Oxford Journal,* both in its blatant editorial bias and (probably) in its fictional nature as well: "Our last accounts from Vienna say, that prince Venceslaus of Litchenstein has had one of his finest seats . . . destroyed by fire, of which a Jew is said to be the author, in revenge of the prince's refusing to renew an advantageous lease of a farm he was possessed of, which is a fresh instance of the implacable revenge so natural to that people; and this natural disposition of theirs shews how necessary those strict injunctions were, which we have in the gospel against resentment and revenge." [11] Another of the stories is somewhat suspect at best, and I have not seen it confirmed in any trustworthy source.[12]

---

true spirit of Christianity." Yet the magazine did, after all, reprint it—as did the *London Evening Post* and *Jackson's Oxford Journal.*

[8] See *WEP,* 1152:3 (June 29).

[9] *Gent. Mag.,* 1753:384, 385. More seriously intended were the verses in *Gent. Mag.,* 1753:436, and *Scots Mag.,* 1753:247.

[10] *Gent. Mag.,* 1753:482.

[11] *Lond. Mag.,* 1753:342; cf. the version in *LEP,* 4006:1.

[12] Following a familiar pattern, it tells of a young Jew of Copenhagen who had

A more subtle device employed by the *London Magazine* was the distortion, in its list of new publications, of the titles of works defending the Jew Bill. Such works usually attempted to emphasize in their titles the limited scope and the merely permissive character of the Bill, in order to counter the opposition canard that the measure was an unlimited naturalization of the whole Jewish nation. Here are two such titles as they appeared correctly, in the well-disposed (and honest) *Gentleman's Magazine:*

Considerations on the bill to permit persons professing the Jewish religion to be naturalized by Parliament.

A candid and impartial examination of the act permitting foreign Jews to be naturalized without receiving the sacrament.[13]

Here is the way they were listed in the *London Magazine:*

Considerations on the Act to naturalize the Jews.
A candid Examination of the Act for naturalizing the Jews.[14]

In like manner, the *London Magazine* altered pamphlet titles so as to suppress any suggestion of the factitious clamor in which it was taking part. Here are two correct titles:

An Earnest and Serious Address to the Free-holders and Electors of Great Britain, on occasion of the clamor raised against the Bill to permit persons to apply for naturalization, professing the Jewish religion.

Popular clamour against the Jews indefensible. A sermon preached at Huntingdon October the 28th, 1753.

And here is the way they appeared in the *London Magazine:*

An earnest Address to the Freeholders and Electors of Great-Britain on Occasion of the Naturalization of the Jews.

A Sermon in Defence of the Jews, preached at Huntingdon, Oct. 28, 1753.[15]

---

become a Lutheran: "Being invited to sup at a house in the principal quarter of the Jews, he [went] thither, but has never since reappeared. [The King] has ordered the Jews to produce this young man in a certain time, on pain of forfeiting eight thousand German crowns" (also in *LEP,* 4003:4).
[13] *Gent. Mag.,* 1753:447. [14] *Lond. Mag.,* 1753:487. [15] *Ibid.,* pp. 487, 535.

About the correspondence from readers little need be said. The letters were pitched at a higher plane of discussion than those in the *Oxford Journal,* and largely avoided references to political parties or to individuals. Thus they resembled the pamphlets more than they did the letters (genuine and pretended) to the newspapers, and in fact should be considered principally as an adjunct to the pamphlet controversy. The *London Magazine,* for example, carried two long communications in answer to particular pamphlets favoring the Bill.[16] Again, when P. C. Webb published his defense of the Jews' legal right to hold lands, the *London Magazine* printed over a page of excerpts from his pamphlet, together with a reader's translation of a lengthy medieval statute that was thought to refute Webb's arguments.[17] The quotations from Webb were an exception to the *London Magazine*'s usual practice, however; for while the *Gentleman's Magazine* was fair about giving space to both sides, the *London Magazine* all but completely excluded the defenders of the Bill from its columns.

The Polite Weeklies. According to a widely reprinted occasional prologue, written by Garrick and spoken by the comedian Foote,

> The many various objects that amuse
> These busy curious times, by way of news,
> Are, plays, elections, murders, lott'ries, Jews.[1]

This being so, the Jew Bill automatically became a topic for those weekly essay-papers which both reflected and supplied the talk of the fashionable part of the town. To a large extent these papers took the lighthearted and careless view of politics that is implicit in Garrick's lines, and that is so often found in people whose chief interests are those to which these weeklies addressed themselves: fashions, manners, literary criticism, and the theater. Thus in many of their references to the Jews or to the Bill, these papers seem mainly to be exploiting the controversy for its entertainment value: for example,

---

[16] *Ibid.,* pp. 456–458, 523–525.   [17] *Ibid.,* pp. 515–517, 521–523.
[1] *Gray's Inn Journal,* 5:29 (Oct. 27); *Gent. Mag.,* 1753:484; *Lond. Mag.,* 1753:484.

in the frequent use of the code-language, or of fantastic pseudo-Jewish names, as material for wit.

Of course even this helped to swell the clamor and to make it self-sustaining; and the lack of political intent was of small comfort to the Ministry: for the jocular use of a Jewish name when "Pelham," say, was meant, served to reinforce in the public mind the association between the Ministry and the unpopular Bill. Moreover, some of the squibs in the weeklies clearly had a purpose beyond that laid down by a typical paper, of promoting "useful mirth and good humour." [2]

One finds a good deal of the sort of whimsy exemplified by the "Hebrew Journal" from the *Craftsman,* of which a specimen was quoted in the last section. This combination of pleasantry and politics was greatly relished by the public,[3] and when the *Gray's Inn Journal* succeeded the *Craftsman* in the autumn of 1753, the feature was continued in the new paper. There we read that the Lord Viscount Salvadore (in 1853) gave a party where toasts were drunk to "Our present happy Establishment in Synagogue and State, The glorious and immortal Memory of HARRY THE NINTH, the Anti-Christian Prelates," and others.[4] In a similar vein, the *Connoisseur* printed a make-believe letter from a Jewish art collector, listing his recent acquisitions. Most bore such names as "The Triumph of Gideon" and "A Sampson in miniature." He had also bought "Peter denying his Master" and "Judas betraying him for thirty pieces of silver"—"both of which," he wrote, "I design as presents to our two worthy friends the B[ishop]s of —— and ——." [5]

Arthur Murphy, the author of the *Gray's Inn Journal,* went well

---

[2] *Gray's Inn Journal,* [1]:4 (Sept. 29).

[3] It was imitated by the *London Evening Post* and by *Jackson's Oxford Journal.* Referring to an issue of the *London Evening Post* in which the feature appeared, John Yorke wrote to his brother, "I have not yet seen it, as they were all bought up immediately by the wits" (Add. MSS. 35374, f. 92: to Philip Yorke, July 24).

[4] *Gray's Inn Journal,* [2]:11–12 (Oct. 6). "Harry IX" is a reference to Henry, Cardinal York (1725–1807), the brother of the Young Pretender, Prince Charles Edward.

[5] *Connoisseur,* 2:9–11 (Feb. 7, 1754). The two bishops are Secker and Drummond, who had spoken well of the Bill when its repeal was debated. The art collector is Samson Gideon himself (see *DNB*).

beyond this, explicitly avowing his dislike of the Bill, and calling for its repeal. After some dire predictions for the year 1853, he commented (in his assumed character of "Charles Ranger, esq."): "Gay and airy as I am, I seriously wish, that not only [these future] evils . . . but also the apprehension of them may be timely averted, by the interposition of superior power." [6]

Though Murphy's dislike of the Bill seems to have been sincere, partisan considerations clearly had more than a little to do with his attacks on it; in fact, as late as five months after the repeal of the Bill, the *Gray's Inn Journal* was still using the Jews to belabor the Court party. [7] Murphy's strongest single political piece was an attack on Calvert of London, which will be quoted later in a section on the City election. Another squib that was aimed at a specific Court politician was an ostensible appeal for votes and interest that appeared at a time when similar advertisements could be found in every newspaper. Written at Lewes in "1853," it begged the "Gentlemen, Rabbi, and Freeholders of the County of Sussex" to support the candidacy of "Launcelot Gobbo" in the election for the next "Sanhedrim." [8] Again the proper names enabled every reader to identify "Gobbo" as the prime minister; and although there was meant to be humor as well as politics in the little parody, it is likely that Henry Pelham was not greatly amused.

A Political Weekly: The Protester. In the spring of 1753, before the Jew Bill became an issue, a group of politicians of whom the most prominent were the Duke of Bedford and William Beckford, engaged the hack journalist James Ralph to write an antiministerial newspaper. In addition to being paid handsomely, Ralph was given promises of entire liberty to write what he would, and of protection in both Houses of Parliament in case the Ministry should prosecute him. [1] As a result of this agreement a weekly called *The Protester,*

---

[6] *Gray's Inn Journal*, [2]:11 (Oct. 6).

[7] E.g., 31:186 (April 27, 1754).

[8] *Ibid.*, [2]:12 (Oct. 6). Reprinted in *LEP*, 4042:1 (Oct. 9). Launcelot Gobbo is a comic (Gentile) servant of Shylock in Shakespeare's *Merchant of Venice*.

[1] Bubb Dodington, *Diary* (Salisbury, 1784), pp. 235–236. Bedford's part in this soon became known to the Court party (see Add. MSS. 35398, ff. 117, 118). For

on behalf of the People, "by Issachar Barebone, one of the People," made its appearance on June 2. Each number was six pages long, and sold for twopence.

Naturally the Jew Bill became one of Ralph's principal topics. Against it, and against the Ministry, "under [whose] avowed protection the Bill was passed," [2] he offered a grab bag of religious, economic, political, and constitutional arguments whose sincerity was, to say the least, questionable, since Ralph not long before had volunteered his pen to Henry Pelham, who had refused it.[3] Ralph praised the spirit shown by the grand juries and corporations that had formally protested against the Bill, and he implied that Parliament was obliged, as an instrument of the popular will, to respond by repealing it.[4] To those for whom this argument did not suffice, Ralph offered the natural-law doctrine associated with Coke: "According to the maxims of the old lawyers, any law that is against the law of God, or inconsistent with common sense, is void in itself." [5] Or again, the Bill was "palpably irreconcilable with Holy Writ," and so was utterly incompatible with the English Constitution, which was based upon Christianity.[6]

Ralph put forward various practical, as well as constitutional, objections to the Bill, some of them so extravagant that he apparently felt it necessary to rationalize his position in advance. This he did by professing to be greatly shocked that the Bill had been passed at all: since such an occurrence "would have been held impossible, if wantonly surmised before it did happen, so any surmise, how wanton soever, may now pretend to an exemption from absolute disbelief." [7] Thereafter he took liberal advantage of this self-bestowed dispensation from the requirements even of plausibility. We find, for example (in addition to the more usual bugbears), expressions of concern that a board of Jewish farmers-general might be put in charge of the

---

Ralph himself, see the *DNB* and Benjamin Franklin's *Autobiography:* Ralph was an American who came to England with Franklin in 1724 and settled there.

[2] *Protester,* 10:59.

[3] Dodington, p. 237; and a letter from Pelham to Newcastle, July 20, in Coxe, *Pelham,* II, 485.

[4] *Protester,* 2:12, 11:63, 13:78, 20:115.

[5] *Ibid.,* 14:79.   [6] *Ibid.,* 10:57–58.   [7] *Ibid.,* 3:16.

entire revenue, or that a "coalition" between the Jews and the Ministry might be formed—though on just what terms, Ralph thought it too early to predict.[8]

To reinforce his attacks on the Bill, and further to arouse his readers' prejudices and anxieties, Ralph reviled the Jews in such a loathsome manner that a positive effort is required to keep in mind the fact that his real purpose was to injure not them, but the Pelham ministry. Jews, he asserted, "cannot be incorporated with Englishmen, without violating whatever Englishmen hold sacred."[9] "Their very breed," he wrote, "is in general of the lowest, basest, and most contemptible kind, distinguishable to the eye by peculiar marks, odious for that distinction, and what, if once communicated to a family, becomes indelible." If we concern ourselves with the breed of horses and cattle, surely we ought to care about *men*. The consequences of not doing so could be observed in the case of the Portuguese, who had degenerated as a result of mixing with "the impure blood of the Jews." Therefore, concluded Ralph, "the wise politician . . . would most rigidly punish every carnal trespass."[10] (This is one of the very few examples I have found—and clearly the most extreme—of an anti-Semitism that is essentially racial rather than religious.)

One of Ralph's passing comments is interesting on account of its explicit reference to the long-standing argument over immigration policy, and more particularly on account of its assumption that both Nugent's recent proposal and the Jew Bill itself were part of the continuing struggle: "Naturalization-projects are no new things: ever since the Revolution they have been continually promoted by some state-adventurer or other, and never without exciting a national disgust . . . It was but yesterday, as it were, that the controversy was revived on the same basis and with the same success."[11]

---

[8] *Ibid.*, 3:16–17.   [9] *Ibid.*, 21:122.   [10] *Ibid.*, 10:58.

[11] *Ibid.*, 11:63. There is also an explicit reference (21:124) to the short-lived Naturalization Act of 1709. Note that these passages, in addition to demonstrating the continuity of the old split over naturalization policy, also provide support for Namier's view of the politics of this period. For the doctrine implicit here is clearly Tory; indeed, elsewhere in the *Protester* there are even arguments and remarks with

The *Protester* was quite frequently reprinted[12] and was much discussed:[13] it was plainly an influential paper. And the best proof of its effectiveness lies in the fact that the Ministry offered Ralph a pension of £300 a year if he would lay down his pen.[14] The arrangement made, he returned the Duke of Bedford's money, accepted the Duke of Newcastle's, and wrote a final number disavowing what he had written in the others.[15] In it he specifically referred to the Jew Bill as a trifling matter, and spoke of the protests against it as having been "promoted." [16] On that point, at least, he spoke truly, and from certain knowledge.

Satirical Prints. The Jew Bill, as we should expect, was the subject of a number of satirical prints or cartoons. These were quite as caustic as the works of Rowlandson and Gillray a generation later, but were much cruder in both conception and execution. As a rule they were somewhat smaller than a quarto page, and sold for sixpence in black and white, or a shilling colored. A catalogue of prints about the Bill lists twenty-five that appeared before the elections of 1754 ended, and while it is possible that the list is incomplete, I have discovered no omission worth mentioning.[1]

Every one of these prints attacks the Jews, their bill, and its supporters: there is nothing at all on the other side of the argument. Since they all seem to have been printed in London, it is not surprising that some of them are primarily concerned with the contest for

---

Jacobite overtones, such as a sarcastic reference (18:105) to a newly minted coin of George II, "with so many additions of German arms, and German titles on it." Evidently the opposition Whig duke who was paying for this thought of himself more as an "out" than as a Whig.

[12] *Lond. Mag.*, 1753:460; *Scots Mag.*, 1753:313, 329, 369.

[13] E.g., Add. MSS. 35398, f. 150 (Yorke to Birch, Aug. 23): "Pray what is Ralph upon in the *Protester?*" Also *ibid.*, ff. 117, 118, 161, 177, 180.

[14] Dodington, p. 251.

[15] Bedford, John, 4th duke of, *Correspondence of John, Fourth Duke of Bedford* (London, 1842–1846), II, 135–136 (Ralph to Bedford, Nov. 10). Among other excuses for discontinuing the paper, he pleaded "repeated attacks of the gout."

[16] *Protester*, 24:141, 143.

[1] Solomons, "Satirical Prints," 205–233; includes several reproductions.

the City's four seats; but most of these would be perfectly clear, nevertheless, to non-Londoners. The personages most frequently met with in these prints are the Pelham brothers, Sir William Calvert (the London M.P. who had voted for the Bill), and the unfortunate Samson Gideon, who, being the best-known English Jew, was pilloried as the chief promoter of a measure which in fact he had come strongly to dislike.

Many of these prints attempt to associate the Bill and its supporters with other unpopular causes or groups. For example, one print links the Jews with the Deists as allies against Christianity.[2] Perhaps the most ludicrous of these attempted associations appears in a quatrain subjoined to a print entitled "A Prospect of the new Jerusalem [London]":

> The Devil, Infidels! Hereticks! and Turks!
> These can't be English, these are Romish works:
> Some Popish Plot to bring in the Pretender;
> Pray Heaven guard our glorious Faith's Defender![3]

But most of the prints are variations upon a very simple theme: bribery. The most extravagant of them sets the price of the Pelham brothers at £500,000, and that of Calvert of London at £100,000.[4] Another, more restrained, shows Gideon presenting the Pelhams with a purse which presumably contains only the modest £200,000 that is shown, on a list lying at Gideon's feet, as the total amount collected "from the West Indies, Portugal, Holland, Metz, Prague, England &c." Pointing to the bag of money, Gideon says, "Dare Gentlemens, & my very good Friends, Dis be de Puss collected by our Tribe for de great Favour."[5]

Gideon's accent and faulty grammar in this print are interesting as a propaganda trick. He was London-born, it will be recalled, and his

---

[2] *Ibid.,* facsimile facing p. 227.

[3] *Ibid.,* facsimile facing p. 218. Cf. the following couplet, which the *Westminster Journal* (quoted in *LEP,* 4131:1) put in the mouth of an M.P. who had voted for the Bill: "So down with your rights, ecclesiastic and civil;/ And up with the French, with the Jews, and the Devil."

[4] *Ibid.,* p. 219.   [5] See plate, facing p. 4.

few surviving letters show that he wrote correct and spirited English.[6] It is possible, of course, that he spoke with a slight accent; but since he was a Sephardi, that accent could hardly have included the Yiddish-German distortions attributed to him in some of these prints. The most extreme example of this occurs in a print which appeared soon after the repeal of the Bill, and which pictures Samson, thinly disguised as "Noedig ye Dupe," bewailing the waste of the huge outlay of bribes by which he had obtained its passage. "Vat Sall Ik do voor myn gelt," he is made to exclaim, "myn gelt dat is all, myn gelt myn gelt." [7]

What we see here is a clever blending of the two groups of English Jews into a single composite image that suited the purposes of the clamorers better than either real one. By combining the wealth and power of the Sephardim with the foreignness and low social status of the Ashkenazim, they were able to create the perfect propaganda stereotype—one that the ill-informed could both fear and despise at the same time. This confusion, partly fostered by propaganda, but partly the natural result of the public's lack of acquaintance with the two groups of Jews, appears again and again in the controversial literature of 1753–54.

Direct Pressure on M.P.'s: Instructions from Constituents. During the summer and autumn of 1753, over a dozen formal protests against the Jew Bill were drawn up by county grand juries and municipal corporations for presentation to the local Members of Parliament or to the competing candidates. These "instructions," as they were called, made a threefold contribution to the clamor and to its political effectiveness. First, they placed the particular politicians to whom they were addressed under the strongest kind of pressure to denounce the Bill and thus, by implication, the Ministry. Second, when published, the instructions and the usually compliant replies

---

[6] See, e.g., Roth, *Anglo-Jewish Letters,* pp. 131–132; Sutherland, "Samson Gideon: Eighteenth Century Jewish Financier," pp. 85, 88–89; and *Hist. MSS. Comm., Lothian Papers,* pp. 148ff.

[7] Solomons, p. 228.

not only added to the volume of the clamor, but provided yet another kind of evidence to show how intense and how widespread was the opposition to the Bill. And finally, they provided the sort of evidence most likely to convince politicians in general that the outcry against the Bill was a political force to be taken seriously. One could shrug off the drunken mobs, perhaps; but these protests came from gentlemen with votes and interest.[1]

The first of these instructions was dated August 2, and was addressed to the two members for Wiltshire by the sheriff and grand jury of the county, who were met at Salisbury for the summer assizes. It was a lengthy, rhetorical document, composed, according to a Whig friend of the Bill, "with all the virulence and absurdity which a Jacobite country divine (for such the writer seems) can furnish upon such a topic." [2] However this might be, the Wiltshire instruction was obviously drafted with a primary view to its effectiveness as propaganda, and was plainly intended for publication. (This does not mean, of course, that those who assented to it were not genuinely opposed to the Bill.)

It began with an expression of confidence in the sitting members, and then turned to its particular "complaint": for who, it asked, "that has any cordial concern for the religion or commerce of his country, can help complaining, when he reflects on the unprecedented privileges lately conferred on the Jews?" It is surprising, continued the address, "that any man, who calls himself a Christian, should be so fond of naturalizing these Jews, who are the only avowed enemies to the Christian religion . . . [and] the people who crucified our blessed Saviour . . . Let us not so degenerate from our ancestors, as to take these serpents into our bosoms; but let us rather exert ourselves as becomes true Christians and true Britons, to defend our laws, religion, and liberties, from being trampled on by Jewish or foreign tyranny." After much more in this vein, the protest closed with a specific request to the county members: "Our request to you,

---

[1] See Add. MSS. 35398, f. 145 (Birch to Yorke, Aug. 11): These instructions "may render the affair more serious than I at first thought it."
[2] *Ibid.*

gentlemen, is, that you would exert yourselves on this important occasion. If you find it beyond your power to stifle this infant law, yet we flatter ourselves your efforts may prevent its progress; a vigorous opposition to each private Bill may possibly defeat the intention of the publick one already enacted." The instruction was signed by the sheriff and twenty-one others.[3]

The text of the Wiltshire instruction was immediately printed by opposition newspapers both in London and in the provinces.[4] A fortnight later the grand jury of Essex followed Wiltshire's lead. They took the earlier document as their model, but went beyond it to request that their members "use [their] utmost efforts to procure a speedy repeal."[5] Other constituencies followed suit with similar protests, which invariably included a demand for the repeal of the obnoxious Act.

These later protests, too, were widely reprinted and variously commented on. Friends of the Ministry and the Bill deplored their extreme language; Ralph, in the *Protester,* praised them as representing a long-overdue revival of the gallant old English spirit.[6] A letter in the *Oxford Journal* expressed similar satisfaction, and drew a parallel between the resistance to the Jew Bill and that of the seven bishops to James II.[7]

Though the connotations of the words "planned in advance" might be too strong, still it is certain that the opposition had for some time been talking of these protests, at least in a general way. We learn this from a letter written on July 20—that is, two weeks before the date of the Wiltshire instruction—by Lord Dupplin, who was at Scarborough with the prime minister: "In obedience to your lordship's commands I communicated to Mr. Pelham what your lordship men-

---

[3] *Gent. Mag.,* 1753:467–468.

[4] *LEP,* 4014:1; *Jackson,* 15:2.

[5] *Gent. Mag.,* 1753:468–469.

[6] Add. MSS. 35398, f. 151 (Birch to Yorke, Aug. 25); *Protester,* 13:78 (Aug. 25). Of course this is what Ralph had been urging all along: hence the name of his paper. In fact, textual evidence suggests that the Wiltshire instruction was drawn up by someone who had read the *Protester* carefully.

[7] *Jackson,* 26:3.

tioned to me relating to a proposal likely to be made at the ensuing assizes in several counties for petitioning the Parliament to repeal the Jew Bill. Mr. Pelham seems not to think it advisable for the friends of the Government to join in [such] petitions." [8] Six days later another Court Whig wrote a letter of thanks for some suggested arguments in defense of the Bill: "[They] will be of no small service, if any attempts should be made to procure petitions from the Grand Juries, which I am on. It is strongly Mr. Pelham's opinion, that the friends of the Government should not come into any such measure." [9] In effect Pelham was saying to his supporters that whatever their opinion on the merits of the Jew Bill, they should treat the Bill as a party matter, since the opposition was doing so.

The nicer partisan potentialities of the addresses became apparent in the ones that were drawn up in the autumn. In those, opposition to the Bill was made a shibboleth, and candidates were pressed to declare themselves publicly on the issue. Thus the Corporation of Reading on September 29 addressed a public letter to the three borough candidates, condemning the Bill and asking them to state their positions on it: "Our conduct will be ruled by your declarations, such as you shall make publick to us for the good of our country . . . 'Tis hoped you will publickly declare your dislike to that Act; and that you will not only use your utmost endeavours to get it repealed, but to oppose any subsequent Bill in favour of any one of the Jews." [10]

All three men declared in favor of repeal, including the Court candidate, John Dodd, who in his reply dutifully parroted the Corporation's words: "I will use my utmost endeavours to get it repealed, and will oppose any subsequent Bill in favour of any of the Jews." [11] One of the opposition candidates—who, incidentally, led the poll while Dodd came in last—replied much more complaisantly: "I most chearfully embrace this opportunity of declaring my entire disapprobation of the late Act in favour of the Jews, and do assure

[8] Add. MSS. 35606, f. 77 (Dupplin to ?).

[9] Add. MSS. 35351, f. 242 (P. Yorke, in Bedfordshire, to Hardwicke, July 26).

[10] *Gent. Mag.*, 1753:469 (reprinted from the *Reading Journal*).

[11] *Gent. Mag.*, 1753:470, and *Hist. MSS. Comm.*, 11th Rept., App., pt. 7, 206; also, for Dodd's Court allegiance, Add. MSS. 35632, f. 238 (Dodd to ?, July 4).

you no one shall be more ready to endeavour the repeal of it, or more strenuous in opposing any subsequent one of the same tendency." [12]

The instruction from Cirencester, to give a final example, requested that the members work for repeal, reviewed several of the familiar arguments against the Bill, and concluded with this strong statement: "The voice of the people has fully declared itself; that voice, which is in some sense the voice of God: it never, surely, was louder or stronger, or more unanimous. It is with the greatest pleasure and zeal that we have joined it. Your regard, gentlemen, to it, or to us, we cannot doubt of, or of your chearful compliances with our request." [13] The Cirencester instruction elicited the same sort of obliging responses as that from Reading. Both members promised to work for repeal, and one of them added, "I never was a friend to Bills of naturalization, nor did I ever think that the Bill mentioned in this representation was a right one." [14]

There were several more of these addresses, all of which received wide public notice. The *Oxford Journal,* for example, in addition to the four already mentioned, reprinted or reported instructions from Chester, Cheshire, Warwickshire, Exeter, Somersetshire, Middlesex, and London.[15] As something new to print about the Jew Bill, they were especially welcome to Jackson, whose propaganda campaign was showing signs of falling off for want of fresh material.[16] In addition, they provided newspapers with a whole new category of rumors and reports, some of them surely fictitious, saying that this or that place was thinking of instructing its members against the Bill.[17] This, of course, made the opposition to the Bill appear even more widespread than it actually was.

Moreover, the violent language of these addresses served to sug-

[12] *Gent. Mag.,* 1753: 470. The Reading contest will be touched on briefly below.
[13] *Ibid.,* p. 471. [14] *Ibid.*
[15] *Jackson,* 20:3, 22:2, 24:1, 25:1, 26:1, 29:2. *LEP* also reported instructions or petitions from Suffolk (4048:1), York (4054:1 [Nov. 6]), Gloucester (4055:1), Bristol (4059:1), Devizes (4060:1), Haslemere (4068:4), and Great Yarmouth (4063:1).
[16] See *Jackson,* nos. 22–24 (early October).
[17] E.g., Cambridge University, whose chancellor was the Duke of Newcastle—a most unlikely constituency to protest! (*Jackson,* 26:2).

gest that the provinces were as fiercely aroused against the Bill as the metropolis was. This suggestion was clearly false: all the evidence tends to confirm the testimony of the M.P. who reported, on his return from a visit to Cornwall, that the clamor was "much greater in London than among the gross of the people, whom he had met with in his journey, and that its greatest violence [appeared] in the addresses of corporations and some counties to their members." [18]

We should not take these protests at face value, then, as simple and spontaneous expressions of a country-wide abhorrence of the Jew Bill. They should instead be regarded chiefly as propaganda documents inspired by politicians who stated their case with special vehemence, in order both to arouse uncommitted local opinion against the Bill and to create an exaggerated impression elsewhere of the strength of the existing antipathy to the measure. In some places, it is true, local political complications played the largest part in the drawing up of the instructions. At Reading, for example, the Corporation's address was plainly intended to embarrass the local Court candidate, and seems to have succeeded.[19] The protests of certain other constituencies, however, clearly had in view not local politics, but public opinion elsewhere: for several of the public protests were addressed to unopposed incumbents who had already taken positions against the Bill.[20]

We may be certain, too, that this violent language did not always represent the unanimous opinion of the bodies that endorsed these instructions: dissenting views must frequently have been overridden or ignored. A Tory account of the Middlesex meeting indicates the power of intimidation that the clamor placed in the hands of the opponents of the Court: "It is remarkable, that at the very numerous meeting of the gentlemen, clergy, and freeholders of the County of Middlesex, held yesterday se'nnight, when the motion was made, to desire the two knights of the shire to use

---

[18] Add. MSS. 35398, f. 179 (Birch to Yorke, Oct. 27); see also Add. MSS. 35606, ff. 85–86 (H. Walpole, Sen., to Yorke, Sept. 29).

[19] See his reply in *Gent. Mag.*, 1753:469–470; and below, Chapter IX.

[20] E.g., Warwickshire, Wiltshire, and Essex.

their utmost endeavours to obtain a speedy repeal of the late [Act], but three No's were heard against it (a few placemen only excepted) and upon the question being put from the chair, not one of the three had the courage to hold up his hand against it.—A most demonstrative proof of the true sense of the County in general." [21] The total impact of all these instructions on public and parliamentary opinion must have been considerable. When Parliament reassembled in November amidst increasing talk of repeal, the current *Gentleman's Magazine* contained a selection of addresses and answers which filled more than four pages of fine print.[22] This can hardly have failed to make a strong impression on the undecided members—especially those facing possible contests—whether they had been specifically "instructed" by their own constituents or not.

Speech and Behavior: Nonprinted Propaganda. What men said and did—including, incredibly, what they wore and ate—contributed perhaps as much to the clamor of 1753 as what they wrote for publication, though naturally the lack of documentation makes it impossible for these ephemeral phenomena to be discussed at a length proportionate to their importance. Especially in the provinces, the agitation seems to have been spread by word of mouth as much as by the printed page. An interesting letter written in Bedfordshire early in the summer reminds us that both kinds of propaganda had their effect on public opinion, and mentions one specific class of volunteer propagandists that but for this reference might have been wholly overlooked: "We do not talk quite so much about the Jews Bill as you do in town, and yet I find upon enquiry, that people have received the same bad impression of it. How should it be otherwise? The *London Evening Post* is retailed in the *Northampton Mercury,* and the riders who are employed by the dealers in town to transact with the country shopkeepers, bring down with them specimens of their politicks as well as their goods." [1]

As this letter confirms, the clamor against the Bill began in

[21] *LEP,* 4058:1.   [22] *Gent. Mag.,* 1753:467–472 (October).
[1] Add. MSS. 35398, f. 130 (Yorke to Birch, July 12).

London and spread outward over the country. It must not be thought, however, that the clamor in the provinces was sustained wholly in this same manner—that is, by renewed infusions of propaganda from the metropolis. For as the outcry against the Jews and the Ministry made its way into the provinces, it found there, in the parish clergy (or rather in that preponderant part of it which was High Church and Tory in its sympathies), a new and enthusiastic body of recruits.

It is not always easy, in considering a propaganda campaign, to discern the precise point in the chain of communication at which artifice imposes upon credulity. Surely many of these Tory divines joined the clamor in a purely partisan spirit, knowing that the supposed dangerous effects of the Bill were merely an election canard. Others, however, duped by their own party's propaganda, were genuinely disquieted by what they believed about the Bill. Doubtless partisanship heightened the vehemence of their attacks on the measure and its sponsors, but at bottom their concern was sincere, and proved most difficult to allay. Thus the Bishop of Oxford, a firm friend of both the Bill and the Ministry, was forced to call upon the chancellor for assistance in answering some of the objections he had met with in his diocese: "I have done my best to quiet my clergy," he wrote, "and I hope with some success. But in a few points I am at a loss." He then laid before the chancellor some involved questions regarding Jewish legal rights—questions, he added, which had been raised by persons whose intelligence and sincerity could not be denied.[2]

No group was more strategically placed to influence public opinion than the parish clergy, once they were aroused; and in the Jew Bill, Tory vicars had a topic that was eminently suitable for politico-religious exhortation from the pulpit. The principal ingredients of their sermons against the Bill can be easily surmised: the old cry that the Church was in danger, pointed recitals of Biblical accounts of Jewish wickedness,[3] and often, no doubt, overtly political attacks on the Bill and its supporters.

[2] Add. MSS. 35592, ff. 88–89.
[3] This was also a common theme of the pamphlets and the letters to newspapers.

The enemies of the Bill counted heavily on the effect of this clerical propaganda: "I have great dependence upon the clergy in general throughout the Kingdom," wrote "Old England" in a letter to the *Oxford Journal*.[4] The *London Evening Post* and other papers repeatedly pressed clergymen to preach against the Bill, and denounced those who refused to do so:[5] "Oh! then, ye ministers of the gospel [reads one of these exhortations], forget your divisions about words and phrases, and unite, one and all [to oppose this evil law] . . . Let not only your pulpits give this instruction, but set your pens at work, lest [people] should cool in their abhorrence of being united with Jews."[6]

The angry reaction of the Whigs seems to confirm the effectiveness of these political sermons. "The Church would be in danger in good earnest," protested one letter writer, "if the Resurrection and Sacrament were to be set aside to make way for preaching about the election."[7] Another outraged Whig exploded, "What a pretty Christian confession of faith it is, to hear a curate cry, G-d d--n me, I am of the Church of England, and all the Whigs are sons of whores, Jews, and friends of the circumcision!"[8]

Whig partisans were further exasperated by the rather overdone expressions of undying and selfless devotion to the Church by which Tory laymen, as well as divines, attempted to exploit the Jewish issue. As an Oxfordshire Whig put it: "Many of the Old Interest are not pillars of the Church but mere buttresses only. They be strong for the Church, but then 'tis on the outside: they roar for the Church and get drunk for the Church; but then, d'ye see, they never in general come to Church to serve God and learn their duty."[9]

Naturally the Bill was the principal cry at opposition political gatherings. We read, for example, of a Tory rally in an Oxfordshire

---

The story of King Ahasuerus is very frequently met with (see Esther, especially chs. viii–x).

[4] *Jackson*, 8:2.
[5] Add. MSS. 35398, ff. 145, 148 (Birch to Yorke, Aug. 4 and 18).
[6] *LEP*, 3983:1 (May 29). See also *Jackson*, 17:2.
[7] *Jackson*, 50:3.   [8] *Ibid.*, 27:3.
[9] *Ibid.*, 50:3. (The "Old Interest" was the Oxfordshire name for the local Tory party.)

village: "A half hogshead of ale was given to the populace, who were numerous and unanimous in their cries, No Jews; No Naturalization; but Wenman and Dashwood for ever." [10] A passage from one of Horace Walpole's letters suggests both by the story it tells and by the use of the code language of the clamor, how universal was the exploitation of the Bill at these affairs. At Worcester, Walpole set out down the High Street, only to find himself caught in an election riot: "Nothing comforted me, but that the opposition is to Mr. Trevis; and I purchased my passage very willingly with crying, 'No Trevis! No Jews!' However, the inn where I lay was Jerusalem itself, the very headquarters where Trevis the Pharisee was expected";—so Walpole found little peace there, either. [11]

At political dinners the Jew Bill seems to have influenced not only the toasts but even the menu, pork and ham being conspicuously consumed by the zealous defenders of the Church. A humorous account in the weekly *Connoisseur* tells of the public feasts of the Tories in a fictional provincial town. The participants manifested their "truly Christian spirit" by eating as much pig meat of all sorts as they could, "so desirous was every one to prove his Christianity by the quantity he could swallow of that Anti-Judaic food." [12] Apparently this account was not mere whimsical invention, since in the *Gentleman's Magazine* we find a further reference to these devout repasts, in some verses addressed "to a friend in the country":

> Ye mighty trenchermen, priest, peasant, lord,
> Whose ham or pork perpetual crowns the board. [13]

At such affairs men often wore ribbons bearing slogans denouncing the Bill. But better evidence of the intensity of the clamor is

---

[10] *Ibid.*, 35:1. This was the meeting at which the effigy of the "Jew" called Ned was paraded. (See p. 75, above.)

[11] *Letters*, III, 187 (to Bentley, Sept., 1753).

[12] *Connoisseur*, 13:76 (April 25, 1754).

[13] *Gent. Mag.*, 1753:384. In the eighteenth century, men still delighted in this sort of concrete symbolism. It went out about the middle of the next century—probably because of the increase in literacy.

provided by the fact that women took to wearing numbers of crosses or ribbons with suitably orthodox inscriptions, in order to advertise their dislike of the measure.[14]

To conclude this account of the clamor against the Jew Bill, here is an excerpt from the weekly *Connoisseur,* describing a country election in 1754. The piece is fictitious and satirical in tone, but every essential point can be confirmed from other sources. Far better than any analytical discussion could, it conveys an impression of the political "style" of the provincial Tory abettors and exploiters of the great clamor of 1753–54:

I am at present in ———, where the election is just coming on, and the whole town is consequently in an uproar . . . Wherever politics are introduced, religion is always drawn into the quarrel. The town . . . is divided into two parties, who are distinguished by the appellation of *Christians* and *Jews.* The Jews, it seems, are those, who are in the interest of a nobleman who gave his vote for passing the Jew Bill, and are held in abomination by the Christians. The zeal of the latter is still further inflamed by the vicar, who every Sunday thunders out his anathemas, and preaches up the pious doctrine of persecution. In this he is seconded by the clerk, who is careful to enforce the arguments from the pulpit by selecting staves proper for the occasion . . .

The great support of this party is an old neighbouring knight; who, ever since the late Naturalization Act, has conceived a violent antipathy to the Jews, and takes every opportunity of railing at the above-mentioned nobleman. Sir Rowland swears that his lordship is actually circumcised, and that the chapel in this nobleman's house is turned into a synagogue. The knight had never been seen in a church, 'till the late clamour about the Jew Bill; but he now attends it regularly every Sunday, where he devoutly takes his nap all the service; and he lately bestowed the best living in his gift, which he had promised to his chaplain, on one whom he had never seen, but had read his name in the title-page to a sermon against the Jews . . . Every Saturday he has an hunt, because it is the

---

[14] *WEP,* 1143:1 (June 9); *Connoisseur,* 13:77; *Gray's Inn Journal,* [2]:10.

Jewish sabbath; and in the evening he is sure to get drunk with the vicar in defence of religion . . .

The fair sex here are no less ambitious of displaying their affection for the same cause, and they manifest their sentiments by the colour and fashion of their dress . . . I observed the other night at the assembly, that the ladies seemed to vie with each other in hanging out the ensigns of their faith in orthodox ribbands, bearing the inscription of NO JEWS, CHRISTIANITY FOR EVER. They likewise wore little crosses at their breasts; their pompons were formed into crucifixes, their knots disposed in the same angles, and so many parts of their habits moulded into that shape, that the whole assembly looked like the Court on St. Andrew's day. It was remarkable that the vicar's lady, who is a thorough-paced High-Churchwoman, was more religious in the decorations of her dress than any of the company; in a word, she was so stuck over from head to foot with crosses, that a wag justly compared her to an old *Popish* tomb-stone in a *Gothic* cathedral.[15]

If further proof is wanted that the shrillness at least of the seminal propagandists was largely factitious, let it be noted that two of the leading Tory contributors to the clamor, the *Oxford Journal* and the *London Magazine,* were willing to laugh the whole thing off—after the election, of course—by reprinting this paper, which the *London Magazine* candidly termed a "just satire."[16]

[15] *Connoisseur,* 13:74–77.
[16] *Lond. Mag.,* 1754:212–213 (May); *Jackson,* 55:2 (May 18, 1754).

VII

THE OTHER SIDE
OF THE QUESTION

*Being a collection of what hath yet
appeared in defence of the late Act
in favour of the Jews.*

THE title of this chapter is taken from a pamphlet that appeared in September, at the height of the clamor. Its implication is plain enough: namely, that the enemies of the Jew Bill were having all the best of it, and that the defense was merely the "other" side. This implication was correct, as well; and therefore the counterpropaganda on behalf of the Bill can be treated in summary fashion. For the most important fact about the public defense of the Bill is that it was a total failure.

As we saw, the attacks on the Bill invariably rested upon the unargued assumption that the measure was not merely wrong in principle, but was also dangerous and far-reaching in its practical consequences. One of the main tasks of the defenders, then, was to attempt to deflate this exaggeration. They explained that the measure was only an enabling one: it was not even a naturalization act, much less a general naturalization, and furthermore, very few Jews would ever be admitted under its provisions.[1] (Often, however, they undid the effect of such arguments by indulging in the same kind of rapturous prognostication that characterized the defense of the Bill in the May 7 debate.)[2]

Another attempt at clarification had to do with the legal status

[1] See, e.g., "Philo-Patriae," *Considerations*, pp. 1–4; and also the same author's *Further Considerations*, p. 80.

[2] *Considerations*, pp. 36–37; and *Further Considerations*, pp. 16, 35–36, 42–44.

of English Jews, and the extent to which it was affected (if at all) by the present measure. The Wiltshire instruction was typical of the attacks on the Bill in alleging that it conferred "unprecedented privileges" on the Jews; and we have seen how in particular the Bill was widely interpreted as giving Jews, for the first time, the right to own land. The defenders, for their part, insisted that the Bill granted no rights beyond those which native-born Jews already possessed; and in a lengthy and learned pamphlet Philip Carteret Webb demonstrated the Jews' capacity under existing law to hold and inherit landed estates.[3]

Besides rebutting these particular objections to the Bill, its friends reaffirmed the general principles of economic and religious liberalism on which the measure was based. And in addition to their essentially defensive endeavors to explain and refute, the Bill's advocates went over to the offensive, upbraiding and unmasking their adversaries as unscrupulous opportunists who were exploiting the confusion over the Bill in order to further various hidden and selfish designs.[4] Much of this was just and to the point, but sometimes the counterattacks were less than creditable to their authors. Strangely, even some of those who argued feelingly for toleration and charity were not above implying that the enemies of the Bill were Deists, atheists, bigoted Papists, or Jacobites.[5] This sort of abuse only increased the heat of the controversy, of course, and thus indirectly served the cause of those who were working to keep it alive.

The chief burden of defending the Bill was assumed by a small group of Whig intellectuals whose principal members were the Rev. Thomas Birch, Philip Carteret Webb, and the Rev. Josiah Tucker. Birch—the honest, dull Tom Birch of Boswell's *Johnson*—was a loyal

[3] See above, pp. 86–87 and n. 49.

[4] Note, e.g., the following pamphlet title: *Motives to the Senseless Clamour Against the Act Concerning Jews Exposed* (London, 1753).

[5] E.g., Josiah Tucker, *A Second Letter to a Friend concerning Naturalizations* (London, 1753), p. 4; *Considerations*, pp. 29, 30, 53. The stock opposition reply to the charge of Jacobitism was that the Whigs, having formed an alliance with the "seed of Jacob," were themselves Jacobites! (*Protester*, 21:126; *Jackson*, 8:3.)

party man and a client of the Lord Chancellor's family; he also had some influence in his own right, since he was secretary of the Royal Society and had an informal connection with Edward Cave, the editor of the *Gentleman's Magazine*.[6] Though he himself appears to have published nothing in the controversy, Birch played a central role in the defense of the Bill, and is our chief source of information about others' exertions in its behalf. Webb, mentioned previously as the solicitor to the Sephardic community and as a propagandist for the Bill, was an F.R.S., a client and close associate of the chancellor, and a candidate for Parliament in the approaching election.[7] Tucker, a Bristol clergyman, was mainly known as a political economist of advanced views. A prolific pamphleteer, he was an enemy of monopolies, and was also so prominent a friend of naturalization projects that he had been burnt in effigy at Bristol by a mob celebrating the defeat of Nugent's bill of 1751.[8]

From Birch's letters we learn how these men exchanged suggestions about works projected and in progress, and discussed arrangements for publishing and distributing propaganda in favor of the Bill.[9] Birch even corrected the press for an eighty-page pamphlet by Tucker, who was out of town and could not do it himself.[10] Unfortunately we know nothing about the guidance or support, if any, that these efforts received from the top ministers.

Pamphlets and Lesser Occasional Publications. About fifteen pamphlets, leaflets, and sermons were published in defense of the Jew Bill; at least two were by Tucker, and at least two by Webb. Two others were the work of "Philo-Patriae," whose widely circulated *Considerations* was frequently cited above, and whose true identity is not known.

[6] *DNB;* and Birch's letters in Add. MSS. 35398.

[7] *DNB.*

[8] *DNB;* and see the Bibliography. For his burning in effigy, see *Gent. Mag.,* 1751:186.

[9] Add. MSS. 35398, ff. 120, 147, 148, 160–161, 163, 166, 178, 181. (Birch to Yorke, between June 23 and Nov. 3.)

[10] *Ibid.,* f. 160.

Tucker's *Letter to a Friend concerning Naturalizations,* in whose preparation Birch advised and assisted,[11] was a typical and important contribution to the defense of the Bill. In this pamphlet Tucker emphasized the economic aspect of the controversy, arguing that the opposition to the Jew Bill was actually designed to protect the profits and privileges of the monopoly companies: "Religion," he asserted, "[is] only the pretence;—but monopoly [is] the *Noli me tangere,* and the real cause of the clamours."[12] In addition to his free-trade arguments, which included an attack on the alien duties, Tucker spoke out strongly for toleration: "The genius of the Christian religion," he wrote, "is to diffuse peace on earth, and good-will towards men. This is its great and distinguishing characteristic . . . Have we not all one Father? Hath not one God created us?"[13]

But in his *Second Letter,* published soon after the first, Tucker took a very different line, saying little about economics and arguing that the true motives behind the clamor were political. The public cries against the Jews, he asserted, "are known to be words of course, invented purely for the sake of inflaming the unthinking populace against the next general election." The opponents of the Bill, he said, were guilty of perverting Scripture "for the vile purpose of supporting a sinking faction against the next general election." Such tricks, Tucker reminded his readers, were not new. Formerly the cry had been "Church and Sacheverell": but those behind it, notably "the religious Lord Bolingbroke," soon "threw off the mask [and appeared] in their proper colours, *viz,* Deists by profession, [and] Atheists in practice."[14] In the *Second Letter* there were also some specific barbs that were meant, according to Birch, to be "particularly felt by Sir John Barnard and Mr. Fazakerley," the respective leaders of the City and Tory oppositions to the Bill in the debate of May 7.[15]

[11] Add. MSS. 35398, ff. 147, 160 (Birch to Yorke, Aug. 18, Sept. 15).
[12] J. Tucker, *A Letter to a Friend concerning Naturalizations* (London, 1753), 2d ed., p. 20.
[13] *Ibid.,* p. 10.
[14] Tucker, *Second Letter,* pp. 3, 40, 4.
[15] Add. MSS. 35398, f. 181 (Birch to Yorke, Nov. 3). See Tucker's *Second Letter,* p. 35, and pp. 33 and 34, notes.

These defenders of the Bill naturally took pains to see that their pamphlets were widely distributed. A plan of Tucker's for disseminating his (first) *Letter* is particularly interesting, both because of its scope and because it indicates the persons whom Tucker was most anxious to reach with his arguments. "He will prefix his name to the pamphlet," wrote Birch, "which he has some thoughts of sending at his own expence to the mayor of every corporation sending members to Parliament, to the sheriff of every county, and to the residentiary of every cathedral." [16] Apparently some such plan, or an even more ambitious one, was adopted. For the first edition of this pamphlet was soon followed by a more economical second one, and not long after, the *Protester* mentioned this as one of the two defenses of the Bill that had been "distributed by the thousand, gratis, through the Kingdom." [17]

It is probable that the Post Office cooperated in the distribution of this pamphlet, since it was common practice at the time for ministerial newspapers and propaganda to be sent throughout the country, unsolicited and post-free, to coffee houses and even to important private persons.[18] At any rate, we do know that this method was used at least once in 1753, to circulate a brief defense of the Bill by Webb.[19]

A Ministerial Newspaper: The Whitehall Evening Post. While certain opposition newspapers, as we saw, were among the foremost contributors to the clamor against the Jew Bill, the role played by their ministerial counterparts in the attempted defense of the measure was negligible. True, a few papers occasionally inserted brief, unsigned articles by Webb and Tucker, but positive counterblows of this sort were so rare as to be particularly remarked when they did appear. Thus we find Birch reporting to a friend in the country: "Amidst the inexhaustible torrent of ribaldry against the Jews' Bill,

[16] Add. MSS. 35398, ff. 160–161 (to Yorke, Sept. 15).
[17] *Protester*, 21:121 (Oct. 20). The other was "Philo-Patriae's" *Considerations*.
[18] Laurence Hanson, *Government and the Press, 1695–1763* (London, 1936), pp. 109–110.
[19] Add. MSS. 35398, f. 120 (Birch to Yorke, June 23); *Jackson*, 16:2.

which daily overflows us from the press, one of the very few pieces on the other side appeared yesterday in the *Public Advertiser* . . . I hope the *Whitehall,* or *General-Evening* will spread it through the nation to counteract the malice of their rival the *London-Evening.*" [20]

The treatment of the controversy in the ministerial press can be described as the exact opposite of Jackson's: where he inflated and invented, it minimized and suppressed. The *Whitehall Evening Post,* for example, did print the text of the Bill, along with a commentary by Webb.[21] But other than that it carried so few items touching on the Jew Bill that a latter-day reader of the paper would not have the least inkling that the Bill had become the center of a violent public controversy, unless perhaps he were to wonder at the number of advertisements for pamphlets and prints having to do with Jews. The *Whitehall*—to give but one instance of its suppression of inconvenient facts—made no reference whatever to the numerous provincial instructions against the Bill!

The Gentleman's Magazine. Although it published a few pieces opposing the Jew Bill, the *Gentleman's Magazine* was at bottom well disposed toward the measure, and threw the main weight of its influence on the side of the defense. This advocacy of the Bill was not political in its origin, since the magazine was not a supporter of the Ministry. Perhaps Birch's influence with the editor, Edward Cave, was a factor; but most probably the chief reason was simply the magazine's remarkable fairness and good sense.[22]

In its June issue the magazine reprinted a piece by Webb, which

---

[20] Add. MSS. 35398, f. 145 (to Yorke, Aug. 11). The piece was by Tucker; the *General Evening Post* did in fact print it, while the *Whitehall* did not. *Ibid.,* f. 147 (to the same, Aug. 18).

[21] *WEP,* 1150:1 (June 26); attribution to Webb, Add. MSS. 35398, f. 120 (Birch to Yorke, June 23).

[22] These undeniable qualities of the *Gentleman's Magazine* in this period make it all the more deplorable that the magazine should be maligned as a vicious *opponent* of the Bill by historians who must have formed their opinion of the magazine's position on the basis of a nonrepresentative quotation or two in secondary works. Roth, for example, scornfully lists the *Gentleman's Magazine* as one of three publications that "particularly distinguished themselves" by their "scurrilities" against the Bill (*Jews in England,* pp. 218–219).

it called "an irrefragable answer to all that has been or can be said against [the Bill]";[23] occasionally, too, it published letters that defended the Bill and deplored the clamor. An otherwise typical passage from one such letter is interesting on account of its author's questioning allusion to the vaunted rationality of the age: "The extreme ignorance and folly which have appeared in some publick transactions upon this occasion, will for ever stigmatize the present age of moral philosophy, in which every one boasts to detect the frauds of superstition, and to determine all questions by right reason."[24]

The magazine's most valuable and unusual contribution to the debate was the four-page review of the whole controversy, with which it led the August issue. After a thorough examination of the arguments on both sides, with each reason numbered and followed by a reply, the magazine reached the following eminently just conclusion: "Upon the whole, it appears that the reasons for the Bill, upon pretence of publick advantage, are not well supported, and that the objections against it, upon pretence of publick disadvantage, are totally overthrown. The inference is obvious: the Bill was intended for private purposes, which alone it seems calculated to answer, and which may be answered with safety to the public."[25]

Some of the magazine's brief notices of pamphlets bearing on the controversy were also clearly designed to help the cause of the Bill. From one work supporting the measure, the magazine quoted a strong argument and a telling piece of evidence; from several against the Bill, it quoted a bit of bad reasoning or bad English, headed by a scornful comment such as, "of this piece the last two lines are a sufficient specimen"; or, "this piece . . . appears to be written with great zeal."[26]

An Address to a Member. As against the flood of instructions opposing the Jew Bill, we find but a single one on the other side. This was addressed by some citizens of York to William Thornton,

---

[23] *Gent. Mag.*, 1753:278–280.
[24] *Ibid.*, p. 280.
[25] *Ibid.*, p. 354.
[26] *Ibid.*, pp. 447, 346, 494.

M.P., who had evidently supported the Bill and come under attack for doing so. Unlike most of the addresses opposed to the Bill, which were intended to have a wider audience and effect, this one seems to have been purely a part of the local factional maneuverings that resulted not long afterward in Thornton's withdrawal in favor of another candidate in the Whig interest.[27]

Though the York address is an exception to the clamor against the Bill, its defensive tone and equivocal wording actually provide far better confirmation of the political strength of the clamor than would the discovery of yet another instruction denouncing the measure. Here is the material part of the address:

> The law lately passed in favour of the Jews (a most unhappy people, and rather the objects of our compassion than hatred) has indeed raised a general alarm. We don't pretend to give our judgment in an affair, about which the most wise and upright may perhaps differ in their sentiments: But we do venture to give it as our opinion that this great clamor has been rather owing to faction than to any real affection to the Christian religion; and we cannot possibly think that those worthy gentlemen who promoted this Bill, or voted for it, had the least design to hurt or undermine either our religious or civil liberties, but that their conduct on this occasion was the effect of that generous and benevolent spirit, which has ever been the distinguishing character of an English Protestant. The wisest of men may be mistaken, but we have the highest confidence in your integrity, and are therefore firmly persuaded that you will use your utmost endeavours either to continue or repeal this law, (without our recommending it to you) as to your best judgment shall seem most advantageous to this Christian and trading nation.[28]

THE LOSS OF HEART

The York address conveys a sense of the discouragement that was felt by men who sympathized with the Jew Bill but found the strength of the clamor too much for them. Early in the summer a demoralized tone, a consciousness of being the "other" side,

[27] *WEP*, 1220:1 (Dec. 8); and see the first part of the address (not quoted here) in *Gent. Mag.*, 1753:529.
[28] *Gent. Mag.*, 1753:529 (November).

began to appear in the correspondence of the Bill's defenders; and by autumn, feelings of despair were all but universal among them.

For one thing, the personal abuse to which the leading propagandists were subjected can hardly have failed to tell on their spirits. Ralph in the *Protester* called Tucker "this Clergyman-Rabbi" and "the Reverend Jew-Advocate"; the *London Evening Post* called him "a scandal to the cloth." [29] Webb came in for his share as well; his fictional circumcision, for example, was reported in such widely separated publications as the *Scots Magazine* and *Jackson's Oxford Journal*. (Jackson added that Webb was dangerously ill as a result of the operation, and was being "attended by two rabbis of distinction for his ghostly fathers.") [30]

More dispiriting still was the growing awareness that the defense of the Bill was a futile, as well as a disagreeable, endeavor. In October Birch sent a copy of Tucker's latest pamphlet to Philip Yorke, M.P., the friend in the country to whom Birch reported on the counter-propaganda campaign. Yorke's reply was gloomy and philosophical—and also accurate: "The domestic politics of this summer will make but a contemptible figure in history, which can afford nothing else than the art employed by faction to swell a most inoffensive Bill into a national grievance, and the success with which the weak and credulous have been deluded into the grossest of absurdities, more deeply imbibed, I fear, than the ingenuity and reasoning of Mr. Tucker can remove . . . This is a season when nonsense has a better chance than sense; our nation

---

[29] *Protester*, 21:125; *LEP*, 4048:1. Birch wrote of the "daily scurrilities" showered on Tucker (Add. MSS. 35398, f. 181). See also ff. 148, 163, 173: Birch was very conscious of this abuse, even though it was not directed at him.

[30] *Scots Mag.*, 1753:377n; *Jackson*, 15:2 (from *LEP*, 4014:1). In the propaganda of 1753 there are many allusions to circumcision, most of them largely humorous in intention. Even today, surprisingly enough, one still finds the same kind of story, though without the saving humor. Note this "report" by Gerald L. K. Smith, in *The Cross and the Flag* for January 1956, pp. 16–17: "The ultimate in demagoguery is almost unlimited. Occasionally some extravert becomes a champion in the art . . . Believe it or not, there came to my desk some time back a bulletin revealing that Gov. McKeldin [of Maryland] had submitted to circumcision and had been hanging around some synagogues."

in its political capacity has fits of both, and the present crisis is favorable to the former." [31]

In addition to such expressions of despondency, there were other indications that the friends of the Bill felt the propaganda battle to be a lost one. The first of these was the talk among the politicians of suppressing the most effective organs of the opposition. As was mentioned above, the Ministry did in fact purchase the silence of Ralph and the *Protester,* though not solely on account of this issue. It was the Jew Bill, however, that old Horace Walpole had in mind when he suggested that the Ministry's most violent newspaper opponent should be dealt with: "I really think," he wrote, "that after the choice of a new Parliament, something should be done to correct the impudence of the *London Evening Post.*" [32]

A more striking indication of this defeatist attitude appears in a letter of August 15 from the Bishop of Oxford to the chancellor. It was Bishop Secker, it will be recalled, who had reported that many of his clergy were disquieted over the Bill, and that they had raised legal questions about it which he could not answer satisfactorily. In order that he might put up a more effective defense of the Bill, Secker had laid the questions before the chancellor: "If you would . . . furnish me with a little instruction on these heads," he had written, "I should be very thankful for it, and endeavour to make a good use of it." [33]

That was in June. But in August, when Secker next sought the chancellor's advice, his request was concerned not with the question of how to fight back more effectively, but rather with the advisability of continuing to fight back at all; perhaps, he implied, it would be wiser to quit the field altogether:

Dr. Church of Battersea hath very unexpectedly sent me a manuscript, which he hath written to prove, that the Jews' Bill is not prejudicial to

[31] Add. MSS. 35398, f. 168 (Oct. 4). Yorke was Lord Chancellor Hardwicke's eldest son.

[32] Add. MSS. 35505, f. 86 (to P. Yorke, Sept. 29); see also Walpole, *George II,* I, 362. (The Government did in fact move against the *London Evening Post* in 1754; see Hanson, *Government and the Press,* p. 72.)

[33] Add. MSS. 35592, f. 89.

Christianity; and begs my opinion, by which he saith he will be ruled, whether he shall publish it or not. It will make a moderate pamphlet, is written sensibly enough, and with good temper, though not with much spirit or elegance; and as he hath shewn himself in several controversies an orthodox man, and received an honorary doctor's degree on that account, possibly his name might have weight with some persons.

But doth your Lordship think it will be best to bring this matter any farther into dispute; or to try, if it will subside and be forgot? If the former, I shall be willing to suggest to him what occurs to me on the subject, and hath been omitted by him: if the latter, I shall dissuade him from proceeding: but in neither case hint to him, that I have asked advice of your Lordship, or any great person.[34]

Dr. Church's manuscript apparently was never published; but we do not have the chancellor's reply to Bishop Secker, and so can only guess whether the pamphlet was suppressed on Hardwicke's instructions. It is not at all unlikely, however, that Hardwicke recommended this prudent course, especially in view of his cautious advice of two weeks earlier to his son, Philip Yorke: "I have inclosed a printed copy of the Jew-Bill," he wrote, adding significantly, "I suppose it will not be advisable for you to talk publickly in favour of it." [35]

But here we have come to an essentially new topic: the reaction of the Court politicians, great and small, to the unhappy trend of the propaganda battle. It is with this subject that the next chapter will be concerned.

[34] *Ibid.,* ff. 127–128 (Aug. 15).
[35] Add. MSS. 35351, f. 248 (July 29).

VIII

PANIC AND REPEAL

The Panic

The Reaction of the Lesser Politicians. It is clear that the politicians and the men (such as Thomas Birch) who followed parliamentary affairs closely were caught unawares by the clamor against the Jew Bill. For one thing, the Bill had passed so quietly through its first parliamentary stages that probably few of them had given it much thought until the war of the petitions and the final heated debate. But even the excitement of those last few days seems not to have made a great impression on the politicians and insiders, who were much more interested in the dramatic and bitterly personal debates on the Marriage Bill, which was still pending in the Commons. (On May 22, after the angry debate over the third reading of the Jew Bill, 151 members divided; but on the previous day, 249 had voted in a committee on the Marriage Bill.) [1]

Thus when the politicians first really noticed the clamor, they were struck with the full force of a great storm that not only had blown up suddenly and unexpectedly, but had done so while their attention was fixed in another quarter. Consequently they took a serious view of the clamor from the first: in their earliest references to it we find not a gradually dawning awareness and apprehension, but a note of genuine alarm. For example, it was on June 23 that Birch first mentioned the clamor in his weekly newsletters to Philip Yorke—and he was already gravely concerned: "The clamour

---

[1] *Commons' Journals*, XXVI, 829; Walpole, *Letters*, III, 158, 161. For the controversy over the Marriage Bill see Coxe, *Pelham*, II, 263–270, and Walpole, *Letters, passim*, and *George II*, II, 336–353.

against that Act is now evidently designed to influence the election next year; and the rage of the people is scarce governable." [2] The politically minded Bishop of Oxford was also worried by the early progress of the clamor: "I am at present in the midst of my visitation," he reported to the chancellor, "and I find, that the Bill for permitting Jews to be naturalized hath not only raised very great clamours amongst the ignorant and disaffected, but hath offended great numbers of better understandings and dispositions, and is likely to have an unhappy influence on the elections of the next year." [3]

Two weeks later Birch (in London) was deploring the "incessant and increasing clamours," and "the rage and folly of the multitude";[4] and Bishop Secker (still in Oxfordshire) was writing in a similar vein of "that astonishing spirit of rage and bitterness, which is gone forth on this occasion. I will take the liberty of troubling your Lordship with a specimen of it, which I received two days ago. Possibly you may have leisure to cast your eye over it, and smile at it: though on the whole it is by no means a laughing matter." [5]

Court candidates who were facing contested elections did not have to be told that the clamor was no laughing matter. As early as June 23—the date of Birch's first reference to the clamor—the Tory *Oxford Journal* carried two separate pieces, one of them reprinted from the *London Evening Post,* urging electors to use the Jew Bill as a touchstone for parliamentary candidates, voting only for those who would publicly declare their abhorrence of the Bill, and promise to work for its repeal.[6] In the next number, one of the Tory candidates, hoisting canvas, as it were, to catch the friendly gale, inserted a signed advertisement in which he affirmed, "I divided against the passing of this Bill, as I have against all

---

[2] Add. MSS. 35398, f. 120.

[3] Add. MSS. 35592, f. 88 (dated only "June 1753").

[4] Add. MSS. 35398, f. 128 (to Yorke, July 7).

[5] Add. MSS. 35592, f. 102 (to Hardwicke, July 6). What the particular "specimen" was, we do not know.

[6] *Jackson,* 8:2.

general Naturalization Bills hitherto proposed." The advertisement was repeated in the next two issues and was also inserted (and repeated) in the London newspapers.[7]

The Oxfordshire Whigs, of whose opinions the pessimistic letters of Bishop Secker were doubtless indicative, did not hesitate for a moment, but surrendered outright to the clamor. In fact, the very issue of the *Oxford Journal* that contained the Tory articles pressing candidates to speak out against the Bill, also carried unqualified disavowals of the Bill by Whig contributors, and attacks by them on the Tory incumbents for having been insufficiently energetic in opposing it! A Whig partisan who signed himself "An English Christian" wrote, "the Act I know is disliked by Lord Parker and Sir Edward Turner; they are against it; I am no advocate for it." Turner had not been in Parliament when it passed, and Lord Parker, the writer insisted, did not vote for the Bill. It was well known that both men had "over and over declared their disapprobation of it."

Then he turned to the Tory candidates: "But I would fain know how Lord Wenman and Sir James Dashwood have distinguished themselves against the Jew-Bill . . . What were they doing [when it passed]? Not debating against the Bill, not voting against it, not even in the House of Commons, one of them not in London." Then broadening (and lowering) the base of his appeal, "English Christian" went on to assert that the Whig candidates disliked foreigners more than did the Tory candidates, and that the Papists were all in favor of the Tories.[8]

In the same issue there was a letter from "Obadiah" accusing Dashwood of shameful neglect of duty: "Instead of trying to keep out the Jews, thou wert revelling and drunkening with thy Philistians at a tavern in Paul's Church-Yard." [9] Finally an advertisement repeated the same points. It was "absolutely false" that the Whig

---

[7] *Ibid.*, 9:4; *WEP*, 1153:2; *LEP*, 3998:4. The other Tory incumbent, having been absent from the debates, could not join in this declaration.

[8] *Jackson*, 8:3.

[9] *Ibid.*

candidates were for the Jew Bill, and the Tories against it: "Neither Lord Parker nor Sir Edward Turner ever approved of that Act, but on the contrary, upon all occasions, have declared their utter dislike to it; nor did Lord Wenman or Sir James Dashwood vote against that Bill." [10]

In default of a division list, the argument over this point of fact was never settled. This was probably well for the Whigs, who were thus enabled to go on insisting, however incongruously, that they, and not their Tory rivals, were the real enemies of this unpopular Court Whig measure. It was an uncomfortable, indeed an almost untenable, position; but it was about the best they could do.

Almost everywhere else the Court politicians ran for cover as they had done in Oxfordshire. Some insisted that they had heartily disliked the Bill from the first. Others said that heretofore they had never read the Bill or given it much thought but that now, having considered the matter, they were in favor of a repeal.[11] Hardest of all was the lot of those who were publicly on record as having favored the passage of the Bill, and now found it necessary to recant. One unfortunate candidate had even signed one of the petitions in favor of the Bill. In an open letter to the corporation of his proposed constituency he prudently declared that he had entirely altered his sentiments; henceforth, he promised, he would "zealously oppose all naturalizations whatsoever, so disagreeable to this nation." [12] We have already noted the enthusiastically compliant disavowals of the Bill in the candidates' responses to the instructions and addresses. These replies, and newspaper advertisements to the same effect, were so common that they became an object of humor. For example, when Arthur Murphy launched his *Gray's Inn Journal* in September, his announcement took the form of a parody of a candidate's appeal for votes and

[10] *Ibid.*, 8:4.

[11] See, e.g., *Gent. Mag.*, 1753:470; Add. MSS. 35398, f. 179 (Birch to Yorke, Oct. 27); and *Hist. MSS. Comm.*, 15th Rept., App. VI, 207: Ord to Carlisle, July 17 (quoted below).

[12] *Gent. Mag.*, 1753:452.

interest. To it was appended this postscript: "N.B. I was always against the Jew Bill." [13]

To judge from the surviving letters, all sorts of rumors must have been current in which the impending doom of this or that particular candidate was foretold. Thomas Birch, for example, substantiated his gloomy view of the clamor by citing specific contests in which he thought it would be decisive. His selection was a curious and unrepresentative one, however; for though it is evident that Birch anticipated a dreadful slaughter among the Whig innocents, he omitted such names and details entirely, preferring instead to dwell upon the one bright spot in the otherwise dismal picture. This was the fact that three Tories had been caught on the wrong side of the clamor and seemed certain to be unseated;[14] and better yet, two of them were men whom Birch particularly disliked.

Of one of these Birch wrote, "The Jews' Bill is likely, among many ill consequences, to have one good effect, in relieving the next Parliament of the oratory of Mr. Sydenham, whose declaring for that Bill has rendered the city of Exeter implacable to him." [15] In a similar silver-lining manner Birch spoke of the troubles of the other two: "But there is this good likely to arise from [the clamor, namely], that M[atthew] Robinson has lost all his interest at Canterbury by assenting to the Bill . . . But better men than he, even of his own party, are in danger on the same account; and Mr. Norb[orne] Berkeley himself has sunk so much in his popularity in Gloucestershire, that he wants only a competitor to exclude him." [16] This Berkeley was a Tory politician of no great importance or merit; he had most probably voted for the Bill because of his personal friendship with Lord Halifax, the sponsor of the meas-

---

[13] *Ibid.*, p. 443.

[14] This fact was cited in an earlier chapter as evidence of the clamor's being unpremeditated. These men had apparently committed themselves to the Bill at some early stage, probably thinking it of no importance.

[15] Add. MSS. 35398, f. 166 (to Yorke, Sept. 29). Sydenham was not returned.

[16] *Ibid.*, f. 151 (to Yorke, Aug. 25). Berkeley and Robinson were both returned.

ure.[17] But apparently Berkeley had committed himself too deeply to retreat gracefully,[18] and a month later Birch reported him still in trouble: "Mr. Norborne Berkeley being attacked at the Gloucester Races for voting for that Bill, frankly owned, that he did it from a persuasion of its being a right one, in which he still continued: But said, that if the County thought proper to name any other gentleman for their representative, he would himself support their candidate, and not attempt to divide the country [sic] or disturb its peace." [19]

Berkeley's difficulties and those of other members were described in a letter of July 17 from Robert Ord, M.P. for Morpeth, to his patron and friend Lord Carlisle. There is a note of amusement in Ord's recital, made possible no doubt by the fact that he sat for a pocket borough; but the letter still conveys a sense of the concern that was felt over the fate of candidates who were vulnerable on this issue:

I hope matters have gone at York according to your wish; here we are fixing our members everywhere upon the test of their having voted for or against the Jews; and where the candidates have not been members I think they judge by their looks, for a man of a dark complexion is scarce safe in the streets. I don't know Sir Geo. Savile, but I think Lord Downe and Sir Conyers may stand this test very well; and as to the other they may probably answer it as many others do, that they never troubled themselves about the Bill. There is such a spirit in Gloucestershire against Norb. Berkeley upon this account, that though he is otherwise the perfect idol of the country, they are now quite in an uproar against him. Mr. [Philip Carteret] Webb, Lord Chancellor's secretary, stands for Hasle-mere, and thought he had secured almost every vote, but upon their being acquainted that he was solicitor for the Jews' Bill, the tables are turned, and the only chance he has left for it is, that his rival Peter Burrell voted

---

[17] Cumberland, *Memoirs,* I, 160; *Dictionary of American Biography,* s.v. "Bote-tourt"; C[okayne], *Complete Peerage;* see also Owen, *Pelhams,* p. 71n.

[18] The implication may be unfair to Berkeley, but it is consistent with the rest of his public career.

[19] Add. MSS. 35398, ff. 166–167 (to Yorke, Sept. 29).

for the Bill. Mr. Sewell the lawyer thought he had secured Wallingford, but his antagonist acquainting them that he drew and was counsel for this Bill, he too is like to be routed, or be at a very great expence . . . It seems to me something like the Sacheverell madness.[20]

The Ministry's Discussions and Decision. "The Sacheverell madness": as early as mid-July the clamor had risen to such an intensity as to evoke that painful memory. Therefore it is hardly surprising that the Triumvirs had already begun, even before the date of Ord's letter, to discuss the possibility of political countermeasures to prevent a catastrophe similar to that of 1710.

Newcastle and Hardwicke were in London, Pelham at a Yorkshire spa; as a result of this separation, we have four letters in which the clamor was discussed. Unfortunately the correspondence is incomplete, and consequently some of what remains is ambiguous or even unintelligible. But the essential point is clear beyond all doubt: except for a slight initial hesitancy on Pelham's part, the ministers from the first were not at all reluctant to repeal the Act, nor in the least inclined to fight for it. (Their matter-of-fact attitude forms an interesting contrast with that of Birch and Philip Yorke, who, being at bottom intellectuals more than politicians, viewed the controversy primarily as a struggle involving moral principles, and anguished over the triumph of bigotry and ignorance.)

Apparently the matter was brought to a head by an appeal from Lord Parker, one of the beleaguered Whig candidates for Oxfordshire. We know that he wrote to Pelham in early July, and he seems to have written to Newcastle at the same time.[21] Parker and his colleague, Turner, had already disavowed the Jew Bill, it will be recalled, but were still under heavy attack from the *Oxford Journal* on its account. In these letters (which are lost) Parker apparently suggested a ministerial declaration promising either to

---

[20] *Hist. MSS. Comm.,* 15th Rept., App. VI, 207.

[21] Add. MSS. 35606, f. 77 (Dupplin to ?, July 20); Add. MSS. 32732, f. 226 (Pelham to Newcastle, July 13). Three of the surviving Pelham-Newcastle letters were published in part by Coxe, in *Pelham,* II, 467–468, 483–485.

repeal the Jew Bill, or perhaps to pass a law expressly forbidding Jews to vote or to sit in Parliament. (In a letter to the chancellor on July 6, the Bishop of Oxford, who was assisting Parker's and Turner's campaign, had recommended just such a step, however supererogatory, "for the sake of quieting people.")[22]

At this point Pelham was inclined—though not strongly—to oppose the granting of concessions: "The alarm of the Jew Bill has not yet reached this country, at least not to any degree. I wrote Lord Parker word, that whatever was your opinion, and Lord Chancellor's, I should acquiesce in, but my own thoughts were, that bargaining with clamour was a dangerous expedient, especially in a case where the Government *had* no interest, nor could not [sic] be supposed to have."[23] Newcastle took a more serious view of the danger than did his brother. In part, no doubt, this reflected the duke's timid and worrisome nature: in these very letters, for example, he was urging the suppression of the *Protester,* while Pelham recommended ignoring its attacks. But more important, probably, was the fact that Pelham was in distant Yorkshire, where as yet "very little" was heard of the Jew Bill,[24] while Newcastle and his mentor, Hardwicke, were in London, where the clamor was shrillest and where intelligence from the rest of the country was most available. Newcastle's reply to Pelham, in other words, must be viewed against the same background that produced Robert Ord's letter referring to the "Sacheverell madness," which by coincidence was written in London on the same day as this letter of Newcastle's: "I hear also, the Jew Bill is more extensive than you seem to imagine; they will call it an act of the Administration; but the worst of all is, that the country is ready to receive a disadvantageous impression. It was the case, formerly, of the Quarantine Bill; which, as Lord Chancellor says, was repealed—and that may become necessary in this case also."[25]

[22] Add. MSS. 35592, f. 102.
[23] Add. MSS. 32732, ff. 226–227 (to Newcastle, July 13).
[24] *Ibid.,* f. 303 (Pelham to Newcastle, July 18).
[25] *Ibid.,* f. 299 (to Pelham, July 17, copy). For the Quarantine Bill, see below.

Henry Pelham's answer of three days later showed him now completely willing to repeal the Bill if the clamor did not subside: "I have the same thought of the Jew Bill, that I have of the *Protester;* let them take their course, and if you find it gives a real uneasiness, repeal next year, as a matter of no consequence in itself; but if it gives disturbance to weak minds, it is right to indulge them." [26] On the same date Lord Dupplin, who was with Pelham in Yorkshire, wrote a letter in which he gave a similar account of the prime minister's views regarding repeal. According to Dupplin, Pelham was of opinion that friends of the Government ought not to join "in petitions to Parliament for the repeal of a law passed in the very last session merely upon account of an unreasonable clamour which has no real foundation. But as the Jew Bill was not at all a measure of Government, and is in itself a matter very indifferent, if the dislike to the Bill be so general as to make the repeal of it proper, he will have no objection to a motion for that purpose in the next session." [27]

So by mid-July the Ministry had come to the point of accepting repeal as likely, unless the propaganda battle should take a turn for the better by November, when Parliament was to reconvene; and having reached this conditional decision, the Triumvirs apparently put the Jew Bill on the shelf and turned to other problems. But since the final decision was still open, no public announcement was made, and the general debate over the likelihood and advisability of repeal continued, both in public and in private. Old Horace Walpole, writing to Philip Yorke on September 29, stated the problem in his usual partisan and outspoken manner, even though he was unsure of the answer:

That a motion will be made at our next meeting to repeal the Jews'–Bill I don't at all doubt; but whether it ought to be withstood by the Administration, is a question not too clear with me. A Bill passed with all imaginable formality and deliberation in the House of Lords, without the least murmuring or opposition within doors or without, calculated

[26] *Ibid.,* f. 324 (to Newcastle, July 20).
[27] Add. MSS. 35606, f. 77 (Dupplin to ?, Scarborough, July 20).

purely for increasing wealth and commerce in the nation, without the least apparent publick ill, relating to liberty, property, or peculiar privileges; received at first in the House of Commons as so innocent a thing, that no debate was expected from it, until the Jacobite part of the Common Council takes it up, and by their incendiary the *London Evening Post* scatters terrors all over the nation . . . Now if a Parliament is to be frightened by the Common Council of London, and an infamous libeller, to cancel immediately their own laws, will not this be a strange weakness in Government? But I shall submit mine to greater and wiser opinions.[28]

Writing at the same time as Walpole, General Sir Charles Howard, a Court Whig member, expressed a similar concern for the dignity of Parliament. Though his tone was more temperate than Walpole's, his conclusion was more definite: "I . . . am not a little hurt at the spirit and disturbances shewed in many parts of England against a law passed after many considerations and debates by the Legislature. What is our prospect if they are to set themselves up for judges whether we do right or wrong? I take for granted we shall have some amendments next sessions, but not give up the Bill." [29]

Philip Yorke also deplored the fact that the Government was "exposed to these popular gusts"; but he was less sanguine than General Howard about the chances of saving the Bill: "I see the Common Council [of London] have instructed their representatives to obtain a repeal of the Jew Bill, and if such a motion should be made, it will be pretty difficult to withstand it, as many of the Whigs will be afraid of risking their elections, just at the eve of a new representative. I consider our Government in a state very near anarchical." [30]

In more or less accepting the likelihood of repeal, and in emphasizing the influence of the approaching elections on the final result, Yorke was rather more realistic than Howard. He was also

---

[28] *Ibid.*, f. 85.

[29] *Hist. MSS. Comm.*, 15th Rept., App. VI, 208 (to his brother, Lord Carlisle, Sept. 28). Howard sat for the safe constituency of Carlisle.

[30] Add. MSS. 35398, f. 169 (to Birch, Oct. 4).

closer to the line of thought that more than two months earlier had led the Ministry to accept repeal, unless the clamor should abate.

Certainly nothing happened between July and the November reconvening of Parliament to induce the Triumvirs to reverse or even reconsider that conditional decision. Instead of subsiding, the clamor had in many respects grown stronger as November approached. Some of the more powerful attacks on the Bill, such as Romaine's widely disseminated *Answer,* were launched in the autumn; and the instructions in particular added new vigor to the clamor in August, September, and October. The instructions had been expected, it is true, but that fact did not prevent them from practically completing the demoralization of the politicians and propagandists who had hoped to save the Bill.

Quite by themselves, then, the events of the summer and autumn would have tended to harden the Ministry's early inclination into a definite resolve. But to their particular impact was added the influence of certain historical precedents, most notably the controversies over the Sacheverell Case and the Excise Bill. These two greatest clamors of the first half of the eighteenth century came often to mind in 1753,[31] and for the politicians—especially for practical politicians of the school of Walpole—they conveyed, when placed in conjunction, a plain and pertinent lesson. Both were occasioned by unpopular actions undertaken by Whig administrations, and both were followed within a year by general elections. In the first instance, the Government persisted in spite of the clamor, and was overwhelmed in the election; in the second, the obnoxious proposal was withdrawn in time, and the Government won the election handily.

A third precedent for repeal, wholly forgotten today but frequently cited in 1753, was the short-lived Quarantine Act of 1721. It had been passed in order to prevent an epidemic then raging

[31] The former more frequently, of course; but for the excise see a "letter" to Pelham in *Jackson,* 17:3. Pelham and Newcastle had taken part in the excise controversy. Interestingly, both had scoffed complacently at the rising clamor against the excise—a mistake that they took care not to repeat in 1753 (J. H. Plumb, *Sir Robert Walpole: The King's Minister,* London, 1960, p. 254).

in France from spreading into England. As soon as public anxiety about the plague began to wane, the opposition fomented a clamor against the act on the grounds that it placed unconscionable restrictions on the liberty of the subject. The measure was a purely temporary one: it would have lapsed in three years in any event. But the public protests were so insistent that the Government thought it prudent to repeal the act forthwith, by which action the clamor was effectively silenced. Moreover—and this was of particular interest to the worried politicians of 1753—the concession was not generally interpreted as indicating a weakness in the Government of which further advantage might be taken by the victorious clamorers.[32]

We do not know when the ministers finally determined to give up the Bill; probably they simply drifted into the decision without much further discussion. At any rate, in their next surviving letters on this subject (which date from early November) we find the chief ministers taking the repeal of the Bill completely for granted. What is more, we find them planning to steal the opposition's thunder by bringing forward on the first day of the new session their own Government bill for repeal, instead of merely acceding to the inevitable motion from the minority.

This plan apparently grew out of a suggestion made by the Archbishop of Canterbury in a letter to Newcastle on October 30. The Bill, wrote Archbishop Herring, was "innocent at least, if not useful in policy," and was "totally unconnected" with religion or the Establishment. "However," he went on, "faction, working upon the good old spirit of High Church, has made wild work in the nation. As the obtaining the Bill was really worth no hazard, so the repealing it seems hardly worth a debate, unless any danger may arise from the Government giving way to a most unreasonable

[32] *P. Hist.*, VII, 928–935, and XV, 101. The latter is Hardwicke's speech for repealing the Jew Bill. For other references in 1753 to the Quarantine Bill, see Add. MSS. 32732, f. 299 (Newcastle to Pelham, July 17, quoted above on p. 141), and Add. MSS. 32733, f. 239 (Halifax to Newcastle, Nov. 12). Both Newcastle and Hardwicke (then Sir Philip Yorke) had taken part in the debates on the earlier Bill.

popular clamour. I could wish the ticklishness of the time would admit of so much delay, as that repealing might be the volunteer act of the Administration." [33]

The plan began to take shape in the following week. On November 6 the archbishop and the chancellor discussed it,[34] and two days later Hardwicke sent Newcastle a draft of the new bill. Since the measure was simply an outright repeal of the earlier Act, only the preamble offered any difficulty: "You may certainly do it," wrote Hardwicke,

without any recital, except of the title of the Act repealed, but that will read oddly, and has hardly a precedent. I have in the draught, proposed the alternative of two different short recitals. For my own part, I like the general one, which stands in the text, best, because every body, who is for repealing it, supposes that some *inconveniences* of one kind or another may arise from suffering it to continue, and no objection can be made to that general word. The words proposed in the margin express *our* sense of the inconveniences apprehended, but then I foresee that some amendment or other will be offered in the House of Commons to those words. If a debate upon such an amendment be not thought worth attending to, or of any consequence, then I think that some recital to that particular effect may be taken.[35]

It was characteristic of Hardwicke to recommend the weaker expression; but the final text of the bill, presumably reflecting Pelham's influence, took the stronger line, asserting that the repeal had become necessary not because of any defect in the original Act but because "occasion [had] been taken from the said Act, to raise discontents and disquiets in the minds of many of his Majesty's subjects." [36] As the chancellor had predicted, the opposition was not to accept this without a struggle.

It had been decided fairly early that the repeal should be introduced in the Lords, where the rules of procedure, unlike those

---

[33] Add. MSS. 32733, f. 163.

[34] *Ibid.*, f. 195 (Abp. Herring to Newcastle, Nov. 6).

[35] *Ibid.*, f. 213.

[36] *P. Hist.*, XV, 131. A paper that appears to be an early draft of this preamble in Henry Pelham's hand, is to be found (out of place) in Add. MSS. 32995, f. 1.

of the Commons, allowed bills to be read and debated on the first day of the session, without previous notice. And at some point during the week before the opening of Parliament, the Duke of Newcastle and the Bishop of Oxford were agreed upon as mover and seconder of the Bill, respectively.[37]

Everything appeared to be settled. But on November 13, only two days before Parliament was to meet, Bishop Secker, in a letter to the chancellor, insisted upon returning to an important objection which he had evidently raised before without success. Might it not be advisable, Secker asked, to exempt from the repeal, and so leave on the statute book, that clause of the original Act by which Jews were forbidden to present to livings? His arguments were drawn both from principle and from practical politics; the political ones are of particular interest, on account of the light they shed on the role of the bench of bishops in the mid-century House of Lords:

I must intreat your Lordship to indulge me a few words more about Jewish patronages: for indeed the longer I think of them, the less I am reconciled to them. They are unfit in themselves: and will be a dishonour to the Church of England, such as no other Church in any Christian country suffers, or ever did. We have laws against Popish patronages: and though the danger from Jewish may not be so great, yet the shame of them is much greater. It was not known before, that there were such in the nation: but now it is universally known: and persons will either fear or pretend fears, that the Jews may set themselves to purchase more advowsons, either for profit or revenge. The Parliament, and the Bishops in particular, have been treated very injuriously for passing this Act. But new reproach will fall upon us and with such appearance of justice, that those of our Bench will not be able to hold up their heads under it, if we concur without necessity in repealing a clause, which everybody owns to be a good one, and which many think the only good one.

Besides, if the preservation of it be not proposed by the Administration, or by us, it will certainly be proposed by the opposition. If their proposal be accepted, they will have the merit of it: If it be contradicted, the

[37] Coxe, *Pelham,* II, 291; Add. MSS. 32733, f. 213 (Hardwicke to Newcastle, Nov. 8); *ibid.,* f. 255 (Bp. Secker to Newcastle, Nov. 14).

Bishops must divide against their friends; the members of the House of Commons will be, in proportion, under the same difficulties about this part of the Act, which they are now under about the whole; and the disaffected will have what they wish, a handle for continuing their clamour.[38]

This counsel prevailed, and the bill presented by Newcastle specifically exempted the advowson clause from the fate of the rest of the original measure.

On November 12, while the Ministry was arranging the last details of its surprise move, the Earl of Halifax, who had introduced the Jew Bill in April, collected his thoughts on the Bill and the clamor in a long letter to the Duke of Newcastle. Halifax was in the country, recovering from a nervous collapse caused by grief over the death of his wife in October. Consequently he had taken no part in the Ministry's deliberations earlier in the month; nor did he feel able to come up to London for the debate.[39]

Newcastle nevertheless had sent Halifax a draft of the repeal, together with an account of the Triumvirs' plans for its surprise introduction. In his reply Halifax thanked Newcastle for the letter and assured the duke that but for his enforced absence he would willingly have supported the repeal in the Lords. But while loyally deferring to his chiefs' decision to give in to the clamor, he also included a lengthy recital of his own earlier views, which clearly showed that if the choice had been his to make, he would have stood firm. Of course Halifax's advice was merely academic even when it was written; but his letter is interesting, both for what it reveals about the original proposer's attitude toward the Bill, and for its clear exposition of the contrary arguments that the Triumvirs must have weighed, however briefly, before coming to their decision to repeal: "From the clamours that have been raised

---

[38] Add. MSS. 35592, ff. 192–193.

[39] Add. MSS. 32733, ff. 95–96 (Dupplin to Newcastle, Oct. 18); *ibid.*, ff. 236–237, 239 (Halifax to Newcastle, Nov. 12).

. . . I never doubted but that a repeal of the Jew Bill would be moved in the House of Commons soon after the opening of the next sessions, and from the general poison that has been infused into the minds of the populace, at whose mercy one branch of the Legislature so manifestly lies at present, I as little doubted of its passing there: but I must confess, my Lord, I had my doubts whether it ought to find the same disposition in the House of Lords." In fact, though many "false and wicked" arguments had been advanced against the Bill, no "solid objection" could be made to it: "If therefore the House of Commons at this juncture of time should find it necessary to retract their opinions in complaisance to the clamours of the infected multitude, I had hopes that a disagreeable civility of that sort might have been there, and there only paid. If material objections lay to the Bill, I grant the whole Legislature would be concerned, but as the opposition to it is merely an engine of faction directed against one part of it, I flattered myself that it would not have been found necessary that the other parts of it should be likewise made retracting parties."

His entire concern, however, was for the dignity of Parliament and not for the Bill, though he himself had introduced it:

As to the Bill itself, my dear Lord, I never thought it a matter of moment whether it passed or not, nor do I now think it a matter of moment whether it be repealed or not, but for the consequences that may attend a precedent of that sort . . .

The worst consequence that I apprehend may attend the repeal of an Act so reasonable and unexceptionable in itself, only because it has been the object of faction, is that the authority of Parliament may seem lessened by it, and it may be a precedent for the same unjustifiable means being used upon a like juncture to obtain a repeal of the best laws that have been passed throughout the course of a session. If those means prevail now . . . it is difficult to say how far the same spirit may extend even during the course of the approaching session.

"A victory gained in one quarter," Halifax warned, "will give [the clamor] fresh vigour in another"; the Marriage Bill would surely be the next object of attack. "It is difficult to say how far precedents

of this sort may go," he continued, "or how far future Parliaments may by faction and clamour be obliged in their last session to repeal the best Acts they have made for six years before." He did grant, however, that the repeal of the Quarantine Act had been followed by no such ill consequences.

"I believe you will not think [these points] entirely groundless," concluded Halifax, "though I make no doubt but what you have determined is right. If the clamour without doors is not to be withstood in the House of Lords, the taking the start of the House of Commons the first day of the sessions, and making the repeal an act of Government I am heartily glad to hear is a measure resolved on." He hoped that in the debate notice would be taken of "the outrageous manner in which Law and the Legislature have been attacked." And he particularly requested Newcastle to do him justice if anyone brought up the unfair accusation, often raised in the public clamor, that the managers of the Jew Bill had "smuggled" the measure through the Lords in the spring.[40]

The Repeal

The mood and expectation of the members as they came up to London for the November 15th opening of the final session of Parliament are amusingly conveyed by an essay in the weekly *World*. At this time of year, it begins, one always asks a friend newly arrived from the country, "Well, sir, what brings you to town?" And usually the answer is a particular or personal one: "To see the new bridge," or "To hear the new opera." But "this year . . . ask whom you will what he is come up for, he draws up all his muscles into a most devout gravity, and with an important solemnity answers you, 'to repeal the Jew Bill.' This religious anxiety brings to mind the political zeal, no less warm or universal, in the year ten." [41]

---

[40] Add. MSS. 32733, ff. 236–240.

[41] *World*, 50:299–300. The *World*, though essentially nonpolitical, was well disposed toward the Jew Bill. The paper's chief contributor, Lord Chesterfield, was a friend of the measure.

Since no one knew which way the Government would throw its influence, there was much speculation both on this point and on the outcome of the inevitable debate. The *Gray's Inn Journal* of October 27, in a dispatch purporting to come from White's Chocolate House, stated that "the odds upon all bets relating to the Jew-Bill have been considerable for a long time past, the knowing ones laying ten to one that it would not be repealed." But today, it went on, a man bet even money that the Bill would be repealed: "The Jews themselves are to petition a certain great man for a repeal," he had asserted, "and I am sure they have interest enough with him to obtain any thing." [42] Whatever the result, the opposition were prepared to turn it against the Pelhams and keep the clamor alive, if possible, until the election.

The House of Lords. The king's speech at the opening of the session made no reference to the Jew Bill. In fact, his majesty's chief concern was over the recent alarming increase in murders and robberies, for which he hoped his dutiful and affectionate Parliament would find some remedy.[43] After the king and Commons had withdrawn and the Lords had voted the usual Address of Thanks, the Duke of Newcastle arose, according to plan, and moved the first reading of the repealing Bill which he held, already drafted, in his hand.[44]

The duke followed the line taken by his brother in July when they had first accepted the possibility of repeal. He argued that the Jew Bill, though a good one, was of so little consequence in itself that if the people were greatly disquieted by it, it was proper to indulge them by a repeal. At the same time he strongly condemned

[42] *Gray's Inn Journal,* 5:29.
[43] *Lords' Journals,* XXVIII, 161–162.
[44] *Lords' Journals,* XXVIII, 162–163: Bedford, *Correspondence,* II, 138–139 (Richard Rigby to Bedford, Nov. 15). Though Rigby was a bitter partisan, his eyewitness account is the best available source for the debate of November 15. There also exists, in an unavailable private collection, an account of the Lords' proceedings by Robert Nugent (*Hist. MSS. Comm.,* 1st Rept., App., Vol. I, 41). The Lords' speeches on repeal in *Parliamentary History* are of little value.

those who had fomented the clamor, as did Bishop Secker, who seconded the motion on behalf of all the bishops.[45]

Of course the ministerial position in the debate was more than a little ludicrous. First, the Bill that was now dismissed as trifling and inconsequential had been put forward in the spring as a great public benefit; it was unfortunate that the later argument had not been used at the beginning of the controversy. And second, the ministerial speakers spent most of their time attacking as groundless and artificial the clamor to which they were surrendering, and defending as wise and good the measure whose repeal they had risen to support. Thus one Tory peer said of the Bishop of Oxford's seconding speech, "that for some time he thought the Bishop had been speaking against the repeal, having advanced more in favor of the Bill than he had heard before." [46]

Except for a few such taunts the opposition said little on the first day, and the only other speech worth noting was that delivered by Lord Temple, an erratic and trouble-making independent, who attacked the repeal for obscure motives of his own. According to Richard Rigby's account, in indirect discourse, Temple

declared the regard he had always paid to the voice of the people, but that he never would to the clamours of them; owned his amazement at a motion of this kind in that House, where he expected to have heard notice taken of the licentiousness of the press in daring to attack every part of the Legislature in the libellous manner it had done upon this occasion; that, for his own part, he saw no reason to think he had done wrong in giving his assent the last year to the Bill, and would not plead guilty to satisfy the lowest of the people, for such only were alarmed at the Bill; no thinking man had been so but for private purposes, which might answer the intent of another House of Parliament . . . but [which] certainly should [have no weight] with him in the present instance. That

---

[45] Bedford, II, 139; Walpole, *George II,* I, 359.

[46] From the "life" (by B. Porteus) prefixed to Secker's *Works* (London, 1811), I, xxiv; also, Bedford, II, 139–140. The speaker was Lord Westmorland, identified as a Jacobite by Feiling, *Second Tory Party,* p. 73. Richard Rigby remarked that Newcastle's arguments, "which, indeed, it is a great presumption ever to pretend to understand, seemed all to tend for the Bill he meant to repeal."

he was against the repeal absolutely, and should vote against it, and had not heard an argument that was not in support of it, even by those desiring the repeal.[47]

On November 20, 21, and 22, the Bill was hurried through the remaining stages of its passage by the upper house. The debates brought the Duke of Bedford to London a day sooner than he had originally intended,[48] and on his arrival he gave a new turn to the argument by putting his considerable influence behind an objection which had been raised (but apparently not pressed) by two Tory peers in the opening debate. He had always disliked the Jew Bill, the duke said, but he could not support the repeal in its present form: the advowson clause, on account of its implicit negation of the salutary common-law provisions against Jewish landholding, ought to go too.[49]

Bishop Secker, who had foreseen the possibility that the opposition might take this line, defended the clause; but he found little support, and the clause was dropped without a division, leaving the Bill an outright repeal of the original. (It is not unlikely that if the repeal had been brought forward in this form, Bedford and the Tories would have made a show of fighting *for* the retention of the clause, as Secker predicted they would.)[50]

Except for this matter of detail, the Administration backed its bill strongly, with the chancellor and the Lord President (Granville) speaking for it, as well as Newcastle and at least two of the bishops.[51] On November 22 it was passed without a division, although Temple, who had continued his violent attacks to the last, entered a formal dissent. For this action he was honored in the Tory press with the new title, "Temple of Jerusalem." [52]

[47] Bedford, II, 140–141. The paraphrase in Walpole, *George II*, I, 359–360, is very similar.

[48] Bedford, II, 141; *Lords' Journals*, XXVIII, 165.

[49] *Lond. Mag.*, 1754:314–315; Walpole, *George II*, I, 360; see p. 86, above.

[50] *Lond. Mag.*, 1754:314–315; *Lords' Journals*, XXVIII, 166; Add. MSS. 35592, ff. 192–193 (Secker to Hardwicke, Nov. 12).

[51] *Lond. Mag.*, 1754:315; Walpole, *George II*, I, 359–361.

[52] *Lords' Journals*, XVIII, 167; *Jackson*, 30:3.

The House of Commons. Though it was less important than Newcastle's little coup in the Lords, there seems also to have been a ministerial plan for extracting an advantage from the manner in which the repeal passed the House of Commons. Subsequent events, at any rate, suggest that when the Bill came down from the Lords, Lord Parker was to be pushed forward as its manager in the Commons, in hopes that this would help counteract the damage inflicted on him by "anti-Jewish" propaganda in Oxfordshire, where he was a candidate.[53]

The Tories, however, either had got wind of the plan or had ideas of their own about seizing the parliamentary initiative in this cause which their propaganda had made so popular. Thus it happened that at about the time the Duke of Newcastle was presenting his unannounced bill to the House of Lords on November 15, the members of the House of Commons, having trooped back to their own chamber, were treated to a similar surprise. When the motion in favor of the Address was made, Sir James Dashwood, one of Parker's Tory opponents in Oxfordshire, rose—not, he said, to oppose the pending motion, but to request gentlemen to remain in the House after the Address was voted, since he had "a motion of very great importance to make."[54]

When he was again recognized, Dashwood delivered a speech—an unprecedented step for him[55]—in which he took note of the just indignation aroused by the Jew Bill, and moved that the House be called on December 4 to consider a repeal. Since a motion to call the House for a specified purpose was unparliamentary, Dashwood was asked to restate his motion in more general terms, which he did.[56] Parker seems to have been caught off balance by Dashwood's

---

[53] Parker was at this time sitting for Newcastle-under-Lyme. It will be recalled that an appeal from him seems to have figured prominently in the Ministry's early decision to accept repeal.

[54] *Lond. Mag.,* 1754:314.

[55] Robson, *Oxfordshire Election,* p. 95.

[56] *Lond. Mag.,* 1754:314. Unless it was merely a nervous slip, Dashwood's procedural error suggests that he had not consulted with any important leader of the opposition before making his motion. (It is not at all certain, as Robson implies, p. 94, that Dashwood knew about Newcastle's motion in the other House.)

unexpected move, but he recovered himself sufficiently to second the motion and make a brief speech in its behalf. (According to an opponent, he arose only after being prompted by "many significant looks and gestures in a certain great man," doubtless Pelham himself.)[57]

All this Oxfordshire byplay was rendered nugatory by the arrival of the Government's bill from the Lords on November 23, more than a week before the day appointed by Dashwood. The events of November 15 are of interest nevertheless as an example of a practice that has become much more common in our day—namely, the adoption of parliamentary tactics that are designed chiefly to impress opinion without doors, rather than within. For several weeks afterwards, Oxfordshire Whigs and Tories heatedly argued the merits of the respective parts that Dashwood and Parker had played in this affair.[58]

Like the Lords, the Commons rushed the Bill through as if the safety of the state depended upon its immediate enactment. It was first read when it was received, on Friday the 23rd, and the second reading, committee, and the third reading took place on the following Monday, Tuesday and Wednesday respectively.[59]

At the second reading the repeal was attacked by Thomas Potter, who had been a supporter of the late Prince of Wales and was now an independent opponent of the Ministry. Like Lord Temple, Potter said that he had favored the Jew Bill when it passed, and did so still. He condemned the clamor as bigoted and groundless, and held that Parliament would be compromising its dignity if it "recanted" in the face of such insolence. He also denounced the Ministry for the weakness and inconsistency of its conduct, pointing out, as had others, that the Jew Bill when first debated had not been represented as "trifling and of no consequence." [60]

[57] *Lond. Mag.*, 1754:314; *Jackson*, 30:2, 32:2.
[58] *Jackson, passim.*
[59] *Commons' Journals*, XXVI, 852, 855 (bis), 856.
[60] *P. Hist.*, XV, 119–128.

Sir George Lyttelton made a fine speech in favor of repeal. The temper of the country, he argued, would doubtless discourage foreign Jews from any thoughts of taking advantage of the Act, so that in effect its repeal would be no loss. Then he too turned on the clamorers for fanning that spark of bigotry and enthusiasm which was always latent, he said, in the minds of the vulgar. He defended toleration on political grounds as "the basis of all public quiet," and also on religious grounds, in a noble aphorism: "He who hates another man for not being a Christian, is himself not a Christian." [61]

But the real partisan fireworks began when the repeal was debated in committee—with Lord Parker significantly serving as chairman,[62] to the great satisfaction of his Oxfordshire supporters. A Tory member, Sir Roger Newdigate, opened the debate by moving an amendment to the preamble. In place of the words, "occasion has been taken from the said Act to raise discontents," Newdigate wished to insert, "discontents and disquietudes have from the said Act arisen." The preamble as it stood asserted a falsehood, he said: the Bill had genuinely disquieted people, and not only members of the Established Church, but Christians of every denomination. Furthermore, the original wording reflected unjustly upon the good sense of the people: Whigs of former times believed in the maxim *Vox Populi est Vox Dei;* but the pretended Whigs of this age question that voice, and tell us that it can easily be imposed on or led.[63]

The motion to amend the preamble was supported with similar arguments by several other members of both the Tory and independent oppositions. Naturally these speakers also made good use of this last opportunity to review all the tired "reasons" against the original Jew Bill, from its fearful implicit threat that Englishmen "should soon be all obliged to be circumcised," to the more modest warning that it might have served as a precedent for extending the Toleration Act to "Socinians, Arians, Deists, and other prohibited sects." [64]

---

[61] *Ibid.,* pp. 128–131. This speech, and Potter's, were printed from the authors' own copies.

[62] *Commons' Journals,* XXVI, 855.

[63] *Lond. Mag.,* 1754:315; *P. Hist.,* XV, 131–134.   [64] *P. Hist.,* XV, 161, 158.

The Ministry called upon its best talent to maintain the rather difficult position that the clamor was fully as artificial and groundless as the preamble implied, but that surrender to the clamor was still in no sense undignified or weak. These speakers repeated the argument that the Jew Bill was merely a trifle; that no Jew would now dare to take advantage of it in any case; and that the potential dangers from what William Pitt called "the old High Church persecuting spirit" were still so great that the Government was showing prudence, not weakness, when it moved to calm that spirit with this timely and inconsequential concession.[65]

Henry Pelham made much of the last point, arguing that whenever religion was brought into a dispute, reason invariably gave way to enthusiasm; and once that had happened, he observed, no one could foretell the harm that might spring from what had originally been the most trivial of causes. This was unexceptionable enough; but then Pelham went on to offer a particular illustration, and set off an irrelevant partisan wrangle which strikingly demonstrates the vividness of the old political memories and the vitality that still remained in the old Whig and Tory attitudes and feelings:

Many gentlemen amongst us must remember, and all, I believe, have read of the trial of that otherwise insignificant parson Dr. Sacheverell; could anyone at the beginning have imagined that the prosecution of such a low, insignificant parson was an affair of any importance? Yet from thence occasion was taken to raise the cry of the Church being in danger, and this soon propagated such a spirit among the people against our then excellent ministers, as gave their enemies the courage to supplant them, which put a stop to the war that had been so gloriously, so successfully, carried on by the great Duke of Marlborough, by a most inglorious, I may say, a most infamous peace, when our armies were approaching the very gates of Paris. This has since cost us, as well as our allies, a great deal of blood and treasure: I wish it may not at last cost both of us our independency; but whatever may be the consequence, it is a late proof, that the most signal events may sometimes spring from the most trivial causes.[66]

Back came William Northey with the Tory version of the

[65] *Ibid.*, pp. 154–155.　　　　　　　　　　[66] *Ibid.*, p. 143.

Sacheverell Case, and a detailed defense of the foreign measures of the Bolingbroke ministry. The Sacheverell trial was no small matter, "because in [the Doctor's] person our established Church itself was attacked; for by his prosecution and sentence, one of its most essential doctrines was condemned, and the rebellious doctrines of 1649 revived." (There, indeed, is genuine Toryism: nonresistance and Charles the Martyr!) And as for the Peace of Utrecht, "if there was anything amiss in that treaty, it was occasioned by the obstinacy of our allies abroad, and the perverseness of a party at home." [67]

This was more than old Horace Walpole could bear. After some biting remarks on "that High-Church doctor [and] his ridiculous sermon," he turned to "the pernicious treaty of peace concluded at Utrecht":

I shall not enter into a minute justification of that Administration, Sir, whose wise and steady conduct had brought France to the brink of destruction, nor shall I trouble you with my reasons for condemning the conduct of those who supplanted them; for the former are now universally applauded, and the latter as universally condemned, by the whole nation . . . All the negotiations and treaties we have been since engaged in, were rendered necessary for correcting the blunders of that treaty and the circumstances that Europe was thereby thrown into . . . [For example,] if the war in Queen Anne's time had been carried on, but for two or three years longer, by the same Administration that had before so successfully carried it on, we might have been treated as absolute victors [at Aix-la-Chapelle recently].[68]

When this partisan debate in committee subsided, and the House was resumed, Lord Parker formally delivered the Bill. The next day the House voted by 113 to 43 to retain the original, or ministerial, wording of the preamble, and then proceeded to pass the repeal without opposition.[69]

[67] *Ibid.*, pp. 147–148. In print, Northey's reply to these points is four times as long as the quotation from Pelham above.

[68] *Ibid.*, pp. 152–153.

[69] *Commons' Journals*, XXVI, 855–857. Some accounts say that the division took place on the same day as the debate.

The parliamentary history of the controversy did not end here, however. When the House of Commons assembled on December 4 it heard not Dashwood's now needless motion for repeal which had been scheduled for that day, but another proposal, which was introduced by Lord Harley, a Tory member, and seconded by Dashwood himself. Harley's motion asked for leave to bring in a bill repealing those provisions of the Plantation Act of 1740, under which Jews could be naturalized after seven years residence in America.[70]

In part this was a defensive move forced on the opponents of the Jew Bill by the logic of their position. In the pamphlet war and in the debates on repeal the friends of the Bill had taunted their opponents for having acceded without objection to the act of 1740, which was actually more liberal than the Jew Bill in that it did not require a private naturalization act for each applicant.[71] But mainly, of course, the motion was a propaganda gesture, intended to provide new fuel for the waning clamor, and to give some members a further opportunity to ingratiate themselves with the electorate.[72]

Evidently forewarned, both sides mustered their strength: the opposition in order to make a good showing, and the Administration in order emphatically to demonstrate its determination not to give another inch. Pelham again spoke out sharply against "the intolerant principles of the High Church," and Pitt insisted that a stand be made against the taking away of legal rights that had been solemnly granted: "It is the Jew today," he warned, "it would be the Presbyterian tomorrow: we should be sure to have a septennial Church clamour." In the division the ministerial majority held firm, and the Tory motion was rejected by 208 to 88.[73]

[70] For this move, and the complicated preliminaries to it, see *Lond. Mag.*, 1754:315–316; and Walpole, *George II*, I, 364–367.

[71] E.g., Tucker, *Second Letter*, p. 35; *P. Hist.*, XV, 143–144.

[72] According to young Horace Walpole, some members supported the move only because they were "obliged" to do so in order "to secure their approaching elections" (*George II*, I, 367).

[73] Coxe, *Pelham*, II, 297–298; Walpole, *George II*, I, 364–367. Feiling implies that these 88 stalwarts were all Tories (*Second Tory Party*, p. 57); this is incorrect, and was probably unintentional.

On December 20 the repeal received the royal assent. For London it was a day of rejoicing; and the news was similarly received in the provinces. At Bicester in Oxfordshire, for example, the church bells pealed all day long to celebrate England's deliverance, and most of the town gathered to drink toasts to Dashwood, Harley, "and the rest of that glorious minority [of 88]." [74] The Tory press was ecstatic. This day, declared the *London Evening Post,* "should be gratefully remembered in this island . . . first, because it delivers us from all apprehensions of seeing British Christians tilling and toiling for Jewish landlords; secondly, because it shews the respect of the Legislature for the Publick Voice." [75]

An Oxfordshire Epilogue

As the Ministry had hoped, the repeal effectively ended the clamor almost everywhere. The most notable exception was Oxfordshire. There, of course, the controversy had received a new lease of life from the prominent participation of Dashwood and Parker in the repeal proceedings, and a lively debate broke out in Jackson's columns over the apportionment of praise and blame to the two rivals. In his news accounts Jackson simply ignored the Duke of Newcastle's bill, and made it appear that it was Dashwood's motion in the Commons that had started the repeal on its way. [76] Numerous letters, too, commented glowingly on Dashwood's parliamentary conduct.

More interesting, however, was the attempt of the Oxfordshire Whigs to make the most of the Ministry's and Lord Parker's roles in the repeal. Of course the Oxfordshire Whigs had long since disowned the Jew Bill; but they were now free to join unreservedly in the clamor against it, and they did so with a will. Dashwood's motion for a call of the House on December 4 would actually have delayed the repeal, they argued; and in an open letter to Dashwood, "Moses Ben Amri" (who had previously written only for the Tories!) expressed his gratitude for the intended favor. [77]

---

[74] *LEP,* 4072:4, 4075:1.
[75] *Ibid.,* 4073:1; also in *Jackson,* 34:2.

[76] *Jackson,* 29:2.
[77] *Ibid.,* 31:3, 32:3.

Lord Parker's seconding speech for the motion was highly praised, as was his conduct as chairman. "We cannot help observing," wrote a Whig partisan, "[that] the nation owes the speedy redress of this grievance to the zeal and activity of that young nobleman. —No Jews; no Jacobites; New Interest and Christianity for ever." The same correspondent, emboldened by his new freedom of action, went over to the offensive and reminded the public that a Tory member for neighboring Gloucestershire (Norborne Berkeley) had "not only voted for but even then declared his approbation of the Jew Bill." [78] "Moses Ben Amri" also loosed a shaft at Berkeley: "Our tribes present their compliments to the D[uke] of B[eaufort]," he wrote, "and thank him for putting in nomination in Gloucestershire a friend to our Bill and Nation." [79] There could hardly be a more striking demonstration of the clamor's success, or of the utter collapse, both political and moral, of the cause in which Tucker, Webb, and Birch had striven so manfully.

[78] *Ibid.*, 31:3.   [79] *Ibid.*, 32:3.

IX

THE JEW BILL
AND THE ELECTION OF 1754

THE BILL'S ACTUAL EFFECT

THE general election that took place in April and early May of 1754 remains to be considered. What effect did the clamor have on the results?

The question is easier to ask than to answer. If the opinion pollers and so-called "psephologists" have learned to be cautious in interpreting contemporary elections, certainly historians ought to be diffident about pronouncing on the impact of a particular issue upon an election that took place two hundred years ago. And there is a further difficulty: in eighteenth-century elections considerations of family and connection, together with other purely local influences and interests, counted for so much that one would have to undertake 558 separate inquiries, rather than just one, in order to measure the effect of the clamor.[1]

A few examples may be useful in establishing how necessary it is to get the local details right, before leaping to general inferences about the Jew Bill and the election. One historian puts forward, in partial justification of the Government's nervousness over the election, the fact that "General Oglethorpe, who had supported the Bill, was unseated . . . after sitting for Haslemere for thirty-two years

[1] In this respect—that is, the great importance of personal and local considerations—these eighteenth-century elections resemble those in modern America much more closely than they do those in modern Britain, a fact often overlooked. Consider this statement by the Republican national chairman, William E. Miller: "In 1962, I think we have a very good chance of winning control of the House . . . I think if we can minimize our concern about the big issues and concentrate on winning local elections we will be a lot better off" (*New York Times*, July 24, 1961).

without a break." [2] At first glance this appears to be impressive evidence. It becomes rather less so, however, when we learn that one of the candidates who defeated Oglethorpe was Philip Carteret Webb, who was well known as the Jews' solicitor and as a supporter of their bill, and who figured in opposition propaganda as one of the foremost honorary Children of Israel.[3] Clearly Oglethorpe's defeat at Haslemere is no proof of the Bill's political potency.

And consider the contrasting fates of two other candidates, Robert Nugent and Sir Crisp Gascoyne. Nugent was well known as the promoter of the general naturalization schemes of 1747 and 1751; he had voted and spoken for the Jew Bill when it passed, and some people even accused him of being its author.[4] In the sitting Parliament Nugent represented a family borough (St. Mawes), but in 1754 he stood also as a single candidate in the Court interest for Bristol, which had been solidly held by Tories for the past twelve years.

Now Nugent not only broke into this enemy stronghold, but even led the poll; and he achieved this victory in spite of a great cry against him on account of the Jew Bill. Other considerations evidently outweighed the Bill in the minds of the Bristol electors. One of these was Nugent's well-advertised parliamentary efforts on behalf of Bristol industries and interests, most notably the manufacture of bottle glass. Another was the large amount of money—perhaps as much as £20,000—spent by Nugent's forces.[5]

While Nugent provides an example of a prominent supporter of the Bill who won a striking victory as a result of other issues and influences, Sir Crisp Gascoyne's story is exactly the opposite: he was

[2] Roth, *Jews in England*, p. 285.

[3] *Lond. Mag.*, 1754:247. Allan Peskin, in "England's Jewish Naturalization Bill of 1753," *Historia Judaica*, XIX, pt. I (April, 1957), 3–32, also corrects Roth on this point. (Peskin's conclusions are just, but his account of the Bill is too often inaccurate in particulars.)

[4] *P. Hist.*, XV, 134–136.

[5] L. B. Namier, *The Structure of Politics at the Accession of George III* (London, 1957), pp. 88ff.; Add. MSS. 35592, f. 339 (Nugent to Hardwicke, April 30, 1754); Nugent, *Memoir of Nugent*, pp. 62–68; *WEP*, 1268:2 (March 30, 1754), 1274:2 (April 13, 1754); Walpole, *Letters*, III, 250.

a prominent enemy of the Bill who nevertheless failed of election for a particular reason. Gascoyne was the Lord Mayor who presided over the special meeting that drew up the City of London's petition against the Bill in May. The credit that he won by this action was more than offset, however, by his espousal of the unpopular side of another public controversy of 1753.

This was the sensational criminal case of Canning and Squires, which aroused such excitement in London at the time that Smollett accorded it two pages in his *History of England*. Early in the year one Elizabeth Canning, described by Smollett as "an obscure damsel of low degree," made public a harrowing story of how she had been robbed, bound, and taken off to the country. There she had been held prisoner for a month, isolated and nearly starved, she said, until she finally managed to escape. She identified Mary Squires, an ugly old gypsy woman, as one of her assailants. Actually Squires had a well supported alibi, and much of the evidence against her would not bear close or dispassionate scrutiny. Public sympathy for Canning was so strong, however, that some of the witnesses for Squires were intimidated from testifying; so the gypsy woman, to the great satisfaction of the mob, was quickly convicted of robbery and sentenced to death.

At this point Sir Crisp Gascoyne, convinced of Squires's innocence, courageously intervened in her behalf. He persuaded the authorities to reopen the case; as a result of further investigations, some of which Gascoyne himself conducted, Squires was granted a royal pardon, and Canning was convicted of perjury and transported to America.[6] Canning's partisans remained loyal to the last, however, and Gascoyne was roundly berated for his intervention in the case. He was dubbed "King of the Gypsies"; he was mobbed and pelted, to cries of "No gypsy, no gypsy!"; his coach windows were broken, and a madman threatened to blow out his brains.[7]

[6] Smollett, *History of England*, II, 113–115; *Lond. Mag.*, 1754:317–320, and prints facing p. 236; *Gent. Mag.*, 1753:107–111; and see the indexes of both magazines for 1753 and 1754.

[7] Entick, *History and Survey of London*, III, 83–88; *Jackson*, 53:3; *WEP*, 1208:3, 1249:1 (May 18, 1754); see also Grego, *Parliamentary Elections*, pp. 130–136, and facsimile facing p. 134, for some of the prints attacking Gascoyne on Squires's account.

In the end the triumph of justice was incomplete, for Gascoyne obtained the gypsy's freedom at the cost of his own political career. He had hoped to enter the new Parliament, and made two attempts in the election of 1754, one in the City and one at Southwark, across the river. But such was his unpopularity over the gypsy that he failed badly in both: at Southwark he was at the bottom of the list; and at London, where the election took place simultaneously with Canning's perjury trial, he deemed it wisest to decline before the polling even began.[8] In Gascoyne's case, then, the purely local clamor over Canning and Squires proved to be more important than the general clamor against the Jew Bill.

Before commenting in general terms on the effectiveness of the clamor, I shall discuss, in addition to these cautionary examples, two of the most important contests of 1754—those in London and in Oxfordshire. Then I shall list a few other contests about which further local investigation might turn up something of interest concerning the clamor and the election.

London. In London the opponents of the Ministry quickly turned the general outcry over the Jew Bill into a direct political attack against Sir William Calvert, a City M.P. who had voted for the Bill. Calvert had formerly been a great favorite of the antiministerial livery: in 1747 they had returned him at the top of the poll. Since then, however, he had moved toward an alliance with the Pelhams; and when he voted with the ministerial majority on the Jew Bill, his old supporters turned upon him with especial fury.[9]

There can be no question about the intensity of the campaign directed against Calvert. In the satirical prints, for example, he is as frequently met with as either Samson Gideon or the Pelham brothers. Some of the prints accuse him of accepting bribes in amounts up to £100,000. Others content themselves with gleeful anticipations of his defeat. One of the latter shows several Jews crowding around Calvert and saying, "You have all our interest, for

---

[8] *Lond. Mag.*, 1754:233, 247; *WEP*, 1277:3 (April 20, 1754).
[9] Entick, III, 94.

your zealous support of our Bill." "Confound your Bill," he replies, "now I have no hope left." [10]

In the newspapers Calvert was called "the Jewish candidate," and, with awkward cruelty, "Lord Mountcalvery." Support him, pleaded one ironical letter, and "you may restore yourselves to the good graces of the Jews, and the Ministry." The same note was struck in a piece of so-called "True Intelligence" in an issue of the *Gray's Inn Journal* that appeared four days before the City election began: "At a meeting of several stock-jobbers, children of Israel, &c., held . . . this day, Jacob Zorobabel in the chair, it was unanimously resolved to support the election of a certain candidate, on account of his attachment to our cause in the last Parliament. His zeal upon that memorable occasion, and the contempt he shewed the City-Petition at Westminster, deserve our warmest acknowledgements, and we are therefore determined to procure him as many votes, as we can influence." The notice was signed with several Jewish or pseudo-Jewish names, such as Abraham Salvadore, Josephus Shylock, and Melchizidec Mammon.[11]

Calvert seems to have had little zest for a struggle against such tactics. For several months he delayed the announcement of his decision to stand for re-election, while rumors of his intended withdrawal circulated.[12] And after he entered the contest, he campaigned much less actively than his competitors.

Not everyone thought his situation hopeless. Thomas Birch, for example, noting that there would be six or seven candidates for four seats, predicted that the opposition would scatter its votes and that consequently "Sir William Calvert, by the assistance of the Court, may, after all the clamours raised against him, be rechosen." [13] Philip Yorke did not speak explicitly of victory, but he did express the hope that if "proper measures" were taken, Calvert might "appear with credit on the poll." [14] A particular factor operating in Calvert's favor

[10] Solomons, "Satirical Prints," pp. 219, 229, and *passim*.

[11] *LEP*, 4130:1, 4127:1, 4020:1; *Gray's Inn Journal*, 31:186 (April 27, 1754).

[12] *WEP*, 1250:2 (Feb. 16, 1754); the other candidates had announced over five months earlier (*WEP*, 1191:1).

[13] Add. MSS. 35398, f. 166 (to Yorke, Sept. 29).

[14] *Ibid.*, f. 169 (to Birch, Oct. 4).

was that the church cry raised against him had brought the Dissenters over to his side in a body.[15]

The polling began on April 30 and continued for a week. The contest was the greatest that had ever been known in London, according to one chronicler; almost 6000 persons voted.[16] Unhappily, Calvert from the beginning appeared with very little credit indeed. He was last on the poll on every day but one; by the second or third day the Duke of Newcastle had given up hope and was trying to find a pocket borough for him.[17] At the close of the poll, Calvert, who in 1747 had been at the top, found himself the sixth of six candidates; and heading the list, as everyone had expected, was Sir John Barnard, the most outspoken enemy of the Jew Bill and the principal hero of the clamorers.

Here is the poll for the elections of 1747 and 1754, with the names of the repeating candidates marked with stars; there could be no more dramatic evidence of the alteration that the clamor wrought on Calvert's political fortunes:[18]

	1747			1754	
*Calvert	3806		*Barnard	3553
*Barnard	3781		*Bethell	3547
*Bethell	3146		*Ladbroke	3390
Janssen	3008		Beckford	2941
Lambert	2530		Glyn	2655
*Ladbroke	1986		*Calvert	2650

Soon after the general election the *Gray's Inn Journal* printed, under the title "The Female Parliament," a whimsical summary of the more important results. The piece included a burlesque of the London poll that shows how completely Calvert had become identified with the Jewish issue. At the top of the list were "Lady Betty Allworthy" and "Lady Mary Meanwell," with roughly the

[15] Entick, III, 94.

[16] *Ibid.*, and note; the *WEP* also spoke of the contest as "the greatest . . . ever known" (1277:3, April 20, 1754).

[17] Entick, III, 94n; Nugent, *Memoir of Nugent*, pp. 202–203 (letter, Newcastle to Nugent, May 2, 1754).

[18] *Universal Mag.*, 1754:235–236.

same number of votes as had been won by Barnard and Bethell respectively; and at the bottom, with a vote approximating that polled by Calvert, was "Lady Deborah Gideonite." [19]

The paper went on to say that Lady Deborah would nevertheless be brought in for some pocket borough, through the efforts of "an old Duchess at Court." This report proved well founded: in 1755 Sir William Calvert, though repudiated by the City of London, reentered Parliament as representative for—Old Sarum.[20]

Oxfordshire. The contest for Oxfordshire's two seats was both important and interesting. According to its historian, it was an old-fashioned Whig and Tory struggle—"a party contest in the most exact sense"; Horace Walpole described it as "a revival of downright Whiggism and Jacobitism." [21] In this battle the prestige of both the Court and the Tory remnant was more heavily committed than in any other, and politically minded people all over the country followed the news from Oxfordshire with particular interest.[22]

Because it was so important, I have often referred to this contest— so often, indeed, that little more need be said about it. The Jew Bill was clearly the principal issue in the county election, and the repeal of the Bill was the climax of the campaign.[23] The Bishop of Oxford, as we have seen, repeatedly expressed concern over the damage that the Bill was doing to the local Whig cause; and the rival candidates showed by their actions that they shared his estimate of the effectiveness of the clamor. It will be recalled that an appeal from a Whig candidate for Oxfordshire, Lord Parker, seems to have been the immediate cause of the Ministry's decision to give up the Bill, and

[19] *Gray's Inn Journal,* 34:200–201 (May 18, 1754).

[20] Judd, *Members of Parliament,* p. 140.

[21] Robson, *Oxfordshire Election,* p. 43; Walpole, *Letters,* III, 242.

[22] This fact, and the intensity of the struggle, were reflected in a remark by Philip Yorke, who was unopposed in Cambridgeshire and was heartily glad of it: "The life they have led for this last twelvemonth in Oxfordshire would not suit me at all" (Add. MSS. 35398, f. 174: to Birch, Oct. 18). See also Smollett, *History of England,* II, 158. According to Namier, *Structure of Politics,* p. 203, the Tories spent £20,068 in the contest, and the Whigs "hardly less."

[23] Robson, p. 97.

that Parker and his Tory opponent, Dashwood, carried the county contest into the precincts of Parliament in their efforts to appropriate the credit for the repeal.

That the Jew Bill cost the Whigs some votes is beyond doubt. There was, to give a specific example, the Woodstock clergyman, Benjamin Holloway, who owed his preferment to the Duke of Marlborough, but deserted his patron on account of the Bill. When the duke sent him a present of venison, Holloway "returned him no other answer than that, if it was intended as a bribe, it would be lost upon him." According to Thomas Birch, "the loss of this one vote . . . surprised [the duke] more than that of an hundred others would have done." [24] Marlborough boasted that this was the only vote that the Bill had cost him, but as Robson says in his monograph on the election, every other indication is to the contrary. In Robson's judgment, the impact of the clamor was "seismic," and its effect on Whig electoral prospects was "undoubtedly adverse." [25]

Not quite 4000 persons voted, and at the close of the poll the Tory incumbents led by about 100 votes.[26] So close was this margin, and so many were the accusations of irregularity against both sides, that the sheriff returned all four candidates. Eventually the House of Commons declared the Whigs elected, and they took their seats. It was hardly a shining victory for the Whigs; but they might well have won it outright, in Oxfordshire itself, except for the Tories' success in exploiting the unpopularity of the Jew Bill.

Others. There were a good many other constituencies where the prima facie evidence suggests that the Jew Bill, in spite of the repeal, played a substantial role in the elections of 1754. In a few of these places the Bill seems to have been the decisive factor; in others it figured importantly in the contest without, however, determining the result. Here are a few constituencies where researches by local

[24] Add. MSS. 35398, f. 158 (to Yorke, Sept. 8).
[25] *Ibid.;* Robson, pp. 93, 90, 103.
[26] Robson, pp. 101–102. All but 95 electors voted a "straight party ticket" for one pair of candidates or the other.

historians might shed further light on the political use and effectiveness of the Jew Bill:

Exeter:

Humphrey Sydenham, who had represented Exeter since 1741, was unseated without going to the poll, evidently on account of the Jew Bill. He attempted to counter the propaganda against him, but succeeded only in making himself appear ridiculous: "To acquit himself of Judaism, he dispersed printed papers, justifying his attachment to Christianity, and urging as a proof of it his travelling on Saturdays, when his business required it, and his strict observance of Sundays. This with some other reasonings of the same force induced his friends to persuade him to suppress those papers, which he had not yet delivered." [27]

Wallingford:

Thomas Sewell, an unsuccessful challenger, was said to have had the borough secured until the Jew Bill was raised as an issue against him. In the event, though the Ministry spent £1250 in his behalf, Sewell did not even go to the poll. [28]

Reading:

John Dodd, a challenger in the Court interest, failed of election by a single vote, his opponents receiving 324 and 296 votes respectively, to Dodd's 295. The Corporation, obviously unfriendly, seems to have drawn up its instruction against the Jew Bill with the specific intention of injuring Dodd's candidacy. Apparently the Jew Bill had more weight than the £1000 or more with which the Ministry backed Dodd's campaign. [29]

York:

William Thornton, M.P., retired from the field several months before the election. The Jew Bill clearly had something to do with this. [30]

[27] Add. MSS. 35398, f. 166 (Birch to Yorke, Sept. 29); see also *LEP*, 4009:4. The results of these contests can be found in *Lond. Mag.*, 1754:243–248, and *Gent. Mag.*, 1754:199–203.

[28] *Hist. MSS. Comm.*, 15th Rept., App. VI, 207 (Ord to Carlisle, July 17); Namier, *Structure of Politics*, p. 198, n. 2.

[29] *Gent. Mag.*, 1753:469–470, and 1754:202; *Hist. MSS. Comm.*, 11th Rept., App., pt. vii, 206; *LEP*, 4061:1, 4072:2; Namier, *Structure of Politics*, p. 198 and n. 1.

[30] *Gent. Mag.*, 1753:529; *WEP*, 1220:1; *LEP*, 4054:1 (Nov. 6).

Canterbury and Gloucestershire:

Matthew Robinson Morris of Canterbury and Norborne Berkeley of Gloucestershire were both heavily attacked on account of their support of the Jew Bill. In the event, they were both returned, but for a while it was thought that they would be unseated.[31]

WAS THE REPEAL REALLY NECESSARY?

Although it is evident that the Jew Bill did have some effect on certain contests in 1754, one could hardly maintain that the Government's over-all strength was materially reduced as a result. Actually the Ministry had every reason to be pleased with the outcome of the election; after most of the results were known, Newcastle wrote: "Throughout every part of [the kingdom], elections have gone well beyond our most sanguine hopes." [32] Of course the timely and "voluntary" repeal of the Bill had done much to nullify its potency as an election issue. By seizing the initiative and removing the object of attack, the Pelhams had effectively disarmed the too-successful clamorers; and by not holding the election until five months after the repeal, the Ministry allowed most of the remaining momentum of the clamor to exhaust itself.

Tactically the repeal was an undoubted success. Yet we cannot help wondering whether the concession was really necessary. What would have happened if the Government had stood firm, at least in the Lords, as Lord Halifax suggested? Knowing, along with every schoolboy, about rotten boroughs and unlimited corruption, we wonder what on earth the Pelhams can have been worried about.[33] Did they really believe that an issue could carry a mid-eighteenth-century election, despite the kind of "arrangements" at which they were so adept? Perhaps the unrepealed Jew Bill might

[31] *LEP*, 4018:1, 4020:4; *Jackson*, 19:1, 31:3, 32:3, 51:2; Add. MSS. 35398, ff. 151, 166–167 (Birch to Yorke, Aug. 25, Sept. 29); *Hist. MSS. Comm.*, 15th Rept., App. VI, 207 (Ord to Carlisle, July 17).

[32] Nugent, *Memoir of Nugent*, p. 202 (to Nugent, May 2, 1754). I should mention that Henry Pelham had died unexpectedly on March 6, just before the election.

[33] Note the *DNB*'s simple explanation of Henry Pelham's power: "His parliamentary influence was chiefly maintained by an elaborate system of corruption" (concise ed.).

have cost them a few seats in the more populous and open constituencies, but surely they cannot seriously have expected to be turned
out.

True, there was the disastrous precedent of 1710, and we can
understand how it must have given them pause. Yet the situations
were quite different. For the clamor of 1753 did not come from a
united and powerful opposition party, ready and able to supplant
the present Government; in fact, the clamor against the Jew Bill
arose out of the opposition's weakness and desperation, rather than
out of its strength.

This is not simply a matter of hindsight, either: there were those
who took a similar view at the time. Old Horace Walpole, for
example, at the very time that the Ministry was conceding the probable necessity of repeal, made light of the clamor: "I do not apprehend it will have any effect of consequence in the general election
against the Whigs, as there is no formidable body of opponents
against the present administration existing." [34] Lord Chesterfield
made a similar estimate of the over-all political situation, and condemned the repeal as a "mean concession to the mob," attributable
to the pusillanimity of the Pelhams: "Yesterday the Parliament met;
and the Duke of Newcastle, frightened out of his wits at the
groundless and senseless clamours against the Jew Bill passed last
year, moved for the repeal of it; and accordingly it is to be repealed.
This flagrant instance of timidity in the administration, gives their
enemies matter for ridicule and triumph." [35]

But while Newcastle's well known timorousness must be taken
into account, probably he arrived at a conclusion different from
that of Walpole and Chesterfield primarily because of differences
between his and their respective situations. Other comments by
Walpole indicate that his estimate of the clamor's potency was
unduly affected by his particular experience in his own constituency,
which, according to his accounts, was almost untouched by the

---

[34] Add. MSS. 35606, f. 79 (to P. Yorke, July 23).
[35] Chesterfield, *Letters,* V, 2059 (to Dayrolles, Nov. 16); and see his letter to his
son on November 26, which says much the same thing (*ibid.,* pp. 2062–2063).

agitation. "None of my constituents have ever said one word to me about it," he wrote; and though he had entertained the heads of both parties at dinner, "not the least syllable even in their cups was mentioned to me on that head directly or indirectly." [36]

Now unlike Walpole's, Newcastle's political purview was general rather than parochial: the duke knew of many places where the intensity of the clamor more than made up for the apparent indifference of Norwich. And his concern, unlike Chesterfield's, was intense, and his responsibility immediate. The earl was all but retired from active politics; with nothing at stake, he could far more easily view the whole scene with Olympian calm than could a campaign manager such as Newcastle, who besides being anxious by temperament was also anxious ex officio, as it were.

Furthermore, even if the "Whig" majority was safe in spite of the clamor, as Walpole and Chesterfield thought, this, to the duke and his brother, was beside the point. Their real problem was not to keep out the Tories, but to keep in power the "present system" —that is, the current coalition, of which they were the contrivers and leaders. And as we noted earlier, the weakness of the regular avowed opposition in the later years of King George II in some ways made this more difficult.

This was because the very vastness of the nominal Whig majority meant that a Government acceptable to the king and adequate to the normal demands of his service could conceivably be based upon any of several different groupings of parliamentary factions and allocations of offices and honors. In such a situation no system could be absolutely secure against the inevitable intrigues, both in Parliament and at Court, in which not only men out of office but even subordinate ministers engaged, attempting either to alter the present system to their particular advantage, or to bring it down altogether, in hopes that when the cards were dealt anew, they would come up with a better hand.

Now admittedly the Pelham ministry was in little danger of

[36] Add. MSS. 35606, f. 86 (to P. Yorke, Sept. 29). Walpole sat for Norwich.

being overthrown or subverted in 1753. The brothers had managed for several years to cope successfully with each threat to their power; and probably their particular system of 1753 was more strongly entrenched in office than any other between the decline of Walpole and the rise of Pitt. Yet for the purpose of understanding their fears of the Jew Bill as a danger in the election, the Pelhams' considerable security of tenure is less significant than one of the principal ways in which they had gone about achieving it —namely, their policy of avoiding contention of all sorts, so far as was possible, and of conciliating their potential rivals, even to the extent of giving them high office.

The paradox in this situation will be immediately perceived: to a certain extent the Pelhams' power was founded upon weakness. The prime minister's strength, in particular, notoriously lay in his skill at compromise, and at making his leadership acceptable, or at least inoffensive, to the largest possible number of influential men. Henry Pelham was, as Chesterfield said, "no shining, enterprising minister," but rather, "a safe one, which I like better":[37] in other words, the sort of man to whom others do not begrudge great power because they are confident that he will not abuse it, or perhaps even exercise it actively. In sum, the Pelham administration was in many respects a sound, sturdy ship, but the measures that had been taken to render it especially seaworthy had in fact so laden it down that its cautious masters felt that they had always to look closely to its trim and to keep it in calm waters and as near port as possible.

If it is true that the Pelhams saw their situation in some such terms, then their fears that the Bill might hurt them in the election become more comprehensible. We must not rule out the psychological factor mentioned by Chesterfield: no doubt it is part of the truth to liken the timid Pelhams to a man who, obsessed with fears for his security, puts five bolts to each door and worries whenever one of

---

[37] *Letters,* V, 2096 (to his son, Mar. 8, 1754). I should say that there were some striking points of similarity between the Pelham administration and that of President Eisenhower.

them begins to show the least sign of rust. But it must also be understood that for the Pelhams to be justifiably concerned over the election prospects, it was by no means necessary that the picture be as dark as it had been in 1710. Even if their refusal to repeal the Jew Bill had caused the loss of only ten or twenty seats, the Pelhams would have thought the cost too great. For what was really at stake—especially in such notable contests as those at London, Oxfordshire, and Bristol—was not just a dozen or so votes on a question of confidence, but rather the prestige of the Pelhams and their present system, and the brothers' future relations and influence both with the harassed candidates and with such men's parliamentary associates and local supporters. If the Pelhams had not done all they could to remove this millstone from the necks of their friends, they would surely have incurred an unwelcome amount of resentment from those who suffered as a result.

Nor would those politicians who lost their elections outright have been the only ones to complain if the Pelhams had done nothing to stifle this controversy which appeared to be infusing new life into oppositions all over the country. Some candidates, though victorious in the end, would nevertheless have been put to extra expense; and in particular, men who had counted on being returned unopposed would have been certain to take it very ill if they had found themselves burdened, on account of the Jew Bill, with the cost, worry, and inconvenience of a contested election.[38]

This, then, is what the Pelhams feared from the Jew Bill when they weighed its probable effect on the general election. It was not a question of their being turned out by an adverse majority—that was all but impossible; nor was it a question of the loss of seats as such.

[38] Note the anguished cry of one incumbent: "I think a contested election one of the greatest evils that could befall me: and therefore by delivering me from such a calamity your Lordship will add very greatly to the infinite obligations I already lie under" (Add. MSS. 35592, ff. 186–187: Thomas Clarke to Hardwicke, Nov. 2). Clarke's reference was to a particular intrigue, and not to the Jew Bill; but see the letter quoted at length above (p. 140), in which Robert Ord described the troubles of Thomas Sewell, against whom the Jewish issue had been raised: Sewell "thought he had secured Wallingford," but was now "like to be routed, or be at a very great expence."

Rather, the brothers, as heads of a coalition, feared a more subtle and general weakening of their power and influence, a weakening that would surely make their management of the new Parliament more difficult.

Of course since the Pelhams preferred not to risk this and so decided for repeal, we can never know for certain whether their estimate of the danger was a just one. Lecky ventured the opinion that if the ministers had not repealed the Bill, "it is probable that the election . . . would have proved disastrous to their power." [39] Surely the word "disastrous" is far too strong; but at the same time, I am convinced that Lord Chesterfield wrote both inaccurately and uncharitably when he implied that the danger was inconsiderable, and that the repeal of the Act was merely a further proof of the Duke of Newcastle's want of courage. For against the personal part of Chesterfield's assertion stands the fact that a good many others besides Newcastle—and men who had far less at stake—shared the duke's forebodings. And against Chesterfield's implied belittling of the potential danger of the clamor, one can set the facts and arguments offered above: first, that even after the repeal, the clamor did have an effect on some contests; and second, that for various reasons the Pelhams were more vulnerable than the size of their pre-election majority would seem to indicate.

In sum, one may regret that the Pelhams gave in to the pressures for repeal with so little reluctance; but—given their obviously sincere belief that the Bill was of no importance—they cannot reasonably be blamed for their decision.

[39] Lecky, *England in the Eighteenth Century,* I, 286.

X

CONCLUSION

FOR the historian, the real interest and significance of the controversy over the Jew Bill of 1753 lie in what the episode tells us about mid-eighteenth-century men and manners, rather than in the effect that it had at the time. Actually that effect was slight—indeed surprisingly so, when we consider the volume and vehemence of the controversial literature that has come down to us.

On the law the episode left no mark whatever: the Act was removed from the statute book without having been invoked by a single petitioner for naturalization. Nor did the episode leave much more of a trace on the politics of the time. It did affect the careers of a few individual politicians; but by no means can the clamor be said to have set its general impress on the composition or conduct of the new Parliament. Sir William Calvert, once of London and now of Old Sarum, must have frequently recalled the clamor and its unhappy effect on his political fortunes; but it is unlikely that a leader of the Commons ever had occasion to cast a desperate eye over the House, and curse the day that the Pelham government became entangled in the Jew Bill.

Yet this transitory episode, which was so inconsequential in itself, sheds a great deal of light on the mid-century political scene. Much of what it reveals is, naturally enough, more or less familiar to students of the eighteenth century. It gives us another opportunity to observe the characters and political methods of the Pelham brothers; it calls our attention once again to the appallingly low ethical and intellectual standards of most mid-eighteenth-century political journalism.

But the history of the Jew Bill goes well beyond mere confirmation of the familiar: it also affords us, as does almost no other contem-

poraneous event, a glimpse of what lay beneath the placid (or even
stagnant) surface of the politics of the Pelham era. "Politics," I have
said: for when we examine the controversy of 1753 closely, we see
that at bottom it was not, as it first appears, a singular and isolated
outburst of anti-Semitic passion as such, but rather a renewal—albeit
a somewhat artificial one, aimed at an approaching election—of a
long-standing dispute over immigration and naturalization policy.

Of course the Jew Bill was merely a technical measure, not a
substantial act of policy. But once it had been inflated into an object
of public controversy and seized upon for election purposes, the Bill
became in effect a doctrinal issue in the old Whig and Tory tradition.
It was attacked and defended by the same opposing factions as had
fought over earlier naturalization bills;[1] the arguments employed by
both sides, too, were the standard, familiar ones, with incidental pro-
and anti-Jewish variations which unquestionably added to the intensity of the controversy but did not alter its essential nature as a
dispute over immigration and naturalization.[2]

That naturalization was the main issue, rather than the particular
position of the Jews as such, becomes clear enough once we penetrate
beneath the topical anti-Semitism of the clamor. We recall the
generalized Tory attacks on "this Bill . . . [and] every Bill that has
the least tendency to let in a swarm of *foreigners, especially Jewish
foreigners*"; also the Tories' patriotic scorn for "naturalized Jews,
or any other foreigners." [3] The phrasing of the politicians' public
statements on the Jew Bill also indicates that they considered naturalization to be the central issue; for after denouncing the Bill they
usually went on to demonstrate their zeal not against the Jews, but
against naturalizations. Thus one Tory member affirmed, "I divided
against the passing of this Bill, as I ever have against all general

---

[1] The Bedford Whigs were an exception, of course.

[2] At least one pamphlet was reissued that had originally been occasioned by one
of the earlier naturalization controversies, and that consequently contained no reference
whatever to the Jews: *Some Thoughts upon a Bill for General Naturalization:
Addressed to Those . . . who act upon Whig Principles* (London, 1751); advertised
in *LEP*, 4017:3 (Aug. 16, 1753).

[3] *Jackson*, 6:4; *P. Hist.*, XIV, 1405–1406; my emphasis.

Naturalization Bills hitherto proposed . . ." Another candidate, after recanting his former support of the Bill, promised further, not that he would see that henceforth the Jews were kept in their place, but that he would "zealously oppose all naturalizations whatsoever, so disagreeable to this nation." [4]

Another fact is generally overlooked by those who see only the anti-Jewish aspect of the clamor, and so tend to regard the whole affair as an isolated explosion of anti-Semitic bigotry, instead of a renewal of an older and more fundamental political quarrel. This is that, strange as it may seem, the English Jews were, on balance, gainers, rather than losers, by the legislation of the year 1753 as a whole. The repeal of the Naturalization Act left them precisely where they had stood before, of course; but both the Turkey Act and Hardwicke's Clandestine Marriage Act contained specific exemptions in their favor. [5] What is more, there seems to have been no serious public complaint on these heads, even at the height of the clamor occasioned by the Naturalization Act. [6]

First of all, then, the controversy over the Jew Bill of 1753 incidentally calls our attention to the existence of a continuing Whig and Tory doctrinal disagreement of many years' standing, on the subject of immigration and naturalization policy. The individual skirmishes in this running battle are known to students of the period; but the thread of continuity connecting them all has somehow been overlooked. Nor has much notice been given to the direct way in which the question of naturalization touched upon one of the most fundamental Whig and Tory doctrinal differences, namely, the relation of Church and State. For, *the Jews quite apart,* the question of naturalization was *in itself* partly a religious one—one that affected the position of the Church both in principle and in substance. It did so in principle, because a more liberal naturalization policy meant a further reduction in the comprehensiveness of the sacramental test;

---

[4] *Jackson,* 9:4; *Gent. Mag.,* 1753:452.

[5] For the Turkey Act see Chapter IV; for the other, see Roth, *Jews in England,* p. 246.

[6] See, for example, the good-natured story in *Jackson,* 51:1.

and it did so in substance because any appreciable influx of non-conformist immigrants was bound to weaken the position of the Established Church within the State.

The second major lesson to be learnt from the Jew Bill is closely related to the first. It is that there was more potential vitality in the old two-party division than is generally recognized by modern students of the eighteenth century. It is true that the traditional Whig and Tory doctrinal differences were usually irrelevant to the substantive political problems and possibilities of the 1750's. Yet the old loyalties and zeal, sustained largely by memories of past struggles, were still alive and ready to be called forth whenever an issue touching on the old politico-religious disputes arose—or was manufactured.

The Jewish Naturalization Act, once the circumstances of its passage had made it notorious, was just such an issue. Furthermore, the fact that the particular beneficiaries of the Act were members of such a distinct and controversial religious minority served to emphasize the religious aspect of the question, and so laid the measure even more open to a propaganda attack by the Church party. The Jew Bill, then, by providing an excuse for a church-cry, infused new life into the old Whig and Tory conflict, the Tories in particular being wondrously reinvigorated by the opportunity to stand forth once again in jealous defense of the Establishment. As of old (except for a topical variation) they cried for "Church and King, without mass, meeting, or synagogue!", and described electoral contests as struggles between the Church party on the one hand and the Presbyterians and the Jews on the other.[7]

Of course the episode of 1753 was but a minor and momentary flare-up whose importance must not be exaggerated. It by no means requires us, for example, to modify the Namier interpretation of the fundamental structure of mid-eighteenth-century politics. But it does require that we give greater recognition to the continuing existence, in the 1750's, of Whig and Tory attitudes and loyalties which, though

[7] Add. MSS. 35398, f. 164 (Birch to Yorke, Sept. 22); *Jackson*, 26:1.

usually dormant and usually irrelevant to the real issues of the day, were still strong enough to rally men at least briefly around the old party standards. Perhaps the most dramatic proof of this is the heated exchange over the Sacheverell Case and the Peace of Utrecht that interrupted the Commons' debate on the repeal of the Jew Bill. In short, it is clearly an error to suppose that the words "Whig" and "Tory" were wholly devoid of meaning or of emotional potency, even in the Pelham era.[8]

In particular, the vitality and trouble-making potential of the Tory remnant are worth remarking. In pamphlets, in newspapers both in London and in the provinces, in protests drawn up by county grand juries, and from rural pulpits all over the kingdom, Tory anathemas were roared forth against the Jews and the Pelhams. But since the Tories were so completely lacking in leadership and in practical purposes, all this noise should be regarded more as mere sound and fury than as a demonstration of effective political strength.

The Tories' (and other opponents') sense of frustration is apparent in the wildly inconsistent constitutional arguments put forward against the Bill. There were lofty appeals to the supremacy of natural law, and half-serious references to the royal veto;[9] then, quite at the other end of the scale, there were appeals to democratic arguments. The latter were very common: the phrase *Vox Populi, Vox Dei,* for example, appears in every sort of attack on the Bill, from speeches

---

[8] Indeed, many mid-eighteenth-century men positively welcomed their few opportunities to let off partisan war whoops. Some of the angriest Tory attacks on the Jewish Naturalization Act convey a sense of something very like exhilaration. And Whigs, too, could take pleasure in the prospect of renewed partisan battle: unwieldy and faction-ridden majorities enjoy recapturing a sense of cohesiveness and purpose almost as much as hopeless minorities enjoy being reassured that they are still in the game. Compare the Commons' debates on repeal and on Lord Harley's December 4 motion with the incident reported in the *New York Times* (May 24, 1959) under the headline "Housing Bill Rallies Liberals in Congress; Rout of Conservatives Comes on a Clear-Cut Social Welfare Test": "Liberalism and party loyalty suddenly came alive in the House Democratic organization this week and President Eisenhower, the Republican minority, and Southern Democrats took a bad licking . . . Along with the victory, the exercise produced a rare spirit of exuberant party loyalty and discipline among the Democrats." (For a further discussion of this point see Appendix A.)

[9] E.g., *Protester,* 14:79; *Lond. Mag.,* 1753:423; *LEP,* 3981:1 (May 24).

in Parliament to the satirical prints.[10] In one of the debates on repeal, a Tory M.P., Sir Roger Newdigate, quoted this phrase, taunted the Whigs for having lost their former faith in it, and went on to assert: "Whatever the late patrons of this law may now think, I believe the people of this Kingdom, to take them in general, are, upon mature consideration, as good judges of their own interest or honour as the majority of either House of Parliament can pretend to be."[11] One may suppose that these appeals to the popular will were mainly an *ad hoc* expedient of a party that had no hope of attaining constitutional power under the existing system.

The same frustration also found expression in attacks—often surprisingly strong—on the supposedly sacrosanct British Constitution itself: a "crazy Constitution," one writer termed it, "unequally and irrationally formed." The counties and cities were under-represented, he complained, leaving the kingdom in the "contemptible, dirty hands" of the venal and perjured borough voters who provided the Pelhams with their majorities.[12] It is especially amusing, in view of the Tories' last ditch resistance to the Reform Bill of 1832, to find them in 1753 poking fun at the anomalies in the borough franchise: "On Monday near 500 persons of both sexes were assembled at the Borough of Garrat, near Wandsworth, to elect two members to represent that place according to a whimsical custom . . . Both men and women, who have performed certain merry ceremonies within two miles of the Borough, have votes. They were sworn four at a time, laying their hands on a brick to be legal voters."[13]

The events of 1753 tell us something, too, about the character and temperament of the public (both enfranchised and not) to which the opposition propagandists made their appeal; indeed, they forcibly remind us of the radical change that the English national character

[10] E.g., *P. Hist.*, XV, 133; Solomons, "Satirical Prints," facsimile facing p. 227; *Protester*, 10:60.

[11] *P. Hist.*, XV, 133.

[12] *Protester*, 20:118–119.

[13] *Jackson*, 56:2. See also P. A. Gibbons, *Ideas of Political Representation in Parliament, 1660–1832* (Oxford, 1914), pp. 24–28.

has undergone since the eighteenth century. Positive statements on that elusive topic are invariably risky; but surely we can say that the extraordinary excitement over the Jew Bill, the near-hysteria over the kidnapping case of Canning and Squires, and the election violence, are wholly out of keeping with the generally accepted stereotype of the phlegmatic, stolid, and fundamentally fair-minded Englishman of our own day.

The contemporary historian Smollett, however, thought these phenomena to be so characteristic of the English nation that he paused in his narrative for 1753 to emphasize the point in general terms: "The genius of the English people is perhaps incompatible with a state of perfect tranquillity; if it is not ruffled by foreign provocations, or agitated by unpopular measures of domestic administration, it will undergo temporary fermentations from the turbulent ingredients inherent in its own constitution. Tumults are excited, and faction kindled into rage and inveteracy, by incidents of the most frivolous nature." [14] Even to one familiar with eighteenth-century England, this unqualified generalization comes as something of a shock. Perhaps if it were more widely known, we should be spared some of those facile arguments that rest upon the assumption that the English (or any other) national character is distinct, easily delineated, and constant.

The final major conclusion to which the history of the Jew Bill leads us is a matter of emphasis and degree rather than of plain fact. It is that the Parliament of Great Britain during the last years of George II was in reality far more sensitive to public pressures than such familiar terms as Whig "supremacy" or "trusteeship" imply.

The arguments over the Bill do, it is true, include several striking expressions of the aristocratic Whig belief in the absolute supremacy and independence of the legislature. Both Lord Temple and Lord Halifax, as we saw, thought that the upper house should have ignored the public demand for repeal. The Commons, in their view,

[14] Smollett, *History of England,* II, 113. The specific reference is to Canning and Squires.

might indeed be forced to bend before the storm and pay what Halifax caustically termed a "disagreeable civility" to public opinion; but the Lords were in no way obligated to concur unless they were convinced that the Bill was objectively unsound, and not merely unpopular. Another Whig aristocrat, General the Hon. Sir Charles Howard, M.P., put the question of principle in its baldest possible form: "I . . . am not a little hurt," he wrote to his brother, Lord Carlisle, "at the spirit and disturbances shewed in many parts of England against a law passed after many considerations and debates by the Legislature. What is our prospect if they are to set themselves up for judges whether we do right or wrong?" [15]

Yet against all this brave talk of independence must be set the plain fact that the people had their way in the end: the repeal of the Jew Bill, exulted the Tory *Oxford Journal,* "shews the respect of the Legislature for the Publick Voice"; *"Vox Populi, Vox Dei,* or the Jew Act Repealed," boasted one of the satirical prints.[16]

Of course this particular triumph of the populace (and the opposition) does not warrant our speaking of the eighteenth-century Constitution as "democratic." What it does show is that the popular will, in T. H. Green's *negative* sense of "the measure of what the people will really tolerate," [17] was able to prevail, once the people were sufficiently aroused against some particular measure. The entire initiative in public affairs lay with the king's Government, which normally carried on its functions in an untrammeled manner quite in keeping with the Whig theory of independent "trusteeship." But when a Government went beyond the bounds of the public's patience—as in the Sacheverell Case, the Excise Bill, and the Jew Bill—it persisted at its peril.

[15] *Hist. MSS. Comm.,* 15th Rept., App. VI, 208 (Sept. 28). The complete quotation is on p. 143, above.

[16] *Jackson,* 34:2; Solomons, "Satirical Prints," facsimile facing p. 227.

Cecil S. Emden, in *The People and the Constitution,* 2d ed. (Oxford, 1956), pp. 42–43, 50, reaches a different conclusion, rejecting the repeal of the Jew Bill as satisfactory evidence of the power of public opinion; but his discussion of the affair is sketchy and inaccurate, and seems to me unduly colored by ideological bias.

[17] Quoted by Lord Radcliffe in *The Problem of Power* (London, 1952), p. 87.

EPILOGUE

Compared with either the later Stuart period or the second quarter of the nineteenth century, the reigns of the first two Georges were remarkably barren of significant legislation dealing with fundamental political or social questions. These were years when, broadly speaking, most members of the politically articulate classes saw no pressing need for substantial change, and when furthermore—the distinction is a real one—many among them entertained a strong and positive antipathy toward almost any kind of innovation.

The latter attitude seems to have contributed materially to the opposition to the Jew Bill. Lord Egmont, for example, in his speech on the third reading, asserted that the measure was prompted by "nothing but a wanton spirit of innovation, with changing the old laws of England, and setting up for every novel institution (the very disease of the times)." [18] We find even Samson Gideon using similar expressions to explain his disapproval of the Bill. In his letter of resignation from the synagogue he described the measure as "directly contrary to my declared sentiments, and my dislike to all innovations"; in another letter he wrote that the affair "does not in the least concern me, having always declared my sentiments against any innovation." [19]

Given this almost reflexive resistance to change, it is hardly surprising that most attempted "reforms" that failed of passage or went sour in some way were not soon accorded a second hearing. Thus a census bill that passed the Commons in 1753 but was rejected by the Lords as a scheme of "very dangerous tendency," had to wait until 1801 for its principle to be vindicated.[20]

The Jew Bill, having burnt the fingers of so many politicians, had to wait even longer. The loss was not serious, however; for under the old (and not truly grievous) restrictions, the Jewish community

[18] *P. Hist.*, XIV, 1423. Cf. this Tory toast of 1753: "Old Stile! Old Faith! and Old England, for ever" (*LEP*, 4012:1).

[19] Roth, *Anglo-Jewish Letters*, p. 131; Sutherland, "Samson Gideon: Eighteenth Century Jewish Financier," p. 85.

[20] *P. Hist.*, XIV, 1317–1365; Williams, *Whig Supremacy*, p. 118; Smollett, *History of England*, II, 111–112.

in England continued to prosper and increase, undiscouraged by the setback of 1753. In fact only three years after the repeal of the Naturalization Act, one Baron d'Aguilar, a person of the very sort whom the measure had been ostensibly intended to attract, removed from Vienna to London, bringing with him his twelve children and, it was said, an immense fortune.[21]

Finally, in 1825—seventy-two years after the great clamor over the Jew Bill—Parliament completely abolished the sacramental test as a requirement for naturalization, whether for Jews or anyone else, and so put a period to the whole argument.[22] There was no public out-cry; and, in spite of the dire predictions that were so industriously propagated in 1753, both Church and State still stand.

[21] Picciotto, *Sketches,* pp. 96–97.
[22] Henriques, *Jews and English Law,* p. 245.

APPENDICES

BIBLIOGRAPHY

INDEX

APPENDIX A

The Bearing of the Naturalization Controversies
on the Namier School's Interpretation
of Mid-Eighteenth-Century English Politics

TO have conferred a measure of intellectual respectability upon the study of the politics of England in the 1740's and 1750's is surely not the least remarkable of the late Sir Lewis Namier's achievements. Before his *Structure of Politics at the Accession of George III* appeared, the age of the Pelhams was usually dismissed as merely an insignificant, dull, and confusing interval between the fall of Walpole and the rise of Pitt. Namier, however, with his new way of looking at political institutions and the men who make them work, forced us to re-examine our notions about "insignificance" in history, and to admit that in some respects a period in which great leaders and great issues were lacking could for that very reason be especially interesting and rewarding to the student of politics.

But Namier did more than just revive historians' interest in the mid-eighteenth century in a general way: his researches and conclusions also gave a particular direction to that interest, with the result that recent investigation and discussion have been chiefly, indeed almost exclusively, focused on the intricate opportunist maneuverings of parliamentary leaders and factions, and on electoral "arrangements" in manageable constituencies. In the resultant version of eighteenth-century politics all is factions, tactics, and private interests; and if parties, principles, or policies are mentioned at all, as a rule it is only in order to dismiss them as unimportant.

I agree that the Namier interpretation is accurate as far as it goes. But the history of the naturalization controversies of 1747, 1751, and 1753 has convinced me that it is not complete; there is, as I shall argue, a significant dimension of mid-century thought and behavior that it tends

to slight, and consequently there are some episodes—these among them—that it cannot fully describe or explain.

Of course the Namier approach is helpful, indeed essential, to any attempt to understand these episodes. Take, for example, the Bill of 1751, which was defeated principally because of the defection, for factious reasons, of the Bedfords. As I noted in Chapter IV, the party zeal that the Bill had attracted at its early stages faded in the end before the centrifugal tendencies of the politics of the Pelham era, so that "a strong Whig parliament" finally refused to carry this "favourite Whig point." [1]

Here, beyond a doubt, the Namier interpretation scores: for this is just the sort of result that it has taught us to expect to find in this period. But though the "structural" version of politics can explain the *outcome* of these controversies, it is of little use in explaining why they arose in the first place, or the nature and intensity of the feelings they aroused. *These* things must be explained chiefly in terms of party attitudes and traditions—and this is something that the Namier interpretation tends to leave too much out of account.

True, when we historians look objectively or "scientifically" at the behavior patterns of mid-eighteenth-century politicians, what we see most clearly is the confused nonideological melee described by Professor Namier; indeed, most often very little else is discernible at all. But if we look through the eyes of contemporary men, we find that they could also envisage a second political battleground, where the Whig and Tory hosts confronted one another still.

Of course this stirring partisan vision was revealed more vividly to some men than to others. In the minds of some—mostly diehard Tories remote from the center of things—the Whig and Tory aspect of politics seemed far more important, indeed more "real," than that with which Namier is concerned.[2] Doubtless for a few knowing politicians it had no affective reality at all, and counted only as a factor to be allowed for in dealing with less clear-sighted men. Then between these extremes were all those who were in varying degree aware of the uninspiring factional "structure" of current politics, but who believed (and not without reason)

[1] See pp. 37 and 35, above.

[2] Cf. much of Dr. Johnson's talk of Whig and Tory—keeping in mind, however, the qualifications that Donald J. Greene rightly insists upon in *The Politics of Samuel Johnson* (New Haven, 1960).

that what they saw was "abnormal" and temporary, the product of un-usual circumstances; the "natural" and abiding division of English politics, they felt, was (or somehow *ought* to be) along Whig and Tory lines.[3] It is not improbable, then, that most men in the 1750's regarded the two-party cross-division of politics as meaningful and even important —or at least potentially so. Many even of the politicians, who were of practical necessity living and moving in accordance with the rules of the nonparty system that Namier described, seem to have continued, at a certain level of consciousness, to think (or feel) about politics in terms of Whig versus Tory.

Nor were such notions wholly without support. Almost always, it is true, partisan attitudes had little relevance to present problems, and per-sisted chiefly because of memories of past struggles.[4] But there were rare occasions, such as the controversies over naturalization, when the vision of politics as a Whig and Tory conflict was endowed, though but fitfully and imperfectly, with substance and life. When this happened, and "the latent strength of disorganized Toryism"[5] was aroused and given a rallying point, the balance between the parties appeared not quite so hopelessly one-sided as usual, and the so-called "Whig supremacy" was revealed as a constitutional and parliamentary, rather than a national, phenomenon. Certainly the Pelhams and their supporters, by so hastily abandoning the Naturalization Act of 1753, showed a healthy respect for the strength of High Church and exclusionist sentiment out of doors.

But although the Tory awakening of 1753 was thus able to leave at least a discernible mark on the statute book, neither it nor the lesser naturalization controversies can be said to have had any lasting effects on the struggle for power and place: it was mostly noise that they generated, rather than effective political energy. For this reason the modern school, with their almost exclusive concern with *the mechanics of political power,* tend to pass over such episodes and the amount of residual Whig and Tory sentiment they reveal, considering these things irrelevant to the "realities" of mid-century politics. Thus in Sir Lewis Namier's *Structure of Politics,* which deals extensively with the election

[3] See the quotation from old Horace Walpole on p. 30, above.
[4] We should note, however, that these attitudes naturally tended to distort men's perceptions of reality and so were, like most prejudices, partly self-validating.
[5] See pp. 27–28, above, and n. 14.

of 1754, *the Jew Bill is not so much as mentioned,* even though the public talk of the politicians and publicists at the time was of little else.[6] Of course in passing over such matters the new historians are merely being consistent with their particular definition of politics. But certainly that definition is itself open to criticism as unduly narrow—when, for example, it leads to the assertion that "the political life of the [mid-century] period could be *fully* described without ever using a party denomination."[7]

Then did party and party doctrines, as we are told, count for little or nothing in the politics of the 1750's? At the level of "structure" this was essentially and importantly true; but there was another level at which it was not. Did questions of policy and principle make no difference in parliamentary elections? By and large this is also true; yet it is equally true that there were men at the time who *thought* that these things made a difference, and whose actions must to some extent have been affected by that belief.[8]

[6] The same exclusive interest in "structure" appears in the use Prof. Namier makes of the correspondence of Bishop Secker of Oxford (*Structure of Politics,* p. 68, where the Bishop's name is incorrectly given as "Talbot"). In the course of a general discussion of the role of the clergy in county elections, Prof. Namier quotes a letter of Feb. 8, 1753, to Lord Hardwicke, in which Secker expresses regret that he has but little electoral influence to put at the disposal of the Government. But Prof. Namier passes over Secker's later letters to Hardwicke, in which the Bishop repeatedly voices a more particular and more intense concern over the "unhappy influence" of the Jew Bill on public opinion, and so also on the approaching election (Add. MSS. 35592, ff. 88–89, 102, 127–128, 192–193; June to Nov., 1753). Here is another example: Namier quotes a letter in which Hardwicke advises his son on the proper *manner* to assume when addressing meetings of country gentlemen (*Structure of Politics,* p. 71), but Namier ignores the chancellor's letter of a few weeks later, which includes some pointed advice as to *matter:* "I have inclosed a printed Copy of the Jew-Bill. I suppose it will not be advisable for you to talk publickly in favour of it" (Add. MSS. 35351, f. 248, July 29. See also f. 242).

[7] Namier, *Structure of Politics,* p. xi (my emphasis). Of course my only quarrel is with the word "fully." That Namier recognized the existence, though not the occasional importance, of the traditional attitudes is evident from two passing references in *England in the Age of the American Revolution* (London, 1930), pp. 207, 212. These passages seem to be inconsistent with the sentence just quoted—unless, again, the term "political life" is construed in the narrowest possible way.

[8] Recall, for example, this passage from a letter written by an exceptionally intelligent and well connected M.P.: "I see the Common Council [of London] have instructed their representatives to obtain a repeal of the Jew Bill, and if such a

Of course there is a sense in which we moderns are fully entitled to call such men "wrong": for, thanks to Sir Lewis Namier and others, we are able to see the essential structure of eighteenth-century political power more clearly than could most eighteenth-century men. But although our first task is to pierce through the veil of memories and illusions that clouded their vision, so that we may look at things as they really were, we cannot thereafter disregard those illusions altogether, as scientists disregard mistaken eighteenth-century beliefs about, say, phlogiston. After all, those illusions, exaggerations, or misconceptions about politics did themselves comprise a part of "things as they really were."

Phrased thus generally, this assertion will hardly seem novel; yet in the present state of eighteenth-century studies, such a reminder is needful. For so dazzling has been the achievement of the Namier school in exploring and interpreting the one aspect of politics which they have made their own, that we are apt to forget that there was another. The mid-century naturalization controversies have a real usefulness as an antidote against this tendency.

---

motion should be made, it will be pretty difficult to withstand it, as many of the Whigs will be afraid of risking their elections, just at the eve of a new representative." (Philip Yorke to Thomas Birch, Oct. 4, Add. MSS. 35398, f. 169.) See also Chap. VIII, n. 72.

APPENDIX B

The Anti-Semitism of the Clamor
and the Tone of Partisan Controversy
in the Mid-Eighteenth Century

AS WE saw in Chapter VI, party politics rather than raw bigotry was the impelling force behind most of the anti-Semitic propaganda of the clamor. The clamor was meant to prepare the ground not for a pogrom, but for a general election; its real targets were the Court Whig politicians, not the Jews; and its violence, at bottom, was that of unrestrained political partisanship rather than anti-Jewish hysteria.

This is not to say that all the expressions of anti-Jewish sentiment were feigned; for it is all too clear that some of the opposition publicists threw themselves wholeheartedly into the task of maligning the Jews. I have quoted enough repulsive examples of their work to leave no doubt of what the Archbishop of Canterbury had in mind when he spoke of being "ashamed for the spirit of our country." [1]

Still, in my opinion, most modern works that touch on the Jew Bill tend to exaggerate both the amount and the intensity of the actual anti-Semitism of the clamor. The reason for this is clear: it has to do with the violent language of the propaganda against the Bill. Heretofore the episode has attracted the close attention only of scholars interested in Anglo-Jewish history. Such men, knowing little about the tone of eighteenth-century political controversy, but being familiar with the language of anti-Semitic bigotry in all ages, naturally tend to see, in the extravagant and cruel attacks on the Jews and their bill, conclusive evidence that England in 1753 went through a period of rabid anti-Jewish hysteria.

Of course genuine anti-Semitic feelings added to the heat of the

[1] Add. MSS. 32733, f. 163 (Abp. Herring to Newcastle, Oct. 30).

dispute; but at bottom the violence of most of the propaganda against the Jew Bill simply reflects the normal level of eighteenth-century partisan debate, which was deplorably low. It is the failure to make allowance for this fact, that leads to an exaggeration of the specifically anti-Semitic bitterness of the clamor.[2]

In order to indicate the context in which the attacks on the Jew Bill should be read, I have appended a few examples of the kind of coarse and bitter personal and party abuse that characterized so much mid-eighteenth-century political disputation. The first is an attack on Sir Edward Turner for requesting a scrutiny of the Oxfordshire poll; it is taken from the *Oxford Journal:*

> Neddy, the more thou stir'st corruption's sink,
>   The more, thou know'st, 'twill throw about its stink,
> Then, Neddy, as the stink is all thy own,
>   Pr'ythee be warned and let the sink alone.[3]

The same issue of the paper carried an elegant little piece in which the Whig candidates for the county were made to bewail in retrospect the futility of their electioneering efforts. One couplet reads,

> [We] find, after all, we might every bit
> E'en as well have let down both our breeches and sh-t.
>   [Refrain:] *Derry Down,* &c.[4]

That the Oxfordshire Whigs could be fully as vulgar and abusive as their rivals is apparent from the following verses on the Tory candidates:

> "Every Man in His Humour"
>
> A gentle knight, brimfull of hope,
>   (Knight of the Shire also)
> To gain the Papists, pleas'd the Pope,
>   And humbly kiss'd his toe.
>
> Poh! cries his colleague, in a pother,
>   That's but a simple farce;
> And that he may outdo his brother,
>   He's gone to kiss his a-se.[5]

---

[2] See also pp. 75–76, above, and n. 7.
[3] *Jackson,* 53:3.
[4] *Ibid.*
[5] *Ibid.,* 48:3.

A Tory sympathizer returned the compliment in the next issue:

> What a kiss-mine-a-se pother, of a knight and his brother,
> By a kiss-mine-a-se fool is here written!
> With his jangling farce, fit to wipe but my a-se,
> Poor booby! he seems to be smitten.
>
> Not only at Rome,—but here too at home,
> If he'd know the right road to promotion,
> The levy's the farce, where W[a]l[po]le's broad a-se
> Has been slobber'd with p[rie]stly devotion.
>
> Make then no ado about the Pope's toe,
> Let not popery be the determent!
> Since Whigs we know all, to bum-worship will fall,
> And smack any a-se for preferment.[6]

Finally, here are some excerpts from a Whig description of a "typical" Tory: "A True Blue is a monster with an English face, a French heart, and an Italian conscience; a creature with a brazen forehead, a prodigious mouth, a swollen paunch, and no brains . . . A True Blue is as fond of slavery as others are of liberty . . . he envies the happiness of canvas breeches and wooden shoes, and extremely admires the mercy of the Inquisition . . . His Church is a drinking parson, his prayers, noise, his morality, drunkenness, and his trust in a bottle." [7]

Clearly, then, the intemperate tone of the controversy over the Jew Bill was quite in keeping with the level to which eighteenth-century partisan debate often sank, and should not be regarded as peculiar to the anti-Jewish clamor. The same general warning applies to several smaller points, too. For some of the more extravagant canards of the clamor that are often cited as evidence of anti-Jewish extremism were actually no more than clichés of partisan abuse.

There is, for example, the oft-repeated tale that the Jews had turned St. Paul's into a synagogue—or soon would—and that Queen Anne's statue in the churchyard was to be thrown down to make way for one of Samson Gideon, Pontius Pilate, or "Henry IX." [8] This is fairly strong stuff; but before ascribing it specifically to anti-Semitic bitterness, we

---

[6] *Ibid.,* 49:3.

[7] *Ibid.,* 27:3. This, too, was answered in kind in the next issue (28:3). For a seventeenth-century version of this lampoon see David Ogg, *England in the Reign of Charles II* (Oxford, 1934), II, 609.

[8] E.g., *Jackson,* 19:1–2. Mentioned by both Hertz, *British Imperialism,* p. 85, and Roth, *Jews in England,* p. 218. For "Henry IX" see above, p. 105, n. 4.

should note that the same story is to be found in an earlier anti-Jacobite piece by Henry Fielding, called "The Imaginary Journal of an Honest Tradesman after the Jacobite Conquest." One entry reads: "Jan. 3. Queen Anne's statue in St. Paul's Churchyard taken away, and a large crucifix erected in its room." [9]

Finally, we noted the opposition's use of fraudulent advertisements, signed with Jewish names, asking support for certain Court candidates. This low device, too, was not peculiar to the clamor of 1753, as we see from the following handbill circulated in the famous Westminster by-election of 1749:

AUX ÉLECTEURS TRÈS DIGNES DE WESTMINSTER.

Messieurs:

Vos suffrages et intérêts sont désirés pour le Très Hon. mi Lord Trentham,

Un Véritable Anglois.

N.B. L'on prie ses Amis de se rendre à l'Hôtel François dans le Marché au Foin.

To My Lord Trentham:

The King of France (my most glorious Monarch) being touched with a lively sense of the obligations he owes your Lordship, for the powerful protection you have given to his subjects in England, honours you with his thanks, and commands me to assure you, that your Lordship shall be the Chief Manager of his Playhouse in England, as soon as your Lordship and your Friends have brought those insolent rascals, the English, under his dominion, being satisfied the measures your Lordship and Friends now pursue cannot fail of your desired success.

I have the honour to be

Your Lordship's most obliged humble servant,

MIREPOIX.

N.B. Translated from the original French.[10]

So standards of polemical decorum were different two hundred years ago; and we must also allow for different notions of what constitutes proper matter for humor, or we shall overlook (or misinterpret) another

---

[9] Quoted by Abbey and Overton in *The English Church in the Eighteenth Century,* II, 391–392n.

[10] Quoted by Grego in *Parliamentary Elections,* p. 122. Mirepoix was the French Ambassador.

aspect—the purely comic—of the uproar over the Jew Bill. For eighteenth-century men looked at politics partly as a form of entertainment; and while a few regarded the drama of 1753 as unrelieved tragedy, most—including men who wished well to both the Ministry and the Bill—were in some measure amused by the affair, as well as exercised. Some of the exaggerated attacks on the Bill were essentially whimsical and facetious, rather than simply venomous and bigoted. Many Tory speakers and writers, aware that politically they had got hold of a very good thing, exploited it not with cold efficiency, but with an air of exhilaration and exuberance, like a card player thoroughly enjoying an unaccustomed run of good luck. Many Court politicians, too, seem to have been able to appreciate a clever trick, even when played on them; now and then one senses in their mood a measure of professional admiration and amusement, as well as of partisan indignation.[11]

Of course our moral and aesthetic sensibilities reject as too cruel, or too crude, much that our eighteenth-century ancestors thought diverting or witty. But whatever *our* reaction, we ought to recognize that a good many contributions to the clamor of 1753 were, by the standards of that day, innocently intended and innocently enjoyed. That was true, surely, of the pamphlet entitled *Seasonable Remarks on the Act,* when it affected to deplore any encouragement to Jewish immigration on these grounds (among others): that "as Jews claimed to be of older lineage than the great English families, duelling would increase"; and that "Britons would suffer in lotteries and on the turf, as the Jews were skilled in astrology and prophecy." [12] And I should place in the same category these verses, which appeared in the *London Evening Post:*

The following SONG is recommended to be sung by the few Christians that may be remaining in this Country One Hundred Years hence; and in the mean Time will be no improper Entertainment at the next General Election.

> When mighty Roast Pork was the Englishman's Food,
> It ennobled our Veins and enriched our Blood.
> And a Jew's Dish of Foreskins was not understood.
>
> Sing Oh! the Roast Pork of Old England,
> Oh! the Old English Roast Pork.

[11] See the letter of Robert Ord quoted on p. 139, above. See also the satire quoted on pp. 121–122.

[12] In Hertz, *British Imperialism,* p. 74.

. . . . .

To circumcise all is most cruel and fell;
Then such a Desire let us boldly repel;
For but give them an Inch, and they'll soon take an Ell,

    Those Foes to the Pork of Old England,
    Oh! the Old English Roast Pork.

Then Britons be wise at this critical Pinch,
And in such a Cause be not Cowards and flinch,
But the best of your Property guard ev'ry Inch

    From the Foes to the Pork of Old England,
    Oh! the Old English Roast Pork.[13]

[13] *LEP,* 4009:1.

APPENDIX C

A Note on the Marriage Bill of 1753

LORD Hardwicke's act to prevent clandestine marriages deserves the attention it usually receives in general works on this period, because it was a needed and a lasting reform. But the Marriage Bill was not, as is sometimes thought, the object of a political clamor or of widespread popular resentment.[1]

The Commons' debates on the bill were unusually acrimonious, and monopolized for a time the attention of political insiders.[2] But soon, amid the clamor over the Jew Bill, the Marriage Bill was all but forgotten. In the summer of 1753 the newspapers rarely mentioned it. Only in the late autumn, after the clamor had forced the repeal of the Jew Bill, did the opposition press turn its fire on the Marriage Bill. The *London Evening Post* opened the attack on November 29 with a brave trumpet-flourish: "Every objection to the Jew Bill holds, if possible, much stronger against that for preventing marriages." The paper, always resourceful, even managed to make out a connection between these two alarming measures: "There will be a visible propriety in their being repealed, as they were passed, together; because the manifest intent of the L[egislatu]re seems to have been to supply, with adventitious Jews, the

---

[1] Cf. John Brooke, *The Chatham Administration, 1766–1768* (London, 1956), p. 229: "The effectiveness of opposition was more related to the mistakes of the Court than to its own promises. It was only dangerous when it could take advantage of the genuine resentment aroused by the mishandling of a popular question. Walpole's excise scheme, George II's partiality for Hanover, even the unpopularity of Lord Hardwicke's Marriage Bill, had served this purpose during the reign of George II." The point is a very good one; but the Jew Bill should be substituted for the Marriage Bill.

[2] See above, p. 134 and n.

loss of natural-born Christian subjects which was likely to be brought upon the nation by laying restraints on marriages." [3]

A subsequent issue contained a long attack on the Marriage Bill, in the form of a petition to the Archbishop of Canterbury from "Mary Mouthwater, Elizabeth Longfor't, Bridget Bitesheets . . . of the County of Kent, Spinsters." These "distressed damsels" complained that Hardwicke's new law would make it more difficult to find husbands. The piece is serious in part, but most of it is merely whimsical and risqué. It concludes: "Your petitioners, though they have been informed that this Act is the child of a gentleman of great parts (and great parts are very alluring) yet cannot but believe it to be a bastard; because it seems much better calculated for the encouragement of common prostitution, than to make your honest, but poor, petitioners happy mothers of lawful children." [4]

No doubt this brought roars of laughter in the taverns and coffeehouses of London; but it was not the sort of thing that could bring out anti-Government mobs to drink and riot in defense of Church and State. The opposition knew this; and its attacks on the Marriage Bill were sporadic, half-hearted, and ineffectual. The Jew Bill was the only political issue that had a considerable impact on public opinion in 1753.

[3] *LEP,* 4064:1.
[4] *Ibid.,* 4074:1, 4 (Dec. 22).

SELECT BIBLIOGRAPHY

THE basic sources for this work are of three kinds: contemporary letters, both official and personal; pamphlets; and periodicals of all sorts. Perhaps the reports of the parliamentary debates are important enough to make up a fourth category, even though they must so very often be taken with a grain of salt. Particularly important have been the letters of Henry Pelham, Newcastle, Hardwicke, and certain lesser men, in the Additional Manuscripts in the British Museum; among the letters of private persons, the correspondence of Philip Yorke (Hardwicke's eldest son) with Thomas Birch, old Horace Walpole, and others, proved invaluable. Among the modern works that I should single out as especially useful are Henry Henriques' *The Jews and the English Law,* the articles by Israel Solomons and Lucy Sutherland listed below, and Cecil Roth's *Magna Bibliotheca Anglo-Judaica.*

Perhaps a word is in order about some works whose omission might be remarked. There are, in the first place, not a few perfectly sound political biographies—Rosebery's *Lord Chatham* is an example—that touch briefly upon the Jew Bill of 1753 and the part played by their protagonists in the affair, without actually adding anything to our knowledge of the episode. There are also secondary works, such as Campbell's *Lives of the Lord Chancellors,* that give general accounts of the Bill which are often cited in subsequent books, but which are in no sense authoritative, and are often full of errors. (Campbell, for example, quite without warrant, flatly ascribes the Jew Bill to Hardwicke.)[1] Since no account of the Bill until that of Hertz in 1908 was even nearly as thorough as that in Coxe's *Pelham* (1829), it would be not only useless but also misleading if one were to include automatically in a list of authorities either these inadequate secondary accounts or the aforementioned biographies. I have, nevertheless, listed a very few

[1] Campbell, *Lives,* 3d ed. (London, 1849), V, 122.

works of both sorts, in spite of the negligible value of their general comments or information, because they included part of a letter, perhaps, or some other specific fact or reference that I found useful.

MANUSCRIPT SOURCES

Newcastle Papers
Add. MSS. no.:

32731–35	Home correspondence of the Duke of Newcastle, vols. 46–50.
32995	Memoranda on public business, vol. III, 1753–54.
33034	Papers of proceedings in Parliament, vol. II, 1741–1760.
33053	Miscellaneous papers, vol. III, 1751–1783.

Hardwicke Papers

35351	Correspondence of the first Earl of Hardwicke and his son Philip, vol. I.
35374	Correspondence of the Hon. John Yorke with his brother Philip.
35398	Correspondence of the second Earl of Hardwicke (who was at that time the Hon. Philip Yorke) and Thomas Birch, vol. III.
35413–14	Political correspondence of the first Earl of Hardwicke with Newcastle and others (parts of vols. VIII and IX).
35592	General correspondence of the first Earl of Hardwicke, vol. IX.
35606	General correspondence of the second Earl of Hardwicke, vol. II.
35632	General correspondence of the Hon. Charles Yorke, vol. I.

PRINTED SOURCES

PAMPHLETS, LEAFLETS, AND BROADSIDES (A nearly complete list of pamphlets on the Jew Bill is to be found in Cecil Roth's *Magna Bibliotheca Anglo-Judaica*.)

A Brief and Summary Narrative of the Many Mischiefs and Inconveniencies in Former Times as well as of late Years, Occasioned by Naturalizing of Aliens. [London?, 1694?].

Britannia's Fortune-Teller. London, 1733.

The Case and Appeal of James Ashley, of Bread-Street, London: Addressed to the Publick in General. London, 1753.

The Case of Henry Simons, a Polish Jew Merchant; and his Appeal to the Public thereon. London, 1753.

The Case of the Merchants of Great-Britain, Residing at Home, or in the British Factories in Foreign Countries, with Respect to Persons obtaining Acts of Naturalization, without any Purpose of Continuing in these Kingdoms. [London?, 1752].

Considerations, see Philo-Patriae, *pseud.*

Free and Candid Remarks on a Paper Published in Defence of the Jews. [London?], 1753.

Hanway, Jonas, *Answer to the Appendix of a Pamphlet, entitled, Reflexions on Naturalization, Corporations and Companies, &c.* London, 1753.

[——] *A Review of the Proposed Naturalization of the Jews. By a Merchant who Subscribed the Petition against the Naturalization of the Jews.* London, 1753.

An Historical Treatise Concerning Jews and Judaism in England. [London?, 1753].

[Knight, Sir John], *The following Speech being spoke off hand upon the Debates in the House of Commons . . .* [London?, 1694].

A Modest Apology for the Citizens and Merchants of London, who Petitioned the House of Commons against Naturalizing the Jews. London, 1753.

Motives to the Senseless Clamour Against the Act Concerning Jews Exposed. London, 1753.

The Other Side of the Question. Being a Collection of what hath yet Appeared in Defence of the late Act in favour of the Jews. To which is prefixed, a word or two by the Editor. London, 1753.

Philo-Patriae, *pseud., Considerations on the Bill to Permit Persons Professing the Jewish Religion to be Naturalized by Parliament. In Several Letters from a Merchant in Town to his Friend in the Country.* London, 1753.

—— *Further Considerations on the Act to Permit Persons Professing the Jewish Religion to be Naturalized by Parliament. In a Second Letter from a Merchant in Town to his Friend in the Country.* London, 1753.

Reasons for Naturalizing the Jews in Great Britain and Ireland. London, 1714.

Reflections upon Naturalization, Corporations, and Companies; Supported by the Authorities of both Ancient and Modern Writers. By a Country Gentleman. London, 1753.

Remarks on a Speech Made in Common Council, on the Bill for Permitting Persons Professing the Jewish Religion to be Naturalized, so far as Prophecies are Supposed to be Affected by It. London, 1753.

[Romaine, William], *Answer to a Pamphlet Entitled "Considerations on the Bill to Permit Persons Professing the Jewish Religion to be Naturalized."* London, 1753.

———— 2d ed. "Reprinted by the Citizens of London." London, 1753.

Some Remarks on a Late Pamphlet, Intituled, Reflections on the Expediency of opening the Trade to Turkey. London, 1753.

Some Seasonable Queries on . . . a General Naturalization. [London?, 1694].

Some Thoughts upon a Bill for General Naturalization: Addressed to Those of all Denominations who act upon Whig Principles. London, 1751.

The Statesman and Broker. [London, 1753].

Sundry Considerations touching Naturalization of Aliens: whereby the alleged Advantages thereby are Confuted, and the contrary Mischiefs thereof are detected and discovered. [London?, 1695?].

Tucker, Josiah, *Letter to a Friend Concerning Naturalizations . . .* 2d ed. London, 1753.

———— *Reflections on the Expediency of a Law for the Naturalization of Foreign Protestants.* 2 pts. London, 1751–52.

[————] *Reflections on the Expediency of opening the Trade to Turkey.* London, 1753.

———— *A Second Letter to a Friend Concerning Naturalizations . . .* London, 1753.

A View of the Queen and Kingdom's Enemies, in the Case of the Poor Palatines. [London?, 1711?].

[Webb, Philip Carteret], *The Bill, Permitting the Jews to be Naturalized by Parliament Having Been Misrepresented in the London Gazetteer of Friday the 18th of May; and probably Having Never Been Read Either by the Author of That Paper, or by Several Others who Have since Signed a Petition, which that Paper was Calculated to Support: to Remove those False Impressions, the Following Short, but True, State of Facts is Submitted to the Consideration of the Public.* London, 1753. Reprinted in *Gent. Mag.,* 1753:278–280.

—————— *The Question, whether a Jew, born within the British Dominions, was, before the making the late Act of Parliament, a Person capable, by Law, to purchase and hold Lands to him, and his Heirs, Fairly Stated and Considered. By a Gentleman of Lincoln's-Inn.* London, 1753.

BOOKS

Abbey, Charles John, and John Henry Overton, *The English Church in the Eighteenth Century.* 2 vols. London, 1878.

Adler, Elkan Nathan, *London.* Jewish Communities Series. Philadelphia, 1930.

Barnett, Lionel D., ed., *Bevis Marks Records, Being Contributions to the History of the Spanish and Portuguese Congregation of London.* Oxford, 1940– .

Bedford, John Russell, 4th duke of, *Correspondence of John, Fourth Duke of Bedford, Selected from the Originals at Woburn Abbey, with an Introduction by Lord John Russell.* 3 vols. London, 1842–1846.

Besant, Walter, *London in the Eighteenth Century.* London, 1902.

Chesterfield, Philip Dormer Stanhope, 4th earl of, *The Letters of Philip Dormer Stanhope, 4th Earl of Chesterfield.* Bonamy Dobrée, ed. 6 vols. London, 1932.

[Cobbett, William, ed.], *The Parliamentary History of England* . . . 36 vols. London, 1806–1820.

Coxe, William, *Memoirs of the Administration of the Right Honourable Henry Pelham.* 2 vols. London, 1829.

Cumberland, Richard, *Memoirs of Richard Cumberland.* 2 vols. London, 1807.

Dickins, Lilian, and Mary Stanton, eds., *An Eighteenth-Century Correspondence* . . . London, 1910.

Dodington, George Bubb, *The Diary of the Late George Bubb Dodington* . . . *1749 to* . . . *1761.* Henry Penruddocke Wyndham, ed. Salisbury, 1784.

Emden, Cecil S., *The People and the Constitution.* Oxford, 1933.

Entick, John, *A New and Accurate History and Survey of London, Westminster, Southwark, and Places Adjacent; Containing Whatever is Most Worthy of Notice in Their Ancient and Present State.* 4 vols. London, 1766.

Feiling, Keith Grahame, *The Second Tory Party, 1714–1832*. London, 1951.

Forrester, Eric George, *Northamptonshire County Elections and Electioneering*. London, 1941.

George, M. Dorothy, *English Political Caricature to 1792*. Oxford, 1959.

—— *London Life in the XVIIIth Century*. London, 1930.

Gibbons, Philip Arnold, *Ideas of Political Representation in Parliament, 1660–1832*. Oxford, 1914.

Goldsmith, Oliver, *The History of England from the Earliest Times to the Death of George II*. 4 vols. London, 1771.

Grego, Joseph, *History of Parliamentary Elections and Electioneering from the Stuarts to Queen Victoria*. London, 1892.

Hanson, Laurence, *Government and the Press, 1695–1763*. London, 1936.

Henriques, Henry Straus Quixano, *The Jews and the English Law*. Oxford, 1908.

Herring, Thomas, *Letters from the late most reverend Dr. Thomas Herring, Lord Archbishop of Canterbury, to William Duncombe, Esq.* [John Duncombe, ed.]. London, 1777. There is also a letter of Abp. Herring's on the Jew Bill in P. H. Maty's *New Review* for 1782.

Hertz, Gerald Berkeley, *British Imperialism in the Eighteenth Century*. London, 1908.

Historical Manuscripts Commission Reports:
  Carlisle Papers. 15th Rept., App. 6.
  Egmont Papers. Vol. I, pt. 2.
  Lothian Papers, 1920 (correspondence of Sir Thomas Drury).
  Weston Papers. 10th Rept., App. 1.
  Whitworth Papers. 4th Rept., App. 1 (de la Warr MSS.).

Hyamson, Albert Montefiore, *A History of the Jews in England*. London, 1908.

—— *The Sephardim of England: A History of the Spanish and Portuguese Community, 1492–1951*. London, 1951.

Ilchester, Giles S. H. Fox-Strangways, Earl of, *Henry Fox, first Lord Holland*. 2 vols. London, 1920.

Lecky, William Edward Hartpole, *A History of England in the Eighteenth Century*. 8 vols. London, 1878–1890.

Macaulay, Thomas Babington, *The History of England from the Accession of James II*. Charles Firth, ed. 6 vols. London, 1913–1915.

Namier, Lewis Bernstein, *England in the Age of the American Revolution*. London, 1930.

—— *The Structure of Politics at the Accession of George III*. London, 1957.

Nichols, John, *Illustrations of the Literary History of the Eighteenth Century; Consisting of Authentic Memoirs and Original Letters of Eminent Persons*. 8 vols. London, 1817–1858.

—— *Literary Anecdotes of the Eighteenth Century*. 9 vols. London, 1812–1815.

Nugent, Claud, *Memoir of Robert, Earl Nugent*. Chicago, 1898.

Oldfield, Thomas Hinton Burley, *The Representative History of Great Britain and Ireland; Being a History of the House of Commons, and of the Counties, Cities, and Boroughs of the United Kingdom*. 6 vols. London, 1816.

Owen, John B., *The Rise of the Pelhams*. London, 1957.

Pares, Richard, *King George III and the Politicians*. Oxford, 1953.

Picciotto, James, *Sketches of Anglo-Jewish History*. London, 1875.

Robson, R. J. *The Oxfordshire Election of 1754: A Study in the Interplay of City, County and University Politics*. London, 1949.

Roth, Cecil, ed., *Anglo-Jewish Letters, 1158–1917*. London, 1938.

—— *History of the Jews in England*. Oxford, 1941.

—— ed., *Magna Bibliotheca Anglo-Judaica: A Bibliographical Guide to Anglo-Jewish History*. London, 1937.

—— *The Rise of Provincial Jewry: The Early History of the Jewish Communities in the English Countryside, 1740–1840*. London, 1950.

Rubens, Alfred, *Anglo-Jewish Portraits, A Bibliographical Catalogue of Engraved Anglo-Jewish and Colonial Portraits from the Earliest Times to the Accession of Queen Victoria*. London, 1935.

Secker, Thomas, *The Works of Thomas Secker. To which is prefixed a review of his . . . life . . . by Beilby Porteus*. 6 vols. London, 1811.

Smollett, Tobias, *The History of England from the Revolution in 1688 to the Death of George II*. 2 vols. Philadelphia, 1822. These two volumes form volumes V and VI of a nine-volume history of England, the first four volumes being by David Hume and the last three by Robert Bissett. Philadelphia, 1821–22.

Tovey, D'Blossiers, *Anglia Judaica: or the History and Antiquities of the Jews in England*. Oxford, 1738.

Trevelyan, George Macaulay, *England under Queen Anne, Vol. III: The Peace and the Protestant Succession.* London, 1948.

Walpole, Horace, *The Letters of Horace Walpole.* Mrs. Paget Toynbee, ed. 16 vols. Oxford, 1903–1905.

────── *Memoirs of the Reign of King George the Second.* Henry Fox, 3rd Lord Holland, ed. 3 vols. London, 1847.

Warburton, William, *Letters from a late Eminent Prelate to One of his Friends.* Richard Hurd, ed. 2d ed. London, 1808.

Williams, Basil, *Carteret and Newcastle.* Cambridge, Eng., 1943.

────── *The Whig Supremacy, 1714–1760.* Oxford, 1949.

Wood, Alfred Cecil, *A History of the Levant Company.* Oxford, 1935.

Yorke, Philip Chesney, *The Life and Correspondence of Philip Yorke, Earl of Hardwicke, Lord High Chancellor of Great Britain.* 3 vols. Cambridge, Eng., 1913.

ARTICLES

Huehner, Leon, "The Jews of Ireland," *Transactions of the Jewish Historical Society of England,* 5:226–242 (1902–1905).

Sedgwick, Romney, "Frederick, Prince of Wales," *History Today,* June 1961, pp. 410–416.

Solomons, Israel, "Satirical and Political Prints on the Jews' Naturalisation Bill, 1753," *Transactions of the Jewish Historical Society of England,* 6:205–233 (1908–1910).

Sutherland, Lucy, "The City of London in Eighteenth-Century Politics," in *Essays Presented to Sir Lewis Namier,* Richard Pares and A. J. P. Taylor, eds. (London, 1956), pp. 49–74.

────── "Samson Gideon and the Reduction of Interest, 1749–50," *Economic History Review,* 16:15–29 (1946).

────── "Samson Gideon: Eighteenth Century Jewish Financier," *Transactions of the Jewish Historical Society of England,* 17:79–90 (1953).

Trevelyan, George Macaulay, "The Two-Party System in English Political History," in *An Autobiography and Other Essays* (London, 1949), pp. 183–199.

INDEX

HARVARD HISTORICAL MONOGRAPHS

19. Vassi and Fideles in the Carolingian Empire. By C. E. Odegaard. 1945.*
20. Judgment by Peers. By Barnaby C. Keeney. 1949.
21. The Election to the Russian Constituent Assembly of 1917. By O. H. Radkey. 1950.
22. Conversion and the Poll Tax in Early Islam. By Daniel C. Dennett. 1950.*
23. Albert Gallatin and the Oregon Problem. By Frederick Merk. 1950.*
24. The Incidence of the Emigration during the French Revolution. By Donald Greer. 1951.
25. Alterations of the Words of Jesus as Quoted in the Literature of the Second Century. By Leon E. Wright. 1952.*
26. Liang Ch'i Ch'ao and the Mind of Modern China. By Joseph R. Levenson. 1953.
27. The Japanese and Sun Yat-sen. By Marius B. Jansen. 1954.
28. English Politics in the Early Eighteenth Century. By Robert Walcott, Jr. 1956.
29. The Founding of the French Socialist Party (1893–1905). By Aaron Noland. 1956.
30. British Labour and the Russian Revolution, 1917–1924. By Stephen Richards Graubard. 1956.
31. RKFDV: German Resettlement and Population Policy. By Robert L. Koehl. 1957.
32. Disarmament and Peace in British Politics, 1914–1919. By Gerda Richards Crosby. 1957.
33. Concordia Mundi: The Career and Thought of Guillaume Postel (1510–1581). By W. J. Bouwsma. 1957.
34. Bureaucracy, Aristocracy, and Autocracy: The Prussian Experience, 1660–1815. By Hans Rosenberg. 1958.
35. Exeter, 1540–1640: The Growth of an English County Town. By Wallace T. MacCaffrey. 1958.
36. Historical Pessimism in the French Enlightenment. By Henry Vyverberg. 1958.
37. The Renaissance Idea of Wisdom. By Eugene F. Rice, Jr. 1958.
38. The First Professional Revolutionist: Filippo Michele Buonarroti (1761–1837). By Elizabeth L. Eisenstein. 1959.
39. The Formation of the Baltic States: A Study of the Effects of Great Power Politics upon the Emergence of Lithuania, Latvia, and Estonia. By Stanley W. Page. 1959.*
40. Conservation and the Gospel of Efficiency: The Progressive Conservation Movement, 1890–1920. By Samuel P. Hays. 1959.
41. The Urban Frontier: The Rise of Western Cities, 1790–1830. By Richard C. Wade. 1959.
42. New Zealand, 1769–1840: Early Years of Western Contact. By Harrison M. Wright. 1959.

*Out of print